Museums of Influence

Kenneth Hudson

Museums of Influence

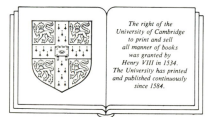

The right of the
University of Cambridge
to print and sell
all manner of books
was granted by
Henry VIII in 1534.
The University has printed
and published continuously
since 1584.

Cambridge University Press

Cambridge
New York   New Rochelle
Melbourne   Sydney

Published by the Press Syndicate of the University of Cambridge
The Pitt Building, Trumpington Street, Cambridge CB2 1RP
32 East 57th Street, New York, NY 10022, USA
10 Stamford Road, Oakleigh, Melbourne 3166, Australia

First published 1987
Reprinted 1988

Printed in Great Britain by the Bath Press, Bath, Avon

British Library cataloguing in publication data

Hudson, Kenneth
Museums of influence.
1. Museums
I. Title
069   AM5

Library of Congress cataloguing in publication data

Hudson, Kenneth
Museums of influence.
Bibliography.
Includes index.
1. Museums – Influence.
2. Museums – History.
3. Museum techniques – History.
4. Museums – Evaluation.
5. Museum techniques – Evaluation.
I. Title.
AM7.M79 1987   069.5   86–24498

ISBN 0 521 30534 9

*Frontispiece: electric trams at the Beamish
North of England Open Air Museum.*

WD

Contents

Preface

Museums of influence, in the context of the present book, are museums which have broken new ground in such an original or striking way that other museums have felt disposed or compelled to follow their example. The process of selection has been fairly rigorous: there are no more than thirty-seven members of the *corps d'élite* for the two centuries with which we are concerned. Originality in itself has not been sufficient to justify inclusion. It must have been significant and worthwhile originality, not mere novelty. This means that each museum, by its existence, its approach and its style, has met a real social need. It will have both echoed a national or international change of mood and encouraged its development. This implies, of course, that the influence of these pioneering institutions has been felt by the general public, by their visitors, and not only by other museums.

In deciding which museums to put on the list and for what reasons, I have relied partly on what I have seen and heard myself in the course of my travels, but even more on the judgement of the considerable number of well-informed people with whom I have discussed the project. This has given me confidence that my final choice is neither arbitrary nor eccentric. There is bound to be a considerable measure of disagreement with the list. Everyone with wide experience of museums will have his own candidates to suggest in preference to those which have found favour with me. If the book does not stimulate controversy, it will have to a large extent failed.

One feature is particularly likely to meet with surprise and possibly criticism. No ethnographical museum as such will be found among the thirty-seven, although many of them have gone to great pains to reflect the crafts and customs of mankind. The Museum of Popular Arts and Traditions in Paris, for example, is by any definition a distinguished and highly successful ethnographical museum. The omission and the apparent paradox are easily explained. The museum world contains a great many collections of the kind which is generally referred to as 'ethnographical', that is, consisting of objects relating to exotic cultures. Some of these are very large and therefore, in professional museum jargon, 'important', but none that I have yet seen or heard of contrives to communicate the essential features of the societies with which the museum or the collection is concerned, in a way that many films, television programmes and even lectures have contrived to do. Visually, these displays are often extremely attractive but, with very rare exceptions, they present the surface of a society. The picture they offer leaves too much to the imagination. The ambitions, the fears, the poverty, the disease, the climate, the cruelty and brutality, the satisfactions and the sufferings of these people are not there to give blood, sense and cohesion to the exhibits. In some ways, the situation is worse than it was fifty or even seventy years ago, because nowadays it is almost taboo to tell the truth about what are euphemistically called 'the developing countries', or even to hint that important parts of reality are not for discussion. Ethnographical museums may collect widely, but they do not dig deeply. The political consequences of doing so would be too serious, or so it is felt.

Meanwhile, there are many technically excellent but, for the reasons just given, anaemic ethnographical displays. As three-dimensional pictures, what can be seen at, for example, the Museum of Mankind in London, the Übersee Museum in Bremen and the Tropenmuseum in Amsterdam, mark a considerable advance on what was available half a century ago and, in pre-television days, they would undoubtedly have stirred the imagination of thousands of people. But I have found it impossible to say that any one of them has 'influenced' the others to any marked extent. They have occurred together, which is another way of saying that social tastes and pressures have brought them into being.

I think it is quite possible that the day of the ethnographical museum has already gone and that, in the years ahead, the habits of man will be presented within a total environment context, in much the same way as one of our chosen thirty-seven, the Noorder Dierenpark at Emmen, is doing. In that sense, what one sees at Emmen might well represent at least one variety of the ethnographical museum of the future. There will certainly be others and clues to their possible character are to be found scattered throughout the following pages.

Chapter One
Fertilisation and cross-fertilisation in the museum world

In the mid-1970s I had the good fortune to be commissioned by UNESCO to travel the world in search of what would strike me as being the most important new ideas in the museum field. When I had accumulated a daunting mass of impressions and information, I did my best to digest it and to produce a book from the results. This appeared in 1977, with the somewhat grandiose title of *Museums for the 1980s: a Survey of World Trends*. Its aim, as printed on the inside flap of the dust jacket, was expressed in the following terms:

> *Museums for the 1980s* has been produced in the hope that it will encourage those who are trying, often under very difficult circumstances, to transform museums into the important social and educational instruments which the modern world demands. It is intended to stimulate experiment and discussion, rather than to serve as an encyclopaedia or a textbook. Many experts and enthusiasts in many countries have been consulted in an attempt to make the work as authoritative and comprehensive as possible, but none of its statements, however confidently expressed, are to be regarded as *ex cathedra*. What is offered is rather a series of examples of the most original, most forward-looking and most constructive views, and their applications, which the author has been able to discover during several years of extensive travel and of determined attempts to see the museum wood for the trees. In ten years' time the picture will no doubt be very different. If museums were to fail to respond to social change and to reflect it, they would indeed cease to justify public support.

Since that time, I have continued to travel a good deal and, in the course of my journeys and of my visits to many hundreds of museums, I have pondered especially on two phenomena. The first is the speed and thoroughness with which a characteristically Western European institution, the museum, has spread itself over the world, for better or for worse, in the course of two centuries. The second is the way in which different countries and different cultures have absorbed the museum and gradually adapted it to their own needs and customs. Imperial power has greatly influenced and accelerated the process. The British planted British-type museums in India, the French created their own distinct types of cultural citadels throughout Africa. What the colonial powers left behind in the form of museums when their empire crumbled were often ill-suited to the real needs and conditions of the newly enfranchised nations, and it has been fascinating, and often sad, to observe the

A not uncommon type of museum in the 17th and 18th centuries: the Collection of Curiosities formed by the Danish scholar, Ole Worm (1588–1644).

efforts which have been made to Indianise and Africanise these remarkable relics of a past age.

There is no reason, however, for Europeans to feel in any way superior about this. There is an extraordinary similarity between the efforts of the Indians to come to terms with the Prince of Wales Museum in Bombay and the love–hate relationship which London's Victoria and Albert Museum has with its building inheritance in the Brompton Road. If these two museums were in a position to start afresh today, one can be sure that neither would choose to encumber itself with a pile of masonry so out of line with their present requirements. The problems created by out-of-date cultural plant are worldwide.

The fact that museums have spread and multiplied is an obvious enough fact. As one of the editors of a world directory of museums which is issued in a revised version every five years, I know all too well what the rate of growth has been: ten per cent every five years. Very often, I have asked myself the reasons for this extraordinary social phenomenon, extraordinary, because in so many instances it defies economic logic and common sense. All five continents appear to be chronically afflicted by very serious financial and political problems, but the number of museums continues inexorably to increase. Why should this be so, and, in particular, why should even the world's poorest countries, some of them poor to the point of destitution and starvation, feel that their self-respect demands museums?

The professional student of museums – and I think I can now modestly claim to be such a person – finds himself faced with other equally puzzling problems. Why should museums not funded by the State or by a local authority – the so-called independent museums – be so plentiful and well-regarded in Great Britain and the Federal Republic of Germany and rare to the point of being considered obscene in Sweden? Why should Finland have by far the highest ratio of museums to population in the world? Why has the Soviet Union, alone among the major countries, never published a comprehensive list of its museums?

The obvious answer to such questions is that museums, like Christianity, take on the colouring of the society in which their activity takes place. A church in the United States is not the same as a church in Denmark or South Africa. A Swedish school is not an Irish school, a Dutch post office is not a Canadian post office. A museum in China does not operate in the same social and political context as a museum in Egypt or Bulgaria. The fact that these institutions share a common generic title – church, school, post office, museum – can be highly misleading. It can produce the wrong expectations, encourage absurd generalisations.

Yet, despite this, it remains true that, just as there is something which one might term the essence of a church, so one can identify without too much difficulty the essence of a museum, a central quality which distinguishes all museums from all flower-shops and all airlines. It is this quality which makes it possible to organise bodies like the International Council of Churches, the International Council of Museums, Interflora and the International Air Transport Association, to say nothing of the innumerable national bodies which function within these various fields. A museum in France has more in common with a museum in Iceland than it has with a petrol station or a printing works in its own country. The international traffic in museology is necessarily different from the country to country movement of ideas and innovations in printing technology.

Yet the ways in which thoughts, improvements and habits are transmitted from one region of the world to another has been studied in only the most rudimentary fashion. In the eighteenth century, the great English agricultural pioneer, Thomas Coke, reckoned that his improvements travelled at the rate of a mile a year and noted that attempts to change the old customs any faster were nearly always a failure. Farmers needed a lot of convincing that it was worth their while to abandon old habits and, not unnaturally, preferred their neighbours to do the experimenting and make the mistakes and suffer the losses.

But in farming, as in most other fields of human activity, change tends to begin at the top and to work downwards. The 'Great Men' interpretation of history is rather out of fashion nowadays, the preference being for Forces and Movements, but there is, nevertheless, a good deal of truth in it. The humble and meek may occasionally riot, strike and protest, but they rarely experiment. Change usually comes from those who have a taste for innovation and the money and security to indulge in it.

For influence to operate and for change to take place, three things are necessary. First, there must be people of exceptional vision and originality of mind to develop the new ideas. Second, the time and the social climate must be right and, third, there must be the means of transmitting the new thinking. If all three factors are not present, any new, let alone revolutionary, proposal is almost certain to fail to meet acceptance, no matter how brilliant or sensible it may be.

One or two examples from the museum field will serve to illustrate the point. The first could reasonably be the Musée Napoléon, created in the Louvre in 1803, and 'born of three parents, republicanism, anti-clericalism and successful aggressive war'.[1] The circumstances of its birth might well be considered disgraceful, although it is not in the French tradition to say so. After the Revolution and the execution of the King, there had been wholesale and systematic confiscation of the art collections of the Royal Family and of the members of the aristocracy, as well as of works of art from churches and monasteries. In 1793, the Louvre was opened as the great national showcase for these treasures and for the next twenty years the collections were augmented by the loot gathered by Napoleon's armies as they overran Europe. In 1803, this enormous accumulation of artistic trophies was honoured with the title of the Musée Napoléon.

So long as the wars were in progress, very few foreign visitors were able to visit the museum, but in 1802 the Treaty of Amiens provided a brief lull in the hostilities and enthusiasts from England flocked across the Channel to enjoy their first sight of what the conquering heroes of France had pillaged from the galleries and collections of Europe. Those who came, often under conditions of considerable discomfort, included the President of the Royal Academy, Benjamin West, and several of his fellow artists, notably Hoppner, Opie, Fuseli and the young Turner. Among the architects, Smirke and Flaxman made the pilgrimage and so did Charles James Fox, the writers, Maria Edgeworth and Fanny Burney, and Kemble, the distinguished actor. Most of them were stupefied by the sheer quantity and magnificence of it all. Turner, however, was not impressed, believing that such an overwhelming concentration on the past would divert attention from the artists of the present, who should, in his opinion, be the main object of public concern.

English visitors to the Musée Napoléon in the Louvre in 1802. From left to right:

Benjamin West (by G. Stuart, 1786)

Henry Fuseli (by J. Opie, date unknown)

John Flaxman (by G. Head, 1792)

Frances D'Arblay, 'Fanny Burney' (by E. F. Burney, c. 1784–5)

John Opie (self-portrait, c. 1785)

Maria Edgeworth (artist unknown, c. 1845)

J. M. W. Turner (by C. R. Leslie, 1816)

John Philip Kemble (attrib. Sir Thomas Lawrence, c. 1800)

Turner, as it happened, was right. The first half of the nineteenth century was marked throughout Europe by an all-consuming cult of the Old Masters, which had been fuelled, if not actually started, by the exciting happenings at the Louvre. It was a complicated process, the result of an alliance, holy or unholy, according to one's point of view, between the dealers, the patriots and the more establishment-minded among the artists. The dealers had played an important part as middlemen in the Napoleonic looting process, especially in Italy and Spain and, to a lesser extent, in the return of property to its rightful owners once the wars had come to an end. Over a period of more than twenty years, they had established themselves as a class of people to be reckoned with and their specialist knowledge was to prove invaluable during the 1820s as national art museums began to be founded outside France. The British Institute in London, which organised a celebrated series of exhibitions of Old Masters in the years after Waterloo, very probably came into existence as a direct result of the extremely strong impression made on Benjamin West by his visit to the Musée Napoléon.

It would, of course, be a ridiculous over-simplification to say that the Prussian State Gallery in Berlin and the National Gallery in London were founded because the French had already done the same thing at the Louvre. Public opinion had to be favourable, the political climate had to be right, and there had to be influential and determined people to drive the plan through to a successful conclusion. But, in 1815, as in 1945, the defeat of an all-powerful dictator, after many years of widespread suffering on the part of his victims, stimulated nationalist movements and brought about social change more rapidly than would otherwise have occurred. A more sinister development was the wish, not always subconscious, to beat the toppled tyrant at his own game. Imitation is often the most potent form of revenge. The Musée Napoléon knocked its first generation of visitors off their feet mainly because it was so monstrously big. It brought together more items of painting and sculpture from more countries than anyone had ever seen before. Once it had happened, nothing could be the same again. The Louvre, with its huge building and its huge collections, provided a new yardstick by which future art galleries would be judged. With France defeated at Waterloo, England and Prussia had an equal duty to surpass her on the museum front. There could and should be no limit to their growth.

But, as one has seen so often during the past 200 years, the big museum comes to be respected and envied not only for what it is, but for what it does and how it does it. During the course of the research for this book, I asked the Director of the British Museum, Sir David Wilson, what he thought the influence of his museum had been. 'Very great', he answered, 'and mostly bad.' I took this to mean, for instance, that once the British Museum was seen to have a classical portico, every large provincial city in Victorian England had to have one, even if it brought itself close to bankruptcy in the process. This, however, was not, in Sir David's opinion, the most important aspect of the matter. What he had in mind was something much more

pernicious and far-reaching, the determination of the Bradfords, Manchesters and
Birminghams to have the same organisational structure as the British Museum, the
same panoply of Departments, Keepers, Research and Publications, whereas, given
the smaller scale of their activities, what they really needed was something much
more flexible and readily adaptable to change.

Until well into the present century, there were remarkably few museums outside
Europe and the United States. The great world growth of museums did not begin
until after the Second World War, although there had been some expansion earlier
within the territories ruled by the major colonial powers: England, France, Portugal,
Belgium and the Netherlands. This meant that, for someone who wished to keep
himself properly informed of interesting new museum developments, world travel
was quite unnecessary. Visits to Europe and America were all that was required and,
until the 1920s, there was little point in progressing beyond the eastern part of the
United States.

It would hardly be an exaggeration to say that until the 1880s the museum world
consisted of four countries: France, Germany, England and Italy. There were, of
course, collections elsewhere, including some of great importance, but little innovation was taking place outside these four countries. This is where the museums of
influence were to be found and even there the places of pilgrimage were confined to
a handful of major cities. But – and the point is an important one – it was necessary
to travel in order to become aware of what was happening abroad, or even in other
parts of one's own country. Journals aimed at members of the museum profession
did not exist and the general run of newspapers and periodicals only rarely contained
descriptions of new developments in museums and art galleries.

It was possible, of course, for the assiduous student to glean a good deal of information from travellers' published accounts of their journeys and visits. One day,
perhaps, we shall have an anthology of some of the more interesting of these comments, under the title, perhaps, of *Museums through the eyes of travellers*. Such a work
would certainly include the comments from members of the general public, including those made by William Hutton, a Birmingham bookseller, on his visit to the
British Museum in 1794. He had not found it easy to obtain one of the much-prized
entrance tickets, but he eventually found someone who was willing to part with his
for the considerable sum of two shillings, and he was able to bask in thoughts of the
pleasures ahead of him:

> Here I shall regale the mind for two hours upon striking objects which
> ever change and ever please. I shall see what is nowhere else to be seen.
> The wonders of creation are deposited in this vast cabinet. Every
> country in the globe has, perhaps, paid its richest tribute into this grand
> treasury.[2]

What actually happened was much less agreeable. As one of a party of ten, Mr

Hutton was hustled through the Museum by 'a tall genteel young man', who refused to give any information about the objects on display and allowed no time to look at anything for more than a few seconds. It was all most unsatisfactory.

> In about *thirty minutes* we finished our silent journey through this princely mansion, which could well have taken thirty days. I went out about as wise as I went in, but with this severe reflection, that for fear of losing my chance, I had that morning abruptly torn myself away from three gentlemen, with whom I was engaged in an interesting conversation, had lost my breakfast, got wet to the skin, spent half-a-crown in coach hire, paid two shillings for a ticket, been hackneyed through the rooms with violence, had lost the little share of good humour I had brought in, and come away completely disappointed.[3]

These reminiscences are no doubt important as a contribution to the history of the British Museum, but Mr Hutton's observations are unlikely to have had much influence on the development of museums, however many people may have read his book or heard about his grievances during conversations. He had attended the Museum as a private individual. His primary concern was with selling books, not with planning or running museums.

The German, Gustav Waagen, was a visitor of quite a different order. Appointed Director of the newly established Royal Picture Gallery in Berlin in 1821, when he was only twenty-five, he was, for professional reasons, an assiduous visitor of foreign museums. During the 1830s and 1840s he made a number of tours in Britain, visiting both public and private art collections. He was concerned partly to locate and list paintings[4] and partly to see how the British displayed their works of art. In professional and academic circles in Germany, and very probably in England as well, his views would have been listened to with respect. He was, one might say, an important carrier of information, a honey-bee of the museum world, returning to his hive in Berlin loaded with foreign pollen. In less metaphorical terms, he was, in the days before museum journals and museum conferences, a leading example of one of the most significant ways in which one museum exercised influence over another.

Connoisseurs and collectors seem to have been pleased to welcome him. At Panshanger, he inspected Lord Cowper's pictures and found most of what he saw very much to his satisfaction.

> The glowing summer's sun had heated me exceedingly, but I was soon revived by the refreshing coolness of these fine apartments, in which the pictures are arranged with much taste. The drawing-room, especially, is one of those apartments which not only give great pleasure by their size and by the convenience and elegance of the furniture, but likewise afford the most elevated gratification of the mind, by works of art of the noblest kind. This splendid apartment receives light from three lanterns, and large windows at one of the ends: and the paintings

of the Italian school are very well relieved by the purple silk hangings. I cannot refrain from again praising the refined taste of the English, who adorn their rooms, which are in daily use in this manner, and thus experience, often from their youth, the silent and the slow, but sure influence of works of art.

I passed here six happy hours in quiet solitude. The solemn silence was interrupted only by the humming of innumerable bees, which fluttered around the flowering plants which, in the greatest luxuriance, adorn the windows. It is only when so left to oneself, that by degrees, penetrating into the spirit of works of art, one can discover all their peculiar beauties. But when, as often happens in England, and as I shall doubtless again experience, an impatient housekeeper rattles with her keys, one cannot of course be in the proper frame of mind, but must look at everything superficially, and with internal vexation.[5]

Waagen would have suffered even worse frustration in public art galleries, at least during visiting hours. For his own private meditations, he was probably careful to choose a time when privilege would allow him to be alone in the gallery. But he was apt to be a severe critic. At Lord Methuen's seat at Corsham, in Wiltshire, for instance, matters were not at all to his liking. The collection, he decided:

very naturally indicates the taste of the time in which it was formed, and the pictures of the later Italian schools accordingly predominate. But it likewise contains a considerable number of excellent works of the better periods of the several schools, the value of which is probably not recognised as it should be, in consequence of the very bad condition in which they are. This condition is caused by that destructive enemy to pictures, the damp; and it may be confidently predicted that all the pictures will be totally ruined in a few years, unless they are soon removed from Corsham House.[6]

It is, perhaps, worth pointing out that Waagen, like nearly every other tourist and traveller until comparatively recently – artists were in a rather different situation – had nothing but words to describe and record what he saw. Anyone in his position today would have been able to take photographs of what came his way, or to buy colour slides of works displayed in art galleries. Most of these items would, in any case, be widely accessible in the form of reproduction. But, in the 1820s, a personal visit was essential and only those who were able to travel were in a position to experience the quality of a work of art or even to be aware of its existence.

Throughout the nineteenth century, museums attempted to overcome this problem, so far as it affected sculpture, by commissioning plaster casts of important works, especially those of the Greek and Roman periods. But few people believed that a cast could be the equal of an original, although it was certainly better than nothing at all. The point was excellently made by Waagen, after he had seen the Parthenon marbles

– the 'Elgin' marbles – in the British Museum, in 1837:

> I never, perhaps, found so great a difference between a plaster cast and
> marble as in these Elgin marbles. The Pentellic marble, of which they
> are formed, has a warm yellowish tone, and a very fine, and at the same
> time, a clear grain, by which these sculptures have extraordinary
> animation, and peculiar solidarity. The block, for instance, of which
> the famous horse's head is made, had absolutely a bony appearance,
> and its sharp, flat treatment has a charm, of which the plaster cast gives
> no notion.[7]

But he disapproved strongly of the lighting. Since the windows were immediately
above the sculptures, 'they unfortunately do not afford any contrasts of light and
shade',[8] and at the National Gallery, in its temporary home in Pall Mall, matters
were even worse – 'The four rooms have a dirty appearance; and with great depth
and so little light, most of the pictures are imperfectly seen.'[9]

One is tempted to ask what useful ideas he might have carried back with him to
Germany, where new museums were springing up at a rate unequalled elsewhere in
Europe. The answer is probably 'none at all'. But he might well have counted his
blessings and felt tempted to agree with Coleridge, who had written, in 1831, these
pessimistic words:

> In this country there is no general reverence for the fine arts; and the
> sordid spirit of a money-amassing philosophy would meet any prop-
> osition for the fostering of art, in a general and extended sense, with the
> commercial maxim – Laissez faire.[10]

Waagen might, however, have learnt some useful lessons as to what to avoid, what
not to do. He might have decided, for instance, that it was dangerous to leave
valuable works of art in private hands, since all too often they would suffer serious
damage as a result of ignorance and neglect. He would certainly have noted the
disadvantages which arose from unsuitable and cramped accommodation and from
insufficient funding. He would have understood, like Coleridge, that organised
culture is unlikely to flourish if those with political power turn their attention and
their energies in other directions.

Had he come to England a little later, however, he would almost certainly have
found more grounds for optimism. By the 1840s, industrialists, financiers and
commercially powerful people – the upper ranks of the middle classes – were
replacing the old type of aristocratic connoisseur as the country's principal art
collectors. These people had the money not only to buy art but to look after it and,
as the character of the art-buying public changed, the attitude to art museums
changed.

Even so, it is very doubtful if any British museum devoted to fine art can be said to have had a strong influence on museum development elsewhere during the nineteenth century. In fact, over the whole museum field, only three museums in the British Isles qualify for inclusion in such a list before the end of the reign of Queen Victoria. They were the Pitt-Rivers Museum at Farnham, the South Kensington Museum or, to give it its later title, the Victoria and Albert Museum, and the Natural History Museum. A number of others were well known abroad because of their collections or for research carried out by members of their staff, but this is quite another matter. As this book defines it, a Museum of Influence is one which breaks new ground, and this the three museums mentioned above certainly did. In this respect, they had no serious rivals in their own country.

It could be argued, however, that the British achievement which had more influence on museums than any other single enterprise, was the Great Exhibition of 1851. No exhibition had previously attracted such a large number of people from so many countries, involved such large sums of money or required such detailed planning, much of it of a pioneering nature. No enterprise did as much to kill the twin myths that the working-class people were not interested in cultural activities and were certainly not willing to pay for them, and that such people were inevitably unruly and likely to resort to drink and violence at the first opportunity. Nothing of such an international nature had ever been accomplished before.

Sir Henry Cole, who was closely involved in the organisation of the Exhibition, and who later went on to be the first Director at South Kensington, described the significance of the Great Exhibition in these terms:

> The history of the world, I venture to say, recalls no event comparable in its promotion of human industry with that of the Great Exhibition of the industry of all nations in 1851. A great people invited all civilised nations to a festival, to bring into comparison the works of human skill. It was carried out by its own private means, it was self-supporting, and independent of taxes and the employment of slaves, which great works had exacted in ancient days. A prince of eminent wisdom, of philosophic mind, sagacity, with power of generalship and great practical ability, placed himself at the head of the enterprise and led it to triumphant success. The Sovereign of that people gave to her husband and subjects her warmest sympathy and fondly watched its progress and witnessed its triumph among a multitude of 25,000 persons, all assembled under one glass roof of 1850 feet in length, an event which had never happened before.[11]

But, as Cole pointed out, the Great Exhibition could not have happened before Sir Robert Peel had ushered in the Age of Free Trade, 'so that it might be in the interests of foreigners to accept the invitation to show us the fruits of their industry'.[12] Everything was right for the exhibition, a favourable political climate, the confidence of British designers and manufacturers that they could stand up to foreign competition,

Bringing the practical arts and well-behaved masses together: the Great Exhibition of 1851.

A grand exterior to make the journey seem worthwhile.

A cathedral-like interior to elevate the mind.

Royal patronage and inspiration in its most active form, a public which was ripe for just this combination of patriotism, art and science. The venture appeared more than justified when the 6,861 British exhibitors won 78 medals, compared with 86 for the 7,076 exhibitors from 30 other countries.

It is very doubtful if the Exhibition project would have come to fruition, however, if the Prince Consort had not been there to motivate and direct it and to give it style and status. When he arrived from Germany in 1840, he brought with him a strong sense, not only of the unity of culture – culture was something in which all classes had a rightful share – but also of the public's right to direct contact with it. He was feeling his way towards a National Museum, a National Culture Centre, in London, after seeing for himself how the Germans were moving towards something of the kind in Munich, Berlin and elsewhere. At South Kensington, he believed, such a National Cultural Centre might one day be achieved. What actually happened – the Victoria and Albert Museum, the Science Museum, the Geological Museum, the Natural History Museum – was a second-best to what he had hoped for, and even that took a very long time to bring into being, but there can be little doubt that without the great success of the Great Exhibition, as a genuinely popular manifestation, even that second-best might never have come to anything.

Perhaps the main value of the Great Exhibition enterprise was that it made the big seem possible. The business of funding and organising exhibitions and museums was increased in scale. But because it was so big and so obviously adventurous, a great many people came to see it, more than six million altogether, all paying their own expenses, and a great many of them from abroad, including large contingents from the United States, France and the Netherlands. If they had not come, they could not have been impressed. And, once they had been and seen what was there in Paxton's great glasshouse, the pattern of their thinking was changed. They had seen marvels and their world was no longer the same.[13]

One of the Prince Consort's main functions was to act as a carrier of ideas between countries. In the days before radio and television, before international conferences and before aeroplanes and mass travel, it was the existence of a relatively few purposeful and dedicated travellers which did more than anything else, apart from war, to prevent societies from stagnating. It is always interesting to ask people who have achieved something new, 'Where did the idea come to you? Was there anyone or anywhere that particularly influenced you?' For the purpose of this present book I have done this frequently, with most useful results. At Beamish, the creator of the great open-air museum for the North-East of England, Frank Atkinson, told me that the source of his inspiration was the museum at Lillehammer, in Norway. The Director of the Museum of the History of the City of Amsterdam said that he owed most to a visit he paid to the Museum of the History of the City of Warsaw, and Kenneth Robinson, who gave the National Motor Museum and the other visitor attractions at Beaulieu their signals for growth and prosperity, answered without the slightest hesitation, 'Disneyworld, Florida', which he had visited for the first time in 1970, when it was new. When I asked him to be a little more specific, he said that Disneyworld had taught him three all-important lessons, that 'in management terms, anything is possible', that 'high quality is costly to create, but it raises the expectations of visitors by giving them something better', and that 'if the level of provision is high, visitors spend more at the shop'.[14] A nineteenth-century Kenneth Robinson would probably have said very much the same after visiting the Great Exhibition.

Journals published primarily for the museum profession did not exist before the present century. They have been an important medium for the circulation of ideas and for making their readers aware of new developments. This is particularly true where the younger members of the profession are concerned. Those in a position of power usually have regular opportunities to travel and to attend conferences: their juniors are not so fortunate and have to broaden their horizons in other ways. It is difficult to realise now how poor communications were in the nineteenth century and how accidental a business news often was.

The *Museums Journal*, the organ of the Museums Association in Great Britain, began publication in 1902, as a monthly. It had correspondents in Germany, the United States, Australia, South Africa, and New Zealand but not, oddly enough, in France, the Netherlands or Scandinavia, which were all areas where interesting things were happening in the museum world. So, within a short time, the *Journal*'s readers were being given authoritative articles on the Zoological Museum in Berlin, the Museum of New York State, the Museum of Science and Art, Edinburgh, and the Museum for National Industries, Stuttgart, all based on personal visits.

In Germany, the quarterly, *Museumskunde*, was performing a similar service, but on a rather more mandarin level. Its first issue appeared in 1905 and its coverage was international from the beginning. America had no similar publication until after the First World War. *Museum Work*, produced by the American Association of Museums, began to appear, twice a year, in 1919. It was not of the same quality as either the German or the British journal, and very parochial. Americans with a desire to find out what was happening in the rest of the world would have learnt remarkably little from *Museum Work*, although for non-Americans it was a rich source of information about American folk ways. In 1924, for instance, an article called 'Campaigning for a New Museum',[15] described in fascinating detail how the citizens of Buffalo were lobbied and organised, by means of talks, posters and meetings, to agree to bonds being issued to finance a new building for the Buffalo Society of Natural Sciences. In 1926 *Museum Work* became *Papers and Reports* of the American Association of Museums, a much more introverted and, to an outsider, less interesting publication.

From a museum point of view, there was no organised movement of ideas around

Spreading information in print: the
birth of national museum periodicals.

The Museums Journal, 1902, the pioneer.
Museumskunde, 1905, 'a rather more
mandarin level'.
UNESCO's *Museum*, bringing the
word to the world.

the world, no systematic exchange of views, before the establishment of ICOM, the
International Council of Museums, in 1946.[16] Closely associated from the beginning
with UNESCO, it described itself as 'a professional organisation devoted to museum
development throughout the world', and said that 'it represents the museum profession internationally and is a technical partner in the execution of UNESCO
programmes in the field of museum development'.[17] The first Conference of ICOM
was held in Mexico City in 1948. There had been no comparable occasion previously
in the museum world. Before the Second World War, delegates from abroad had
attended the annual conferences of the various national museum associations, but a
meeting on this scale, deliberately aiming to bring to a central point representatives
of all the countries of the world, was unprecedented. Without the existence of a
worldwide airline network, rudimentary as this was in 1948, it would have been
impossible. For museums, as for all other forms of human activity, aeroplanes have
transformed the spread of ideas.

The first issue of *ICOM News* appeared in 1946 and its publication over a period of
what is now forty years has provided an invaluable international information service.
The ICOM Documentation Centre in Paris, during the same period, has offered
museum people a collecting and consultation point for the mass of books, periodicals, catalogues and reports which appear each year. Whatever may be said about
UNESCO – and its organisation has been widely criticised – ICOM is a cultural
achievement of which the post-war world can be justly proud.

Its attentions have not been confined solely to the activities and interests of museum
professionals. In 1951 UNESCO and ICOM co-operated to launch their Crusade
for Museums, a campaign on an international scale to create a public awareness of

the educational role of museums. This eventually led, in 1977, to the institution of International Museums Day, which is celebrated on 18 May each year in many countries.

A hundred or even fifty years ago, there was every reason for not knowing what was happening in museums outside one's own country. Today, with the existence of UNESCO and ICOM, together with an impressive improvement in television reporting and in the coverage provided by museum periodicals, there is little excuse for ignorance.

The main international agency for detailed, illustrated articles on museums is the UNESCO quarterly, *Museum*, which first appeared in 1948. The contents of two typical issues show the kind of information service which is now regarded as normal, but which would have seemed extraordinary before the Second World War. One of the 1980 issues[18] was devoted mainly to the museums of China, but it also contained a long article describing and assessing the first ten years' work at the pioneering industrial eco-museum, La Creusot – Montceau-les-Mines, in central France. In 1982, in a single issue,[19] readers were offered these articles:

> Museums of Kiev
> Skansen – a stock-taking at ninety
> Planning the open-air museum and teaching urban history: the United
>   States in the world context
> In Botswana: bridging the ignorance gap

Even the national museum periodicals are far less parochial than they used to be. The *Museums Journal*, the main publication of the Museums Association in Great Britain, can hardly be distinguished, nowadays, so far as the list of its contents is concerned, from UNESCO's *Museum*. In a 1979 issue, for instance, the main articles were these:

> British Museum (Natural History): a new approach to the visiting
>   public
> The Sainsbury Centre for Visual Arts
> The National Museum of Popular Arts and Traditions, Paris
> The Travelling Curator Service in Scotland
> National Museum and Art Gallery of Botswana

There is, of course, a danger in this international approach, that because travel is now so easy and because information is so easily obtainable, museums everywhere will end up by looking and feeling much the same, similarly organised, in similar buildings, eager to approximate to a desirable international norm, much as every Hilton Hotel is constructed and run on the same model and feels the same, whether the location is in Cairo or Dallas, despite minor concessions to a national style of décor. If this happens, as it well may, then what began as influence and example could end up in deadening uniformity.

But, no matter how favourable the circumstances may be, fertilisation and cross-fertilisation in the museum orchard cannot be guaranteed. A classic instance of this is the continued failure to set up a Folk Museum, a National Museum of Popular Arts and Traditions in England. In his Presidential Address to the annual meeting of the Museums Association in 1909, Henry Balfour, Curator of the Pitt-Rivers Museum at Oxford, set out his demands for such a museum.

> What is required is a National Folk Museum, dealing exclusively and exhaustively with the history of culture of the British Nation within the historic period, and illustrating the growth of ideas and indigenous characteristics. Until such an institution is founded, there will remain a very serious *Lacuna* in the list of our museums, and we shall remain open to the fire of just criticism from other countries, on the score of our almost pathetic anxiety to investigate and illustrate the ethnology of *other* races and peoples, while we neglect our own. Others have, indeed, a perfect right to criticize us, since our comparative neglect of national ethnology, in which we have persisted, has in many cases been remedied elsewhere, for in most European countries national pride has found expression in the formation of national collections, and a folk-museum is a prominent and patriotic feature in very many of the Continental cities and towns. I have but to recall those of Berlin, Buda-Pesth, Sarajevo, Moscow, Paris, Helsingfors, Copenhagen, Bergen, Christiania, and last but most important of all, Stockholm. In all these cities (and there are other cases which I do not now recall or with which I am not personally acquainted), a folk-museum exists, either as a separate institution, or as a special department of a more comprehensive museum. These folk-museums and departments are devoted to the preservation of objects of strictly national interest, and serve as repositories in which may be seen and studied not only the domestic and other appliances and the various material relics of bygone centuries, but also characteristic features of the more recent culture and social economy of the peasantry, the backbone of every nation.[20]

The model existed in Stockholm, Balfour told his audience, 'the famous Nordiska Museum in Stockholm, which is not only a magnificent record, but also a splendid monument to its founder and organiser, the late Dr Arthur Hazelius'.[21] But, in the nearly eighty years since Balfour made his appeal, nothing has happened. Precious material has steadily decayed, vanished and gone abroad and there is still no British Museum of Popular Arts and Traditions. Perhaps there never will be. Perhaps there is something in the atmosphere of Britain which prevents it from happening. The moral is presumably that you can take the museum horse to the water, but you cannot make it drink.

Chapter Two
The antiquarians and archaeologists

British Museum, London: *'The most useful institution in the world for savants'*
National Museum, Copenhagen: *'The first step in dispersing the thick fog'*
Pitt-Rivers Museum, Farnham: *'They must learn the links between the past and the present'*
Roman Palace Museum, Fishbourne: *'Keeping the finds on the site where they were discovered'*

'A mere antiquarian', wrote Dr Johnson in a letter to Boswell in 1778, 'is a rugged being'.[1] Of the eight meanings given by Johnson for 'rugged' in his *Dictionary*, the one he intended here was presumably: 'Savage of temper; brutal; rough', which is perhaps another way of saying 'uncivilised', 'unfinished', 'incomplete as a human being'. The immediate occasion of Johnson's remark made at a dinner was the understandable resentment felt by Dr Thomas Percy, the celebrated antiquary and ballad-collector,[2] At Johnson's accusation that he was a narrow-minded person, unable to see his special interests in their wider context. Boswell was able to persuade Johnson that the remark was unjustified and it was later withdrawn, in a fit of generosity which smoothed away the quarrel. After the reconciliation, Johnson admitted to Boswell that 'Percy's attention to poetry has given grace and splendour to his studies of antiquity'. It is a pity that Johnson is not alive and able to make the remark today, since we have been cursed for much too long with the kind of person for whom 'mere antiquarian' would have been a perfect label, people whose interest in the past is totally lacking in the poetic imagination required to give significance and vitality to dead objects. The determination of so many modern archaeologists to see themselves as scientific figures has been in the best interests neither of society nor of themselves. There have been not a few times, when visiting archaeological museums and galleries, that I have longed for the warmth and enthusiasm of the pioneers, who knew so little and felt so much. With the museum situation as fluid as it is at the present time, I think it is very probable that a complete re-orientation of archaeological museums will take place during what remains of the present century, and that we shall see some stimulating new forms of presentation and interpretation aimed at the heart quite as much as the head. It would have been an enormous pleasure to have included such an institution in our select list of Museums of Influence, a museum born out of a successful marriage between humanists and scientists, but it has not yet arrived and so we shall be able to do no more than mention pointers towards it.

It is strange that Johnson's great dictionary, published in 1755, does not include the word 'antiquarian', nor, for that matter, 'archaeology', although both words had been in use since the seventeenth century. 'Archaeologist', however, is a nineteenth-century innovation, a product of the new wish to study the evidence of the past in an organised manner. One is never fully up-to-date in these matters – definitions are slippery things and words are changing their meaning all the time under our very noses – but in 1973 Glyn Daniel felt able to say that archaeology has two meanings, 'the study of the material remains of man's past and the study of the material remains of man's prehistoric past'.[3] This amounts to believing that the archaeologist has most power when he has no competition, when he is dealing with a period in history for which there is no written evidence. In such circumstances, he is on his own, the sole provider of clues as to what may have happened in the past. For Greece, Rome and the Saxon and medieval periods, he has, inescapably, to share the kingdom with the historians.

But the key word in Glyn Daniel's definition is surely 'study'. 'Study' implies something much more than 'discover' or 'collect'. The antiquary or antiquarian may discover and collect, the archaeologist studies, analyses and classifies. For this reason, the words 'antiquary' and 'antiquarian' have for many years had something of a flavour of amateurism and self-indulgence about them, at least among the archaeologists. An archaeologist finds it difficult to regard an antiquarian in anything but a patronising way, 'a mere antiquarian', in fact, although for quite different reasons from those which were important to Dr Johnson. For Johnson, 'mere' meant 'without a poetic, humanising streak', whereas, for the archaeologist, the anti-quarian is 'mere' precisely because he is seen as an all-too-human potterer. There is a delicious irony in the fact that in England the archaeologists' professional body, a body to which I am proud to belong, is called the Society of Antiquaries.[4]

In choosing our Museums of Influence for this chapter we are consequently forced to consider them within two different traditions, that of the antiquarians and collec-tors, and that of the systematisers, the students, the archaeologists. The two cannot, of course, be fully separated. There were plenty of studious, methodically-minded people at work in the eighteenth century and there are archaeological galleries today in which the antiquarians of Johnson's time would have felt very much at home. One might be fairer to both parties by suggesting that the essential difference between an archaeologist and an antiquarian is one of temperament. An archaeologist could perhaps he redefined as a cold antiquarian, and an antiquarian as a warm archaeologist. But there are degrees of heat and cold and a series of fine gradations as the antiquarian shades off into the archaeologist: between, at one end of the scale, those whose prime interest and motivation is collecting and, at the other, those for whom the construction of theories and systems is the aim.

It is, in any case, extremely difficult to deduce motives. The honest historian will admit that he is more likely to fail as a result of attributing the wrong motives to a figure of the past, even the recent past, than for any other single reason. Throughout Western Europe during the sixteenth, seventeenth and eighteenth centuries, people with the money, the time and the inclination were collecting curiosities, works of art and antiquities, but why were they collecting? Were they inspired primarily by greed, by fashion, by a passion for knowledge, by curiosity or by the social cachet which comes from possessions? Or did they bring objects back from their travels in much the same spirit as a modern tourist does, as mementoes of visits to foreign parts?

The Renaissance scholars who revived interest in the classical writers, the dilettanti – 'the people who delighted in the arts' – of fifteenth- and sixteenth-century Italy, the connoisseurs, who filled their homes with Greek and Roman statuary discovered during excavations, the travellers to Italy and Greece who revelled in the antiquities and had as many portable souvenirs as possible transported westwards and north-wards to grace their own houses and gardens, all these antiquarians, at different levels, were operating within a fairly safe and agreed framework. What they dis-covered, bought, moved away and sometimes, perhaps, in the formal sense, studied, could be placed, at least approximately, in time and in relation to known events. Whether such a collector saw a portrait-bust or a piece of carved frieze simply as a work of art or whether it had some sort of archaeological or sociological connotation for him is impossible to say. When, in his London house, he gazed at his Roman statue or his Greek vase, did he say to himself merely, 'This is beautiful', or 'This is valuable', or did it give rise to questions about the kind of society which produced it, questions that he wanted to have answered?

The question is important, because it goes to the heart of what one might call 'the museum problem'. One simply does not know, one cannot predict the effect which any particular object may have on those who see it. Organisers may plan and designers may design, but the public reaction to their efforts can be conditioned only to a limited extent. So, if one says that a given selection of objects, arranged and presented in a certain way, can be reckoned to result, or to have resulted in this or that response from the public, one is behaving with no small degree of arrogance and foolishness. One never really knows what other people think, except in the broadest terms.

I have visited a number of chaotic museums, with not so much displays as a hotch-potch of objects jumbled together, a chaos which the visitors obviously loved, presumably because they felt safe with it. They were free to indulge their fancy and to pick and choose what interested them. Nobody was attempting to influence their thinking or to do their selecting for them. They were their own cultural masters. And I have been, on the other hand, to tightly disciplined, carefully designed museums which frightened customers away, because of the purity and understate-ment of their style. A museum of industry and technology can prove attractive to people who are not in the least interested in industry or technology, but who are fascinated by the shape and complexity of a machine or a piece of apparatus. A costume museum can mean one thing to the person who designed it and something utterly different to a visitor who sees in a display of fashion nothing more than additional evidence of the folly and social irresponsibility of the rich.

Perhaps the main service which a museum can perform for its visitors is to arrange displays which stimulate curiosity. Paradoxically, it does not have to be what the professionals would call 'a good museum' in order to achieve this. Most of the eighteenth-century collections were, in the modern sense of the term, very bad museums. Their owners made little attempt to set out the items attractively or to explain them in any way. That they existed and had been brought together was sufficient to produce a sense of wonder, the excitement of having been brought into contact with the unknown.

It is interesting to observe how important the words 'curious' and 'curiosity' were in the seventeenth and eighteenth centuries, and how their vigour faded during the nineteenth, under the combined pressures of respectability and science. Such a wide range of virtues were reflected by 'curious', which had, before its decline, three different meanings, 'careful, scrupulous, attentive to detail, anxious to produce first-class workmanship', 'eager to learn and to acquire information', and 'likely, by its quality or novelty, to excite interest'. 'Curiosity' was 'painstaking application', it was 'strangeness', it was 'connoisseurship'. The person of intelligence and learning who was not 'curious' was almost impossible to conceive. The fact that today 'curious' means almost exclusively 'strange, odd, queer' tells us a great deal about the culture of our own times. To wish to find out for oneself has become the mark of someone who has chosen to live on the fringe of society.

That the early collectors and antiquaries have not received proper credit is largely, as so often happens, for semantic reasons. When, in 1720, Thomas Hearne published *A Collection of Curious Discoveries by Eminent Antiquaries*, he was giving the highest possible praise to the men who had written these papers. The use of the adjective 'curious' implied that they were painstaking, accurate and eager to discover new facts. In the same way, John Tradescant's Closet of Curiosities, also known as Tradescant's Ark, which became the core of the Ashmolean Museum, did no more than reflect the seventeenth-century assumption that everything was potentially interesting and useful. The formation of such a collection of 'varieties and oddities' was central to the pursuit of knowledge. It was not an eccentric fringe activity.

The Ashmolean, which grew from the Tradescants' bequest, was for many years essentially a Cabinet of Curiosities on the grand scale. Its first catalogue, issued in 1656, makes this conclusion inescapable. Yet, in the form it took after its new building was completed in 1683, it was also the first modern museum, specifically designed to display its collections, organised so that the University could use it for teaching purposes, and regularly open to the public. It was arranged on a tripartite system, with rooms devoted to natural history specimens, antiquities and the inevitable curiosities, and it also had a library, a lecture room and a chemical laboratory. The curators of the different departments were academics, and for nearly two hundred years, the Ashmolean was the main centre of scientific studies in the University.[5]

The museums being created in America towards the end of the eighteenth century were all of the Cabinet of Curiosities type. The Charleston Museum[6] in South Carolina was beginning to assemble its exhibits during the 1770s and within a few years it possessed 'an extensive collection of Beasts, Birds, Reptiles, Fishes, Warlike Arms, Dresses and other Curiosities', by no means all of which had any connection with South Carolina. There were, for instance, a 'Head of a New Zealand Chief', an Egyptian mummy, the bones of an ostrich, a duck-billed platypus, and 'Shoes of the Chinese Ladies, 4 inches long'. Peale's Museum[7] in Philadelphia was not dissimilar. It opened in 1782, primarily as an art museum, but very soon it was expanding into the field of natural history and into strange items of all kinds, including a chicken with four legs and four wings, a turnip weighing 80 pounds, the trigger-finger of a convicted murderer, and a small piece of wood purporting to come from the Coronation Chair in Westminster Abbey.

No matter whether one is thinking of England or America, this was an age in which anything old, exotic or unusual was likely to be interesting so far as the general run of the public was concerned. A museum which contained a good range of exhibits of this kind was on its way to success. There was no point in specialisation, partly because there was insufficient material to make it possible, and partly because most visitors, like most collectors, enjoyed a good spread of interests. Methodical collection, study and arrangement came later, and as a minority taste. Meanwhile, what was old was *ipso facto* interesting.

Glyn Daniel has described the eighteenth-century study of antiquities as 'youthful',[8] and the adjective is well chosen. There was an unmistakable freshness and enthusiasm in the air and a willingness to take new things at their face value, all of which are qualities which characterise the young and incur the suspicion of the old. Victorian England was not youthful, certainly not in the way that Victorian America was, and, if antiquarianism was a natural and appropriate expression of the spirit of the eighteenth century, then archaeology, with its much greater emphasis on order, method and conformity, is a true child of the nineteenth. It would be fair to say that, in its early years, the British Museum had both feet in antiquarianism and one toe in archaeology, a not altogether comfortable position for a national institution to be in, and one which does much to explain the arguments which surrounded it. I do not myself feel able to call the British Museum a Museum of Influence, in the sense that it reflected an original concept and that it had a profound influence on the development and philosophy of other and later museums, but I think it certainly did a great deal to change the attitude of the British public, or at least the London public, towards museums and towards antiquities. Its public impact was considerable, but its influence as an innovator was not remarkable. Its immense size and its position as the unchallenged senior partner in the national museum company have made it difficult for us to assess its achievements in an objective way. Like the Louvre, it is a huge department store, with some departments a good deal more satisfactory than others.

The basic facts about its history are simple enough. The British Museum was created by an Act of Parliament in 1753. Montagu House, in Bloomsbury, was bought for conversion and the Museum opened there in 1759. The great collections of Sir Hans Sloane, together with the manuscripts of Sir Robert Cotton and Robert Harley, Earl of Oxford, formed much of the original basis of the collections. Sloane had wanted them to remain intact and in London, 'where they may by the great confluence of people be of most use'. The money to buy them came, not from the Treasury, but from the proceeds of a lottery. Once the Museum had been founded, Parliament, by providing annual grants on an extremely mean scale, made it difficult to offer a reasonable service to the public. Entry was severely restricted. For many years after the Museum was set up, there was a limit of sixty visitors a day. By 1808 this had gone up to a total of 120, in groups of fifteen, on Mondays, Tuesdays, Wednesdays and Thursdays only, but in 1810 'any person of decent appearance' was admitted between ten and four on Mondays, Wednesdays and Fridays, and permitted to 'tarry in the apartments or the Gallery of Antiquities without any limitation of time, except the shutting of the house at four o'clock'.

Daily opening was not brought in until 1879, and as late as 1836 the Principal Librarian, Sir Henry Ellis, found no difficulty in defending his decision to keep the Museum shut on Saturdays, Sundays and public holidays, on the grounds that it was his duty to keep out 'the vulgar class', such as 'sailors from the dockyards and girls whom they might bring in with them'.

The Porter, the real centre of power at the British Museum.

Without private benefactions, the Museum's collections would hardly have increased at all although, under pressure, Parliament did make grants from time to time specifically for a few exceptionally important purchases, the chief of which were the Greek and Roman vases belonging to Sir William Hamilton, in 1772; the Townley Marbles, in 1804 and 1814; the Lansdowne manuscripts, in 1807; the Greville collection of minerals in 1810 and the Elgin Marbles, in 1814–15. It was the acquisition of the Elgin Marbles which, more than anything else, gave the Museum its international reputation within the field of classical antiquities, although for some time the Marbles had to be kept in a shed in the garden, for want of space to display them.

In the elegant surroundings of Montagu House, the British Museum was hardly a place of popular entertainment. A large part of what was on display consisted of manuscripts, books, coins and medals, although the atmosphere would have been enlivened here and there by such items as Egyptian mummies, a vulture's head preserved in spirits, a cyclops pig, and one of the horns which had grown out of the

A minimum of interpretation: *Tom and Bob in search of the Antique*.

head of a certain Mary Davies, whose portrait, showing her with both horns, was on the wall above. The British Museum was still very much a cabinet of rarities and curiosities.

Until the mid-nineteenth century, such influence as the Museum may have had is likely to have stemmed as much from its new building, the first stage of which was completed in 1823, as from its collections or the way in which it displayed them. A new building was certainly needed. Montagu House had become impossibly over-crowded and the classification and arrangement of the collections was, to put it kindly, chaotic. The British Museum had nothing to teach the world in either of these matters. So far as the collections were concerned, the strength of the Museum was not in art or antiquities, but in manuscripts and books and in natural history. In natural history, however, the Museum was no better than anywhere else in the ordering and display of its natural history specimens. The pioneers there were, as it happened, both museums in Britain, the Hunterian Museum in Glasgow, which was replanned and rehoused by William Stark in 1804, and the Hunterian Gallery at the Royal College of Surgeons, in Lincoln's Inn Fields, which received George Dance's skilled and imaginative attentions between 1806 and 1813.

The new British Museum: Sir Robert Smirke's temple. During 1851, the year of the Great Exhibition, 2½ million visitors passed through this portico.

There was nothing particularly courageous about Sir Robert Smirke's new building for the British Museum, which was carried out very predictably, in the Greek Revival style. This style was gaining favour everywhere at that time, not only in England. It is easy to understand why. Museums had come to be regarded as temples, which existed in order to create a reverent attitude towards their contents. Given this aim, it is not surprising that architects should have attempted to build museums in the form of temples. A recent historian of the British Museum has pointed out that 'the Grecian columns of the British Museum can be matched – in style, not in number – in almost every capital city in the world'.[9] Throughout the nineteenth century, hundreds of classical museums, art galleries and libraries were

A notable British temple of the arts. The entrance hall of the Fitzwilliam Museum, Cambridge.

built throughout Europe and in America, each one confirming the attitude of governments, architects and the public that this was the only proper and fitting kind of design for a museum. The museum building was itself a museum, the essential image of the museum idea.

The most influential early examples on the Continent were both in Germany, the Glyptothek in Munich (1816–30) and the Altes Museum, Berlin (1825–8). The British Museum is only the best known British example of the crop of these temples of the arts which could be found throughout the country by the end of the century. It did not begin the fashion, but it certainly reinforced and encouraged it. The list even of the most prestigious buildings of the temple type in Britain is a long one –

the Hunterian Museum, Glasgow (1804); the City Art Gallery, Manchester (1823); the Ashmolean Museum, Oxford (1841–5); the Royal Scottish Academy (1822–6 and 1932–5); the National Gallery (1832–8); the Fitzwilliam Museum, Cambridge (1937–75); the Scottish National Gallery (1850–7); the Harris Free Library and Art Gallery, Preston (1882–93); the Tate Gallery (1897).

Where the British Museum really was a pioneer in the field of museum architecture was not in its façade or its exhibition galleries, but in the design of its library and reading-room, the parts of the building intended for scholars, not for the general public. The iron-framed Round Reading Room, completed in 1857, was Sydney Smirke's masterpiece.[10] Its efficiency and immense prestige exercised an influence on library planning throughout the world. The Library of Congress (1897) and the Prussian State Library in Berlin (1914) are its most famous children.

A library building cannot, of course, be dissociated from the books it contains and there can be little doubt that the development of the British Museum Library during the middle years of the last century did at least as much to give the Museum its international reputation as what went on in the Museum itself. Its growth was entirely due to the determination, persistence and vision of Sir Antonio Panizzi,[11] who was appointed Keeper of Printed Books in 1837 and Principal Librarian in 1856, a post he held until his retirement in 1866. Panizzi graduated as a lawyer in Italy and came to England in 1823, at the age of 26. When he was first appointed to the Department of Printed Books in 1831, the Library contained 240,000 volumes, many fewer than the Bibliothèque Royale in Paris, and less than the main libraries of Berlin, Dresden, Munich, Copenhagen and Vienna. The Government failed to take the Library seriously. In no year between 1820 and 1824 was the annual pur-chase grant more than £300. Panizzi decided to push and shame Parliament into acting in a way more appropriate to the richest and most powerful country in Europe. In his evidence to the Select Committee on the British Museum, which conducted its hearings in 1836, he said: 'I want a poor student to have the same means of indulging his learned curiosity, of following his rational pursuits, of consulting the same authorities, of fathoming the most intricate inquiry as the richest man in the kingdom, as far as books go, and I contend that the Government is bound to give him the most liberal and unlimited assistance in this respect'.[12] Despite continuous bickering and opposition and immense frustrations, the Principal Librarian lived to see his aims fulfilled. During his reign, the collections of the General Library were greatly increased in size, the organisation and cataloguing overhauled, the develop-ment of the collection of maps, music, newspapers and English and foreign official publications established on sound lines and important foreign sections developed.

In 1861, Thomas Watts, Panizzi's assistant, recalled their policy over the previous quarter of a century. It had been to 'bring together from all quarters the useful, the elegant and the curious literature of every language; to unite with the best English Library in England or the world, the best Russian Library out of Russia, the best

The frame of the British Museum's Reading Room in course of erection in 1855.

Reinforcing the glass-case image. One of the British Museum's ethnography galleries *c.* 1900. If the British Museum presented the collections in this way, how could lesser institutions fail to do so?

German out of Germany . . . and so with every language from Italian to Icelandic, from Polish to Portuguese . . . I have the pleasure of reflecting that every former student of the less-known literatures of Europe will find riches where I found poverty'.[13] A special effort was made to build up the collection of American works, and by 1873 this was acknowledged to be superior to any that could be found in America itself.

What we are discussing is something which would be known today as the image of the British Museum. In the days when Sir Henry Ellis, Panizzi's predecessor, was Principal Librarian, that is, Director of the Museum, the image was unquestionably one of inefficiency, poverty, chaos and élitism, a situation reflected in part by William Cobbett's attack on the Museum in a House of Commons speech as 'a place intended only for the amusement of the curious and the rich', and by Sir Henry's own comment that 'the Museum library is rather too much than too little used'.

But overall progress at the Museum was exceedingly slow. Until the 1960s, there was an atmosphere of almost continual crisis. Money was always desperately short and the building was soon shown to be not only too small but ill-planned for its purpose. Some breathing space was given in 1875 when the natural history collections were moved out into a new building in South Kensington. It was here that the second director, Sir William Flower, was able to institute what the British Museum at Bloomsbury had never had, a logical division into conservation, research and display.

One might say, with considerable justification, that a great deal of both whitewashing and brainwashing has gone on so far as the British Museum is concerned. Much the same has happened in the case of the Louvre. Because it is so big, because its possessions are so enormous and so wonderful, the legend has therefore grown up that it has always been innovative, well-managed, efficient and at the service of the public. Would only that it had been so. There is no doubt that it is a vastly better place today than it was a hundred or a hundred and fifty years ago, but this is not to alter the fact that, museologically and museographically, the most significant changes and improvement have come, not from the British Museum and from museum giants, but from more modest establishments.

This is certainly true so far as archaeology is concerned. The most significant archaeological event of the nineteenth century was probably the development of the Three Age system of prehistory, the division of prehistory into an age of stone, an age or copper or bronze, and an age of iron. The system was established in Denmark between 1800 and 1850 and cleared away the confusion which had previously surrounded the study of all pre-Roman remains. Before this happened, excavators in France and Britain had been digging up great quantities of prehistoric artefacts, without being able to understand their significance or to put them into any kind of time-sequence. The blanket use of words like 'Celtic', 'Gallic', 'Ancient British' and

'Druid' indicated the despairing situation in which even informed antiquaries found themselves at the turn of the century, a situation in which the results of their excavations were stored and set out in museums without any idea of the age of the objects. The British Museum was no worse than any other in this respect.

In 1806 Professor Rasmus Nyerup, the Librarian of the University of Copenhagen, published a book, the English title of which was *A Survey of the National Monuments of Antiquity*.[14] Professor Nyerup had already formed a small museum of Danish antiquities at the University and in his book he recommended that a Danish National Museum of Antiquities should be set up, on a much larger scale than had been within his power to achieve as a private individual. The government agreed and in 1807 a Royal Commission was entrusted with the task of establishing such a museum, with Nyerup as its Secretary. The expanding collections of the new National Museum were carefully studied by scholars, one of whom was Vedel-Simonsen, who in 1813 was the first to publish the new theory of the Three Ages of prehistory,[15] in what has become a classic statement.

'To begin with,' he wrote, 'the weapons and tools used by the earliest people in Scandinavia were made of stone and wood. Later, copper came to be used and, later still, iron. So, on this basis, the development of their culture can be divided into three ages, an age of stone, an age of copper and an age of iron. These ages were not precisely and definitely separated from each other. They overlapped, and there can be no doubt that the poorer members of the community continued to have to make use of stone tools after the introduction of copper, and copper after iron became available.'

In 1816 Christian Jürgensen Thomsen took over the Secretaryship of the Commission from Nyerup and became at the same time the first Curator of the National Museum, a post he held until his death, nearly fifty years later. He arranged the collections, which were very inadequately housed in the University Library, on the basis of the successive ages of stone, bronze and iron. The Museum, the first archaeological museum anywhere to be organised systematically, was opened to the public in 1819. Thomsen himself was always present during the hours when the Museum was open and he spent much time taking visitors round and explaining the collections to them.

After a few years, the collections had expanded to such an extent that new accommodation had become essential, and the museum was transferred to part of the royal palace, Christiansborg, where each of the Three Ages had a room to itself. The establishment of the National Museum, especially in its new home at Christiansborg, was, in Glyn Daniel's well-judged words, 'the first step in dispersing the thick fog, the first step from the ignorance of antiquarianism to the knowledge of archaeology'.[16] Professor Daniel has been a stout defender of the right of the Danes, especially Thomsen and his one-time assistant, J. J. A. Worsaae,[17] to be considered

Thomsen explaining an object from the Museum's collection to a group of visitors (drawing by Magnus Pederson, 1845).

Christian Jürgensen Thomsen, the first Curator of the National Museum, Copenhagen, as he was in 1849 (drawing by J. W. Gertner).

Title-page of the 1836 guide to the National Museum, Copenhagen's collections, subsequently published in England as *A Guide to Northern Antiquities* (1848).

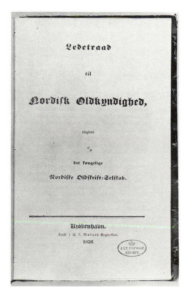

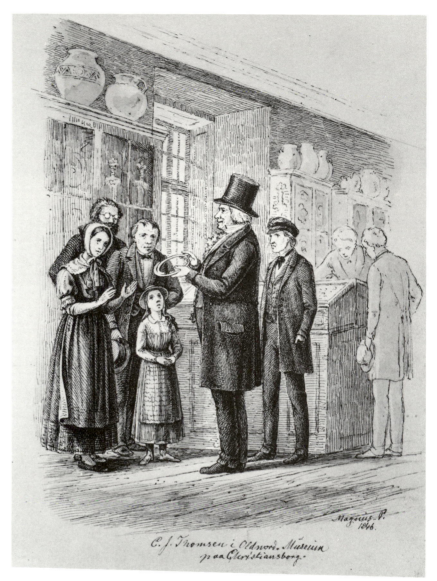

the originators of the Three Age theory. He has no doubt that 'the Copenhagen Museum *Guide* of 1836 and Worsaae's *Primeval Antiquities* are probably the most important archaeological works produced in the first half of the nineteenth century'.[18] The fact that English and German translations of both works appeared soon after the original publication must have greatly facilitated the rapid spread of the new theory, since Danish was not a widely read language.[19]

From the beginning, Thomsen, at the National Museum, paid special attention to

country people who visited the museum – 'peasants', in the terminology of the time
– on the not unreasonable grounds that these were the people who were most likely
to discover prehistoric material, in the course of working their fields. It was therefore
sensible to inspire and instruct as many of them as possible by providing them with
a knowledge of the importance of the discoveries which they might make on their
farms from time to time. It would not be unfair to Thomsen, however, to say that the
main purpose of his museum was to advance the cause of scholarship and that the
education of the general public was secondary.

The first person to establish an archaeological-cum-ethnographical museum, a
museum planned to illustrate the worldwide development of human culture and to
do so specifically for educational purposes, was Lieutenant-General Pitt-Rivers,
born in 1827 and for much of his life a professional soldier. In the course of his
professional duties, he became an authority on rifles and wrote the Army's standard
manual on rifle training. The technical progress in the design of firearms interested
him and he formed a collection of guns, to illustrate their historical development.
Gradually he extended his collection, first to include other types of weapon, then
tools and eventually a wide range of ethnographical material. As his collection grew,
he began to establish a theory, which he called the Evolution of Culture, and
delivered a celebrated lecture on this subject in 1875. He had been much influenced
by Charles Darwin's *Origin of Species*, which appeared in 1859, and became a friend
of both Darwin and of his great supporter, Thomas Huxley.

By the mid-1870s, his collection of ethnographical and anthropological items had
outgrown the accommodation he was able to provide for it in his own house, and it
went, first, to the Bethnal Green branch of the South Kensington Museum and then,
in 1883, to the University of Oxford, where, in the Pitt-Rivers Museum, the 14,000
items were arranged according to the evolutionary principles which he considered to
be central to scientific thinking in these fields.

In 1864, he began to extend his interests to the study of antiquities. This involved a
great deal of excavation, in the first place as a means of refining the 'typology' – the
word was his own – of material culture and of discovering significant new objects to
add to his collection. Very soon, however, he came to realise that the finds which
appeared in the course of the excavations could, and should, be used to throw light
on the culture of the people who had created the sites which he was excavating. Once
that point had been reached, the dividing line between archaeology on the one hand
and ethnology and anthropology on the other had ceased to exist.

In 1880 he inherited the Rushmore Estate, in Cranborne Chase, on the borders of
Dorset and Wiltshire, and spent the remaining twenty years of his life excavating
and studying its rich archaeological remains. Our primary concern here is with the
museum he created on the estate, rather than with the antiquities and research which
fed it, but, since the museum only makes sense within the general context of Pitt-

Rivers' archaeological achievements, it is necessary to indicate briefly what these were.

He was a pioneer in four ways. First, his primary aim, unlike those of his prede-cessors and most of his contemporaries, was to recover information, not to acquire beautiful and valuable antiquities. This view of the archaeologist's task is encapsu-lated in his celebrated remark that 'the value of relics, viewed as evidence, may be said to be in an inverse ratio to their intrinsic value'.[20] By this he meant that clues, however small, to the everyday life of the people who lived on the site were what mattered most. Second, he was careful to record his finds in detail, relating them to accurate plans of the site. Thirdly, he studied and analysed his finds with the sole purpose of building up a better understanding of the life of our ancestors. To this end, he carried out many practical experiments, such as knapping flints, digging with bone and antler tools, and throwing boomerangs. He measured modern animals and their bones in order to be able to make comparisons with the animal bones found during his excavations. And, fourthly, he made his discoveries and conclusions available to everyone, partly in handsome volumes published at his own expense and partly in the museum he created at Farnham, Dorset.

Nothing like the Farnham Museum and its setting had ever been seen before. It contained anthropological and social history collections, as well as archaeological objects from Cranborne Chase and elsewhere, and it was surrounded by the Larmer Grounds, which offered visitors a remarkable range of leisure activities, an art gallery, a bandstand, Indian houses bought from the Great Exhibition, golf links, a racecourse, an open-air theatre, picnic facilities and an enclosure containing exotic wild animals. Everything was calculated to bring people to the museum, often from a considerable distance, in order that they might educate themselves.

Pitt-Rivers made a sharp contrast between his own museum and the British Museum.[21] It would be difficult to better his analysis of the kind of place which the British Museum had come to be. It had begun, he said, as 'pretty much what local museums have hitherto been, a collection of miscellaneous antiquities', then its collections had been 'enlarged and classified in historical grand divisions or geo-graphical areas'. It had always, however, collected on an *ad hoc* basis, 'as opportunity offered', and its displays were in 'rooms that are ill-adapted for displaying them historically, designed in subordination to architectural considerations'. As an educational museum, it was 'simply bewildering', but 'as a large store of antiquities, it is probably the most useful institution in the world for savants, who know what to look for and where to study them, in order to form their own classifications and deductions'. It is a conclusion with which it is difficult to disagree.

Pitt-Rivers put a clear label on the British Museum. 'I call such a museum a Museum of Reference', he said, 'or it might, perhaps, more properly be termed, a Museum of Research'. What he was trying to create on his estate was entirely different, 'an educational museum, in which the visitors may instruct themselves'. In doing this, he was motivated mainly by political considerations, which he took no trouble to conceal. 'We have thought proper to place political power in the hands of the masses. The masses are ignorant, and knowledge is swamped by ignorance. The relative numbers of the educated and uneducated are enough to ensure this. The knowledge they lack is the knowledge of history. This lays them open to the designs of demagogues and agitators, who strive to make them break with the past, and seek the remedies for existing evils, or the means of future progress, in drastic changes that have not the sanction of experience. It is by a knowledge of history only that such experience can be supplied.'[22]

One of General Pitt-Rivers' 'inducements'. Visitors at the Larmer Grounds, Farnham, listening to the Entertainments at the Theatre on Whit Monday, 1899.

Lieutenant-General Pitt-Rivers as a young man.
'My private band' at the Pitt-Rivers Museum, Farnham.

To nip revolution in the bud, the working-man had to be introduced to the principles of evolution, to 'the law that Nature makes no jumps'. He must be shown that all man-made objects follow in an ascertainable sequence, and that improvements are being made all the time. A museum should organise its displays with this and only this in mind. In the Pitt-Rivers Museum at Farnham, opened in 1885 in a building which had formerly been a school for gypsies, the exhibits were arranged in eight rooms, five quite small, about 20 feet by 18, and the remaining three much larger. Four rooms contained miscellaneous ethnographical material, especially pottery, tools and household objects. In the fifth and sixth were 'models of excavations made by me in the locality, the relics from which are arranged in the adjoining cases', together with 'models of ancient monuments, 95 in all, made under my supervision by my archaeological staff'. These models, said the General, 'certainly form the chief feature of the museum, and they are unique'. The sixth room also displayed prehistoric, Roman, Egyptian and medieval implements.

The seventh room continued the archaeological exhibits and the eighth was devoted to agricultural implements and equipment, to the development of locks and keys, and to 'a series of crates carried by country women of different countries on the shoulder, and collected expressly to show the women of my district how little they resemble the beasts of burden they might have been if they had been bred elsewhere'.

The Museum was open seven days a week and admission was free. During 1890–1, the recreation ground, 'where my private band plays every Sunday in the summer months from three to five', was visited by 16,839 people. King John's hunting lodge, 'where any amount of bread and butter, tea and buns can be obtained at slight cost', drew 4,346 visitors, and the Museum 7,000. 'The people', the General noted, 'come from a radius of 20 miles around', many of them by bicycle – 'the enormous distances bicyclists can go by road, especially on a Sunday, has rendered the population of country districts locomotive to an extent that has never been known before'.

The museum world has not known many geniuses. General Pitt-Rivers must certainly be reckoned to be one of them. He was a long way ahead of his time in realising that, in order to appeal to the general public, a museum had to have something more than interesting collections to offer. It had to meet the common man half-way, especially by arousing an interest in the practical aspects of life in the past and in other cultures. And there had to be what the General termed 'inducements'. The museum pill needed to be sugared. 'The outing', he was sure, 'is in itself an important accessory in a visit to a country museum. A pretty country, a pleasant drive in their country carts, an attractive pleasure ground, a good band, and lastly a museum, are the means which I have found to be successful.' The selling-power of A Good Day Out for All the Family is well enough understood today in the museum world – Beamish and Ironbridge depend on it – but it was a great novelty in the 1880s.

As I have tried to show, there are several good reasons for including Farnham in our list of Museums of Influence, but for the much more recent Roman Palace Museum at Fishbourne, near Chichester in Sussex, there is just one. It established a new standard for what an archaeological site-museum could and should be, an extremely popular museum, based on scholarship of the highest quality, which does not talk down to its visitors and which gives every impression of putting their interests first.

Fishbourne was an important Roman harbour, first developed during the period A.D. 43–75 as a military supply base, and occupied until the end of the third century. Between A.D. 75 and 100, a large and sumptuous palace was constructed close to the harbour. Barry Cunliffe, who excavated the site in the 1960s, believes it is probable that the palace was built for a native king, known, in the Romanised form of his name, as Tiberius Claudius Cogidubnus, who helped the Romans during their invasion of Britain and who was allowed to retain his position as a consequence, continuing to rule his people, but within the framework of what had become a Roman province.

The excavation, which was spread over a period of seven years, was sponsored, not by the Government, but by Chichester Civic Society, and financed by grants from a number of bodies, including the British Academy, the Society of Antiquaries and the Ministry of Public Building and Works. It was a shoe-string excavation which would never have happened if an ample supply of volunteer labour had not been available. The professional element in the team was very small.

The entire North wing of the Roman palace is now protected by a modern building, largely paid for by a private individual, Ivan Margary, beneath which the original mosaic floors and the lower part of the walls are displayed, with walkways to allow the details to be clearly seen. At one end of the shelter-building, there is a museum, where all the finds from the excavation are displayed and the history and significance of the site explained. The exhibition was originally conceived and sponsored by *The Sunday Times* in 1968.[23] Ten years later, the display was refurbished and brought up to date by the Fishbourne Executive Committee, which administers the site on behalf of the owners, the Sussex Archaeological Society.

As visitors move around the roofed-over excavations, they are offered explanations, in English, French and German, of the most significant features in front of them. Great care has been taken to make these texts clear and straightforward, while at the same time providing all the essential information. Here is an example:

> A mosaic floor put down at the beginning of the second century over an
> earlier black and white mosaic, which can still be seen in patches
> beneath it (much as some people today lay a new linoleum over old).
> The upper floor has a Medusa head in the centre, surrounded by a
> curious mass of geometric motifs laid out by inexperienced craftsmen.
> As the irregular shapes show, they made many mistakes. The ruts
> running across the floor were gouged by medieval ploughing.

Left The introductory museum at Fishbourne, containing finds from the excavations.

Right Viewing system for the mosaics at Fishbourne.

During its first year, 1968–9, Fishbourne attracted 250,000 visitors, an indication of both its novelty and its quality. In recent years, it has settled down to about half that number, but the figure is still remarkable for such a highly specialised museum. It is always possible, of course, that so many people come to Fishbourne precisely because it is so specialised, so compact and so readily understandable. What might be termed the Fishbourne recipe – making sense of history where it happened and baiting the hook by keeping the finds on the site where they were discovered – has proved extremely attractive in recent years. One can observe the same method successfully applied at, for instance, the Bryggens Museum, Bergen, where part of medieval Bergen has been revealed and interpreted; at Roskilde, Denmark, where Viking ships are on display; and at Pischeldorf, near Klagenfurt, in Austria, where a cluster of mini-museums has been established on the site of a large hillside town. Nowadays, in the mid-1980s, we take this kind of museum almost for granted, ungratefully forgetting the international impact which Fishbourne had as a pioneer in the 1960s. The achievement at Fishbourne falls into three parts – keeping the excavations permanently visible, holding on to the finds, and interpreting everything in a way which would be appealing and intelligible to a wide range of people. It was the combination of all three which made Fishbourne different. Previously it was assumed that all excavation finds would be removed to what might euphemistically be called a host museum, for safety, convenience, conservation and scholarly investigation. So, to think only of one or two British examples, what was found at Meare Lake Village is now in the County Museum, Taunton; the Maiden Castle material is in Dorchester Museum; and what is popularly known as the Sutton Hoo Treasure is in the British Museum. But suppose these places had received the

Reconstruction of part of the Romano-British garden at Fishbourne.

A room at the Palace, reconstructed from evidence gathered in the course of excavations.

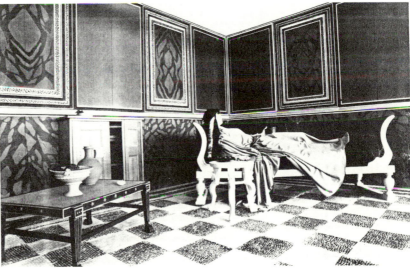

Fishbourne treatment. A really good site-museum at all three would have been inspiring and a splendid tourist attraction. The reason why matters were arranged differently can be stated quite plainly. Meare, Maiden Castle and Sutton Hoo were excavated and the finds removed elsewhere before the Fishbourne concept of site-museums got under way. Since then, however, the situation has changed radically.

It is now recognised that, in museums as in other types of institution, size can no longer be automatically equated with quality. In Victorian times and, indeed, until very recently, it was accepted that big museums had a Divine right to suck in more and more of the world's cultural products and to become steadily larger by the month. They were, in fact, and still are, gigantic warehouses, with showrooms to give customers an idea of what was in stock. It was an atmosphere in which it was almost impossible for site-museums to flourish. The movement of the goods into the warehouses was inexorable and unchallenged.

What, more than any other factor, brought about a revolution in thinking was the growth of the industrial archaeology movement from the mid-sixties onwards. This will be discussed more fully in a later chapter, but for the moment it is sufficient to say that the view of the industrial archaeologists was that, wherever possible, the historical objects and their context should be preserved together, since both were needed for a full understanding of what happened in history. This thinking gradually spread to other fields. A mosaic pavement at Fishbourne would have lost impact and sense if it had been rolled up and taken to London. Outside Nigeria, the Benin bronze has become anaemic and denaturalised, a mere art object. The Elgin Marbles are one thing in the British Museum; they would become something quite different if they were to be returned to the Parthenon.

A surprisingly high proportion of the world's museums could nowadays be described as site-museums. This would certainly not have been the case even fifty years ago. They range from museums in the former homes of the great to museums in coalmines, from cathedral treasuries to water-pumping stations, but they are all, in their different ways, what I have called 'museums of history where it happened'. There are, according to my last count, about 2,200 museums in the British Isles. Of these, about 20 per cent could claim to be site-museums. It is a high figure, but it can be paralleled in other countries and during the next twenty years or so I am sure it will rise. The site-museum is a child of the motorcar and the motorcoach. With rare exceptions, every site-museum is a place of pilgrimage. The people who go to such places have made an effort to do so. They are not there by accident or to get out of the rain or because they can think of nothing better to do and, for this reason, they can be reckoned to be rather above average in curiosity and interest, if not in intelligence and education. Site-museums seem to be most successful when they are located in a pleasant area, where people enjoy going anyway, and when their theme is clear and simple. Fishbourne, like the Viking Ship Museum at Roskilde and the Bryggens Museum at Bergen, meets all these requirements.

One should, however, make a clear distinction between a site-museum and an interpretation centre. The first, in order to be a true example of the breed, must be built around objects discovered on the site or very closely associated with it. The second need be little more than a book taken to pieces and put up around the walls of a room, with no original objects to bring it to life and to give it point and meaning. There are today far too many interpretation centres masquerading as site-museums. Fishbourne is the genuine article. Farnham was half a site-museum and half something else. Its real merits, which were very great, were rooted in the motives of the man who created it.

Chapter Three
Temples of art

Central Art Museum, Paris:	*'Each work was provided with an explanatory text, for the instruction of the people'*
Altes Museum, Berlin:	*'To honour the arts in a museum-palace'*
Victoria and Albert Museum, London:	*'Housed in a museum which was one of its own exhibits'*
Metropolitan Museum, New York:	*'We shall be able to outbid the world'*
Museum of Modern Art, New York:	*'Few Americans care to argue with a hundred million dollars'*

There have always been two main reasons for a private individual to accumulate possessions: a love of the objects themselves and a satisfaction in the social prestige they confer. The two motives are never easy to disentangle but, when in doubt, it is probably wiser to go for the second. Certainly, to regard all, or even a majority, of the more celebrated art collectors of the past four hundred years as connoisseurs would be generous to the point of flattery. Many of them undoubtedly collected simply because, at the level of society to which they belonged, it was fashionable to do so. Others inherited collections from fathers who were more discriminating and more genuinely interested than they were themselves. A few, during the past century, have assuredly considered works of art chiefly as a sound form of investment, with the market value of a painting or whatever as its most important quality.

Most public art galleries have had their origins in private collections, but by no means all collectors have been art-lovers in the sense that Thomas Howard, 2nd Earl of Arundel was. Born in 1585, married to the daughter of Gilbert, 7th Earl of Shrewsbury, one of the most distinguished of the Elizabethan patrons of the arts, he learned Italian as a young man and developed a great fondness for Italy and its culture. He built up a superlative collection of paintings and drawings and, as David Howarth has commented, 'perceived as no other Englishman before that arts and learning added to the dignity of great men'.[1] He was, Howarth goes on to say, 'the first great art collector in this country to see a connection between life and art, manners and actions, collecting and ethics'. The connection had already been noted elsewhere, more particularly in Italy and, to a lesser extent, in France, in the Netherlands and in parts of the German-speaking countries, but it would be rash to generalise and to say that, in well-to-do households, the possession of works of art was necessarily associated with a high level of personal culture. It was quite as likely to have been a mark of social status.

And, in any case, one needs to ask, 'which works of art?' The Renaissance turned

39

for inspiration to Greece and Rome because it was trying to break out of the fetters of the Middle Ages, and to collect the sculpture of these past cultures was evidence that one's thinking and aspirations followed the new pattern. To revere the antique was, paradoxically, to prove oneself modern, and it is by no means impossible that the rediscovery of Roman art and Roman art collections, which included, of course, Greek works, brought with it something of the Roman attitude to art, which was by no means purely aesthetic. As Germain Bazin has observed, 'the position of the Romans regarding works of art can be compared to that of contemporary Americans in relation to masterpieces produced by Western civilisation. To assemble these at great expense constituted an element of prestige associated with power and wealth.'[2]

Art, in other words, represented conspicuous wealth and, in the aristocratic residences of Western Europe and in the town and country houses of the increasingly prosperous middle classes, large art collections were steadily building up during the seventeenth and eighteenth centuries. Quantity was quite as important as quality. The superabundant display scheme prevailed. Superabundance increased the value of the objects.

But, until the twentieth century, in order to form an impressive art collection, one did not need to be super-rich. The main reason for this was that there was not a great deal of spare money about. 'The great fortunes of pre-industrial Europe', Robert Hughes reminds us, 'were land-rich but, relatively, cash-poor.'[3] As the amount of spendable money increased enormously, which it did after the end of the Second World War, rich people began to buy works of art on an unprecedented scale, partly in order to have something to spend their money on and partly as an investment, a chance to profit by inflation. The supply of old paintings and pieces of sculpture rapidly became exhausted, so driving up the price still further, and contemporary works, some by artists of real talent and some by artists of no great merit at all, whom the critics and dealers combined to make celebrated and desirable, were at hand to fill the gap.

'At forty-five', Robert Hughes sighs, 'I am among the last generation that conducted its basic art training in empty museums, without ever thinking about the cost of their contents. And although I am grateful for the volume of scholarly attention that the art market has helped to direct on art, I cannot help feeling a twinge of regret – not to say an occasional surge of nausea – at the way in which the monetary value of museum art has been moved to the forefront of people's experience. Twenty-five years ago it was easier to appreciate works of art in their true quality: what the masterpiece, laden with fetishistic value, has lost today is a certain freedom of access – a buoyancy, an availability to the eye and to the mind. It has been invested with a spurious authority, like the façade of a bank.'[4]

The history of the art museum seems, then, to have passed through these stages.

Beginning as a private collection, formed for reasons of prestige or out of genuine interest, it became a display to which the public had access. At the beginning of the nineteenth century, the items in the museum began to be organised in a systematic way and the general public was invited to participate in the world of art, as seen and analysed by the new race of art historians. Gradually, from about the middle of the nineteenth century onwards, men who had been successful in commerce or industry began to support the arts financially and, aided and abetted by the dealers, to influence the art market to the point at which buying outstanding examples of yesterday's art was entirely a pastime of rich individuals and rich institutions. Coinciding with this phase is the process whereby certain contemporary artists develop into cult figures, with financial consequences which further distort the market and undermine cultural judgement. Finally, the stage at which we find ourselves today, a reaction has set in and a new generation of museum curators attempts to present works of art in a way which will bypass the obsession with money values and make it possible once again to think about a work of art in terms of the artist and of the society in which he lives and works. Within the 200 years during which this process has been taking place, the Museums of Influence could be said to be those which have, for better or for worse, played a major rôle in encouraging change. They will not, of course, have been solely responsible for directing art museums in a new direction. It is fairer, indeed, to regard them as the agents or servants of society at a particular time. A museum, like a politician or a playwright, responds to the public mood, yet it may well intensify and give respectability to that mood.

The Musée Français, later to be renamed the Musée Central des Arts or Musée Napoléon and later still the Musée du Louvre, has already been mentioned in Chapter 1.[5] The fact that it existed at all was a consequence of the Revolution, which had nationalised the property of the Church and religious establishments, and of Napoleon's campaigns, which swept the artistic treasures of Europe into the booty-waggons of the conquerors. Paintings, in general, were preferred to sculpture, because they were lighter, more portable, and less likely to be damaged in transit. But these acquisitions had to be legitimised and justified, and this was achieved by emphasising the educational purpose of the Museum. To begin with the paintings were arranged according to what were known as 'Schools'. 'School' is not an unsatisfactory term when it relates to the pupils or disciples of a particular artist – 'the School of Rubens' has a certain reasonableness and validity – but it is unhelpful and makes little sense when it is made to refer to a whole country, as in 'the Spanish School', or 'the French School'. To lump all Spanish painters together in this way is as peculiar a habit as it would be to pretend that all Spanish writers have some marked feature in common, some unmistakable quality which distinguishes them from all French or Bulgarian writers. However, the Louvre, if we may use the Museum's more convenient and widely understood modern name, decided to organise and display its paintings according to four Schools, the Italian, the Flemish,

41

the Dutch and the French. Because Napoleon had failed to cross the Channel, there was, of course, no English School. So far as the Louvre was concerned, English painting did not exist.

Under the Directory (1795–9), a more systematic approach was followed, but still within the general framework of the four Schools. Each work was given an explanatory text, which gave information about the artist and the subject. This was an entirely new procedure. No previous museum had attempted to present and interpret its pictures in this way, because it was assumed that all visitors were well informed, or would pretend to be, and because it was felt that the impression a painting made, either individually or as part of the overall effect of a mass of pictures covering a wall, was the most important thing about it.[6]

Another innovation was to prepare and put on sale a cheap catalogue and guide which helped members of the public to find their way around the Museum and drew attention to some of the more important and interesting things to be seen in it.[7] The Louvre took its new duties very seriously. It was to be a 'people's museum', which everyone was entitled to visit as a right and without charge, in contrast to the usual practice hitherto of restricting entry to educated people, whose interest and good behaviour could be assumed. Everything possible was done to make clear that the new Museum was a public institution, not a private collection. Administratively and legally, it formed part of the State education system.

The new system was, one should remember, confined for the time being to Paris. There were no mini-Louvres in Lyon, Bordeaux or Marseilles. But the size and range of the collections in the Louvre, together with the deliberate and painstaking educational and democratic approach, made Paris for a while, probably until the 1820s, the museological capital of the world. In more ways than one, the Louvre was a revolutionary establishment.

Ironically, one of the most profound and widespread influences of the French Revolution and its aftermath concerns something which was never put into practice. Between 1790 and 1820, French architects devoted a great deal of attention to the development of a style and type of building which would relate specifically to museums. Many designs were made and published.[8] None were actually built – they were purely theoretical – but they were, even so, known about and discussed by architects in other countries, especially Germany, and they undoubtedly influenced museum-building elsewhere. The designs had certain common features. All of them were single-storeyed, cross-shaped and windowless on the outside walls. All made provision for both art and scientific collections.

The German contribution to the development of art museums during the nineteenth century was very strong and in some ways regrettable. In the eighteenth century, art collections had been concentrated in the princely Residences in the autonomous territories, with Berlin and Vienna in the lead. The picture galleries were arranged in such a way as to make each wall present an agreeable design. Towards the end of the century, they began to be reorganised according to Schools, but without abandoning the design principle.

In the 1780s and 1790s, Prussia had to forget museum-building for a while, because its finances had been severely weakened by war. Meanwhile, the Romantics were beginning to regard art as a religion, or at least as an element of religion. A typical expression of this attitude is to be found in a work by Wackenrode and Tieck, published in 1797. 'A picture gallery', they said, 'appears to be thought of as a fair, whereas what it should be is a temple, a temple where, in silent and unspeaking humility and in inspiring solitude, one may admire artists as the highest among mortals.'[9]

'Temple of art' – 'Tempel der Kunst' – was a phrase frequently employed by adherents of the new movement. It did not correspond at all to 'Church' – 'Kirche', which embodied an old-fashioned concept of what religion was about. It expressed a secular attitude, in which a reverence for art combined with a new feeling for the national past, and it foreshadowed the sanctification of nationalism which was to characterise Europe during the later nineteenth century and which was to lead eventually to the tragedy and horror of the First World War, a cataclysm for which the Franco-Prussian War and the Boer War can now be seen as dress rehearsals.

It is interesting to observe that the German names selected for the new type of art-centre museum had no Christian or indeed religious associations at all. The Romantics developed their own vocabulary for the new buildings – Glyptothek, Pinakothek, Kunsthalle, Kunstgebäude, Neue Eremitage, Gemäldegalerie. 'Museum' itself was added to the list, at least on the Continent. In England, throughout the nineteenth century and into our own times, a clear distinction was made between an art gallery and a museum. The English usage did not allow a museum to contain paintings, drawings or modern sculpture, but in Germany and France, thinking was different.

One can argue as to whether the German or the French influence was the stronger in creating the philosophy that national fervour and respect for art were indissolubly mixed, that one could and should stimulate the other. Lenoir's Musée des Monuments Français, created during the early years of the Revolution, was indistinguishable in spirit from what was beginning to appear in Germany at about the same time, institutions which were devoted partly to art and partly to national history. The art, one might say, was used to raise the emotional level of the museum and to give a dimension of spirituality to the nationalism. The historical aspects of this crusade are discussed in a later chapter, but it is necessary to point out here that, in early nineteenth-century Germany, nationalism did not mean quite the same thing as it did in France or England. In Germany, as in Italy, the political entity was the

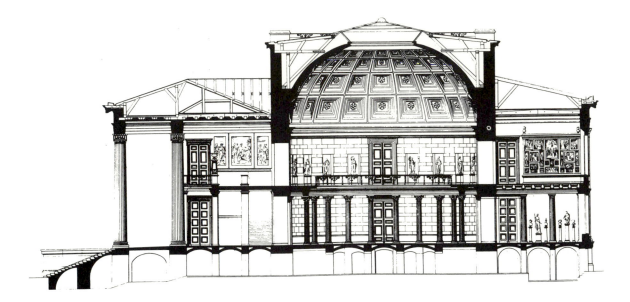

Museums as temples. Three of Karl-Friedrich Schinkel's early nineteenth-century dream-designs (*Sammlung arkitektonischer Entwürfe*, 6 Heft, 1825; 17 Heft, 1831).

autonomous kingdom or princely state, whereas in England or France it was the country as a whole. For those who lived in the German-speaking world, 'German history' was a phenomenon which crossed political frontiers. 'English history' or 'French history' was significantly different.

An important consequence of this was a quite different relationship between the national past and the national future. The concept of German-ness – Deutschtum, 'a German soul in a German body' – looked forward to the eventual unification of all the territories in which German was the mother-tongue and to the national fulfilment and national political power which would characterise such a colossus. This dream led straight to Hitler and to the Second World War. During the years when Napoleon dominated Europe, France basked in the temporary sunshine of controlling a continent by force and in the success of its armies. After Waterloo, there was comfort and encouragement to be obtained by looking backward. 'La Gloire' has been a powerful element in sustaining French morale for not far short of two centuries now. France still idolises its army in a way which is unique in western Europe.

Patriotism in Britain has followed a different course. Despite the distinctly mediocre quality of its eighteenth-century rulers, it contrived to preserve its monarchy and to stave off revolution and, with the help of a long-lived and popular Queen, determined builders of an overseas Empire, and successful manufacturers and merchants, it was able to establish itself as the political and military leader, not only of Europe,

but of the world. 'Great Britain', which originally implied no more than the political union of England, Scotland and Wales, acquired a strongly patriotic flavour, yet one which was quite different from that of Groß Deutschland. 'Grande France', curiously enough, never appeared, and one wonders why.

But, although throughout the Victorian period God was always assumed to be on the side of the British and to favour them more than any other people on earth, religion and museums were kept strictly apart. Ruskin and William Morris might speak and write of the ennobling qualities of art in a manner which recalled Wackenrode and Tieck, but Nelson and Wellington were not driven forward to victory by thinking of the British Museum, and it was not the National Gallery which made the 1851 Exhibition such a success and which caused so much of the map of the world to be coloured red.

In Germany it was otherwise. The Germanisches Nationalmuseum was set up in Nuremberg, on the inspiration of Lenoir. The first of the new-style monumental museums was the Glyptothek in Munich, built between 1816 and 1830 and paid for by Ludwig I of Bavaria. The king of Bavaria commissioned three palace-museums, each designed in the classical style, around a new square, the Königsplatz, so as to make it clear that Munich was henceforth to be regarded as the cultural capital of Europe. The museum attendants were dressed in magnificent liveries, in order to encourage public respect for art and antiquity. In the earliest of these, the Glyptothek, dedicated to sculpture, both the King and his architect, Wittelsbach, were anxious to avoid accusations of being didactic or over-intellectualised. Atmosphere was to be more important than facts, so there were no labels and no catalogues, and from time to time the King himself offered special guests refreshments in the museum and led them on a torchlight tour of the galleries.

Frederick William III of Prussia followed a similar policy. In 1815, when construction of what came to be known as the Altes Museum in Berlin was about to begin, he made it known that his aim was to bring about what he described as 'the honouring of art'. The collections of paintings and statues were to be housed and presented in a manner which would produce among the public 'a mood of sacred solemnity'. Practical measures were taken to achieve this. In the Rotunda of the Museum, for example, classical statues were placed on exceptionally tall pedestals, so that visitors had to crane their necks in order to look up at them, a practice which had already been instituted at the Musée Napoléon in Paris.

The main purpose of a collection of works of art was therefore seen to be the awakening of a spirit of reverence and devotion. Museums were temples and their directors and assistants priests. In an age when the power and appeal of ecclesiastical religion had faded, art was destined to take its place. But there was another aspect of the Altes Museum, overshadowed at the time by its priestly claims, yet of much greater importance in the long run. It established from the beginning a systematic buying policy which would allow it to build up a fully representative collection of works of art and, by arranging it systematically, to educate the public in the history of art, as the German academic art historians conceived it. The other museum-palaces of nineteenth-century Europe[10] followed the lead of Berlin, so that it became accepted international policy that art museums should be controlled by art historians, not by artists, and that visitors to such museums should be regarded as people preparing themselves for some unspecified examination in art history. Until recently, this automatic subjection of art museums to the academic mode of thinking has very rarely been questioned. It is so firmly rooted that most people are unable to realise that there could be alternative and radically different ways of going about the task. And for this the Prussian influence, as typified and publicised by the Altes Museum in Berlin, must be held largely responsible.

In the field of the applied arts, the art historian has never exercised the power that he has had over the fine arts, largely, no doubt, because it is more difficult to construct a mystique around a teapot or a chair than it is around a painting. The fact that items which come under the heading of the fine arts have a much greater rarity value also, no doubt, has something to do with the difference. So, too, does snobbery. What is beautiful, but useless, has for at least two thousand years tended to have a higher prestige than what is beautiful, but practical. One of the greatest crimes of the nineteenth and twentieth centuries has been to drive a wedge between the artist and the craftsman, and to pretend, very effectively, that the first is a superior order of person to the second or, in the dangerous words of Wackenrode, to see the artist as 'the highest among mortals'. Every artist of any competence at all is first and foremost a craftsman. In this respect, there is no essential difference between a painter and a carpenter or a plumber. Both work with their hands, both are skilled in using tools and materials. The point was well understood in pre-industrial times but the development, first, of machinery and, later, of mass-production, as the means of making everyday articles, left the artist marooned.

In these circumstances, the creation of the South Kensington Museum in London can be seen as a heroic gesture, an attempt, in an increasingly ugly environment, to make good design seem both possible and normal, to build a series of bridges between the artist and the new technology. The whittling down of the grand concept, at the end of the century, so that a single, all-embracing cultural centre in South Kensington eventually became a group of autonomous institutions – the Victoria and Albert Museum, the Science Museum, the Geological Museum, the Natural History Museum and, nearby, Imperial College, the Albert Hall and the Royal College of Music, with the National Gallery in another part of London altogether – was a sad, though perhaps inevitable, anticlimax to a courageous and imaginative idea.

Prince Albert, who was the moving force behind the whole idea, must have realised that what was taking place in Berlin, Munich and elsewhere in Germany was not necessarily possible in Britain. The cultural centres which he had seen being created in German cities were concerned with history and the fine arts, not with industrial design. They had the support of a ruling class which had a profound belief in the value of culture and the necessity of the arts. This was not the situation in Britain at all. 'In the nineteenth century', wrote Lord Clark, in one of his more intensely pro-French and anti-British moods, 'the only man who had this belief was a foreigner, the Prince Consort, and the upper classes considered him ridiculous. Power was in the hands of men like Lord Palmerston, who thought learning and the arts were an absurd interruption to the pursuit of politics. Even Lord Salisbury declined to give a grant to the South Kensington Museum, on the grounds that it was no concern of Her Majesty's Government to provide people with luxuries.'[11]

Perhaps the main value of the Great Exhibition of 1851 was to prove to the British people, if not to the British Government, that art, in the form of industrial design, could be good business. The Great Exhibition was a manufacturers' exhibition, presented on a scale and in a manner which would ensure a large attendance, both from home and abroad. If the Exhibition had not been so successful, South Kensington would not have come into being. As things turned out, it made a profit of £186,000 – a large amount of money for the time – and this was used to buy the site in South Kensington on which the Museums and other cultural and educational buildings now stand.

An official interest in industrial design, albeit somewhat lukewarm, existed long before the 1851 Exhibition. In 1835, Parliament appointed a Select Committee on Arts and Manufactures, 'to enquire into the best means of extending a knowledge of the Arts, and of the Principles of Design, among the People (especially the Manufacturing Population) of the Country'. Among the recommendations made by the Committee was one to the effect that 'the opening of public galleries for the people should, as much as possible, be encouraged'. Nothing, however, was done to implement this until, in 1852, with the unchallengeable success of the Great Exhibition still in the air, the Government set up the Department of Practical Art – a title changed in the following year to the Department of Science and Art – under the control of the Board of Trade. The new Department had the task of administering the existing art school and of establishing 'museums, by which all classes might be induced to investigate those common principles of taste which may be traced in the works of excellence of all ages'. By consent of the Treasury, £5,000 was made available in order to buy, from the stock resulting from the Exhibition, objects which were to be 'selected without reference to styles, but entirely for the excellence of their art or workmanship'. This provided a small group of contemporary products around which other items could be assembled in the course of time.

The new Museum of Manufactures opened, in Marlborough House, in 1852. The collections were increased by means of purchases and loans, and the items arranged according to the materials from which they were made – wood, metal, ceramics, and so on. In a short time, the name of the Museum was changed to the Art Museum and then again to the Museum of Ornamental Art.

In 1857, the Museum was moved to its present site as the first instalment of the complex to be known as the South Kensington Museum. Its collections at that time comprised 'a miscellaneous collection of British sculpture, architectural casts, animal products, food, models and patented inventions, educational aids, the nucleus of the National Art Library, a circulating art library, and construction and building materials'.[12]

A notable feature of the Museum's temporary buildings was the restaurant, which was referred to as 'a daring innovation'. South Kensington was the first museum in the world to provide such an amenity. The restaurant remained in use until 1868, when new refreshment rooms were opened in the main building.

Sir Henry Cole, K.C.B., the first Director of the South Kensington Museum.

South Kensington soon outgrew its original accommodation and extensions were added piecemeal until 1884, by which time it had shed its science and certain other collections, which had been transferred elsewhere. The steady expansion of the art collection, however, made new buildings essential. Queen Victoria laid the foundation stone of the Brompton Road façade building in 1899, her last important public ceremony, and on that occasion she graciously consented to rename the Museum the Victoria and Albert Museum, trusting that 'it will remain for ages a Monument of discerning Liberality and a Source of Refinement and Progress'.

In attempting to assess the influence of the Museum, one has first to decide to which stage of its development one is referring. In its original, cramped accommodation at South Kensington, it was immensely popular with the general public, who arrived in great numbers to see the combined artistic and scientific displays, which included the newly arrived Sheepshanks Collection of 233 paintings by British artists.[13] It was much the same kind of public that had flocked to the 1851 Exhibition. South Kensington, one might say, carried on from the point where the Great Exhibition had left off. It provided ample evidence that, whatever the situation might be at the upper levels of British society, the working and middle class were extremely curious to see new inventions and examples of good craftsmanship. It showed, as the Great Exhibition had done, that the way to the average man's heart was through practical matters, a simple and obvious lesson which most twentieth-century directors of art museums have shown themselves strangely unwilling to learn.

Secondly – and this was true even before the Museum moved into its 1909 building – the collections and the classes in art and design associated with them have been of great value to generations of students. This part of the dream of the Prince Consort and of the Museum's inspired first Director, Sir Henry Cole, has at least been realised. What is, alas, much more dubious is whether the taste of the general public has been influenced in the slightest by the examples placed before it in the Museum.

The plaster cast of Trajan's Column, Rome. Made for the South Kensington Museum in 1864 and now a feature of the Victorian Plaster Cast Court.

A third possible influence has come from the size and quality of the collections themselves, divided as they are into Departments of Metalwork, Ceramics and Glass, Sculpture, Furniture and Woodwork, Textiles and Dress, and Prints, Drawings, Photographs and Painting, with a separate Indian Section and a Far Eastern Department.[14] The Victoria and Albert Museum and its predecessors have undoubtedly, over a period of more than a century, played a large part in convincing both the public, the British and other Governments, and local authorities throughout the British Isles, that it is as reputable and rewarding to collect the practical as the unpractical arts, and that, by any standard, must be counted a great achievement. Whether it would have happened if the dealers and auction-houses had not become as interested in what one might call Victoria and Albert material as in National

Gallery or Tate Gallery material is a nice question. What is certain is that, given the values and snobberies of the past hundred years or so, if the Victoria and Albert had not been big, its influence would have been greatly reduced.

The fourth influence stems from the new building itself, cursed for its inconvenience by the generations of staff who have had to work in it, but of immense importance as a permanent advertisement for craftsmanship of the highest order. By a stroke of genius, Cole organised a Museum of Construction, with its own catalogue to encourage the public to study the new buildings as they went up. The Catalogue tells us what the Museum of Construction contained – 'samples of building stones and marbles; specimens of all the best cements and asphalts; examples of the numerous applications of ceramic manufacture to the purpose of construction, more especially in this country and in France, such as tiles for roofing and flooring of the newest and most approved form and clays; bricks, hollow, solid and moulded, of various sorts; examples of many ingenious applications of these materials which are made in France, such as lintels, jambs, exterior and interior cornices, mouldings, window dressings, etc.; specimens of French fire-proof floors for private houses. To this list may be added ornamental tiles for interior wall decoration from England, France and Spain, and a great variety of hip and ridge tiles and crest ornaments, principally intended for edifices in the Gothic style. Some bricks decorated after the manner of majolica and samples of ornamental slate and other imitations of marble may be classed with this description of material.'[15]

The site and the area surrounding it was a hive of activity. 'Minton's[16] had to set up a manufactory near the Albert Hall; students were painting ceilings, modelling majolica, or engraving layers of coloured cement on the abyss-like east wall of the Henry Cole Building. Here Cole created a ladies' mosaic class, into which he pressed members of his family to cope with all the work in the Museum and the Albert Hall,[17] and even lady convicts at Woking were making mosaic floors.'[18]

Most of this do-it-yourself designing and manufacturing at South Kensington unfortunately came to an end in 1870, when the First Commissioner of Works decided that the Office of Works, not the Department of Science and Art, should control building work for the new Science Museum. But at the Victoria and Albert, as at the Natural History Museum nearby, generations of students and apprentices have come to admire the construction work and other decorations. Until the outbreak of the Second World War, apprentice-bricklayers were regularly brought to the Quadrangle of the Victoria and Albert to study the quality of the façade of the Museum's Lecture Theatre.

The passion for decoration at South Kensington was normal among those responsible for the creation of public buildings in the nineteenth century.[19] All types of building, churches, theatres, law courts and banks, were enhanced by appropriate artistic decorations. The section of the Louvre known as the Musée Charles X, built

The original Refreshment Rooms at South Kensington, adjacent to the Brompton Oratory. The first museum restaurant in the world. Watercolour by Anthony Stannus.

in 1827–33, has a series of ceiling paintings illustrating the civilisations of antiquity, and in the Neues Museum, Berlin (1843–55) there were paintings of Teutonic myths. The Neue Pinakothek in Munich had frescoes on the outside of the building, with representations of modern painters, sculptors and architects, while the earlier Alte Pinakothek (1826–36) had an impressive series of frescoes illustrating the development of European art in the Middle Ages and the Renaissance.

It is important to give the Victoria and Albert Museum credit for the right achievements. It was not the only or even the leading museum of what was called industrial art in nineteenth-century Europe. Throughout the second half of the century, the German-speaking world was spawning such museums at a great rate. The influence of the architect, Gottfried Semper, on their construction and arrangement was very strong.[20] The first to be built was the Museum of Art and Industry in Vienna (1863). This was followed by the Museum of Applied Art in Berlin, in 1867 and, outside Germany, by Brno in 1873 and Budapest in 1874. During the 1870s, Dresden, Frankfurt, Hamburg, Kassel, Kiel and Leipzig all established museums of industrial art – a phenomenon which was repeated nowhere else in Europe – and by the end of the century nearly every important city in Germany had been equipped with such a museum or with a department of industrial art in a general museum.[21]

The second Refreshment Room in the new building at South Kensington, designed by James Gamble. Photographed in 1917.

The new restaurant at the Victoria and Albert Museum, opened in 1985.

These new museums were primarily intended to guide and inspire craftsmen and designers, by providing examples of good design and by illustraging technical processes. They nearly all observed the principles laid down by Semper,[22] that museum collections of industrial art were most effectively classified and arranged according to materials and techniques, rather than in historical sequence. By the end of the century this approach was seen to be no longer useful. Fewer craftsmen and designers were visiting the museums each year and interest was falling off among the general public as well. The new philosophy, which aimed to attract the public back to the museums, was to present craftsmanship as part of cultural history, which amounted to abandoning the sense of practical purpose which had motivated Semper and his disciples.

One can see, with hindsight, that much of the enthusiasm and appeal of the South Kensington Museum and the corresponding German museums in their early days was due to an agreeable amateurism among the organisers and administrators, an amateurism which members of the general public found easy to share. In 1851, and for perhaps thirty years afterwards, it was not too difficult to present science, technology and art in the same museum and for the same public. By 1900, however, increasing specialisation within both the sciences and the arts and a considerable improvement in scholarship had made the splitting up of the South Kensington collections inevitable. When Queen Victoria renamed the Museum in 1899, in memory of the efforts which her late husband had put into creating it, Albert's dream of a comprehensive culture had already evaporated. The great integrating label, 'industrial art', had faded with the dream, to be replaced during the present century by 'applied arts' and 'decorative arts', which have a quite different force and flavour, and a different clientèle.

If one is looking for an American equivalent of the Victoria and Albert Museum, it can only be the Metropolitan Museum of Art in New York, although this vast empire, established at a time when the Victoria and Albert was suffering from severe growing pains, is perhaps best regarded as a museum stew, with the British Museum, National Gallery and Victoria and Albert Museum as its ingredients, and well stirred. Its influence has been enormous and worldwide, not always, alas in beneficial ways.

Its history does much to explain both its good and less good qualities. In the 1860s, more than a few people were making a great deal of money out of the Civil War. New York was, to use Leo Lerman's graphic phrase, 'bustling rich'.[23] There was money to spend and among the newly rich the interest in art was rising fast. The time was clearly ripe for the establishment of new art galleries, and New York was the obvious first choice. The moving spirit behind a museum which would do credit to the nation's most important city was John Jay, Minister to Germany and President of the Union League Club. He entrusted the development of the museum idea to the Club's Art Committee. A launching meeting, held in 1869, had the influential

William Cullen Bryant, the poet and editor-in-chief of the *New York Evening Post*, in the chair. In the course of the meeting, Dr Henry W. Bellows, who was in charge of All Souls Church, put this rhetorical question to the powerful New Yorkers who formed his audience: 'Who is to say when we, through the redundant wealth with which our property threatens to possess us, shall be able to outbid the world in any market for those great, recondite works of Art which are so necessary for the cultivation of every people.'[24] Dr Bellows' prophecy, as we well know, has come horribly true.

The meeting decided to set up a Metropolitan Arts Museum Association. As a guide to the kind of museum which they had in mind for New York, they discussed the virtues of existing museums in Nuremberg, Leipzig, Berlin, Paris and London, where the Victoria and Albert was 'extolled'. Trustees were appointed and the Metropolitan Museum of Art received its Act of Incorporation from the Legislature of the State of New York in 1870. The new museum was to be 'located in the City of New York, for the purpose of establishing and maintaining in the said city a museum and library of art, of encouraging and developing the study of the fine arts, and the application of arts to manufacture and practical life, of advancing the general knowledge of kindred spirits, and, to that end, of furnishing popular instruction and recreation'.[25]

It was a generous brief, which gave the Trustees almost unlimited freedom of action,[26] and the first Annual Meeting,[26] held a few weeks later, adopted a recommendation of the Policy Committee that the Museum 'should be based on the idea of a more or less complete collection of objects illustrative of the History of Art from the earliest beginnings to the present time'. A 'complete collection' is a daunting prospect and one wonders what the Policy Committee intended it to mean. What they possibly intended to imply was that the Museum should eventually contain examples of every type of art which had been created anywhere in the world, but even that was a fairly tall order. Large sums of money would obviously be needed and so an appeal was launched, mainly in order to allow the Museum to make purchases on the European market, where the most desirable items were to be found. It was a good time to buy, as the organisers of the appeal reminded those who might welcome the opportunity to get rid of what Dr Bellows had called 'redundant wealth'. The appeal was worded in a way that was likely to make good sense to businessmen. 'There is now an opportunity', it said, 'made by the political and social changes in Europe, to buy works of art of all kinds and at low rates.' The 'political and social changes' referred to were mainly the results of war and revolution, which had resulted in the impoverishment of many aristocratic and landed families.

The Museum's first collection was got together in this way and early in 1872 part of it was put on public exhibition in a rented house at 681 Fifth Avenue, the Metropolitan's first home. In the following year it moved to 128 West 14th Street where, after a short time, an admission charge of 50 cents was imposed. Attendances dropped significantly and, on sound business principles, the amount was reduced to 25 cents, with free admission on Mondays and Thursdays, which had hitherto had the fewest visitors. This had an immense effect. In 1874–5, free-day admissions averaged 577, which at the time was considered to be a very respectable figure for an art museum.

It should be remembered that the Metropolitan was wholly dependent on private finance for its operations, as most museums in the United States have always been. If it were to develop, it had to pay its way and at the same time raise capital. This meant that it had to find ways of attracting and pleasing visitors and at the same time persuading moneyed people to support its work with gifts, subscriptions and legacies. The Metropolitan was, in fact, running a business, and the methods by which it proved itself so successful in carrying out this task have provided ideas for a great many other museums, both inside and outside America. It was, for example, a pioneer in revealing the possibilities of extracting sums of capital from members of the public in exchange for certain privileges. Very early in its career, the Museum instituted a system of Fellows and Patrons, for those who could afford to subscribe hundreds or thousands of dollars, together with, a little later, a new category of Annual Member. This cost ten dollars a year, for which the Member received a season ticket for two and invitations to all receptions. It was an excellent bargain for both parties, the greatest advantage to the Museum being that it brought in a steady flow of ready cash. There were, in 1876, 600 Annual Members, and the total rose steadily year by year.

Another useful innovation was the loan exhibition, for which private individuals lent items from their own collections. The public relations value of this was considerable, since it allowed the Museum to push out further roots into the well-off sections of the community, while at the same time enriching the displays available to the public, at no cost to the Museum, which, in the first few years of its existence, had very little of its own to offer members of the public who had paid for admission and expected something fairly substantial in return. The first of these loan exhibitions took place in 1873, with 112 items from 32 separate collections.

In 1880, the Metropolitan was able at last to move into a new building, which was to be its permanent home. This, too, was an excellent deal. The City of New York owned the building – it still does – maintained it, and leased it to the Museum. This was a pioneering arrangement, which had considerable influence elsewhere in America. The new accommodation arrived only just in time, since both the collections, and their value, were increasing very fast, mainly as a result of gifts.

Sunday opening came in 1891, in the afternoon only, after fierce opposition from religious organisations and traditionalists, and three years afterwards the Museum continued further along the road of giving the public what it wanted by opening its own restaurant – this was in 1894 – and providing visitors with a room in which to store their bicycles. These new facilities coincided with the opening of the North

Wing. At this point the Metropolitan became, so far as its buildings were concerned, as large as the British Museum.

In discussing the Metropolitan Museum one finds oneself repeatedly returning to the word 'large'. This is not accidental: from the beginning, the Metropolitan set itself the task of beating Europe at its own game and, in so far as money could achieve this, it succeeded wonderfully well. There was simply so much money in America and the Metropolitan made sure of getting its fair share of it. It had two great strokes of luck. In 1901 Jacob S. Rogers, the owner of a locomotive works at Paterson, New Jersey, died and left the Museum five and a half million dollars. He left directions that the capital was not to be touched, leaving the income from it to be used for purchases. And then, in 1904, John Pierpont Morgan became the Museum's President. One by one, he filled the Board with fellow tycoons, in order to be able to achieve a perfectly simple aim. 'He would gather for America an undreamed of collection of art, so great and so complete that a trip to Europe would be superfluous. And he would give this vast and splendid compendium of art to the Metropolitan Museum.'[27] It is small wonder that J. J. Rorimer, the Museum's Director from 1955 to 1966, felt able to declare shortly before he retired, that he had the privilege of administering 'the greatest treasure house in the Western Hemisphere'.

Buying presents at the Metropolitan Museum.

...the ideal way to buy your presents from The Metropolitan Museum

Every three months—four times a year—the Museum will announce by mail remarkable new replicas—exact copies of Museum originals: sculpture, decorative objects, tableware, and ornaments.

The variety will be extraordinary: ancient jewelry in gold and silver; Oriental and European porcelain; early American glass in crystal and rare colors; bronze from Egypt, Greece, China, and the medieval world; silver, pewter, brass, and pottery from Colonial America.

These copies, often produced by the same techniques used for the originals, are made by artist-craftsmen working under the Museum's direct supervision. The care taken in production frequently limits the quantity, and the majority of replicas can be bought only by mail or at the Museum. (Above: Hippopotamus, brilliant blue faience decorated with lotus flowers. Length 8", $10.75 plus $1.25 shipping.)

To receive all of the advance announcements to be issued during the next year, send the coupon below with one dollar to cover mailing.

On September 1, you will receive the first of these, the 116 page Christmas Catalogue. A brilliant array of new presents includes an ancient Egyptian necklace of blue lotus flowers; golden stags, panthers, lions, and griffins from the Scythian treasure hoard; needlework kits of a tiger from a Chinese ceremonial banner, and puppies and kittens from a New England rug; a tree and a star in stained glass; a book of Persian miniatures in full color and gold; a bronze Etruscan acrobat; art nouveau stationery; a new cookbook, *To the King's Taste*, and next year's engagement calendar, *Secret Gardens*. In addition, there is an unparalleled selection of Christmas cards.

THE METROPOLITAN MUSEUM OF ART
255 Gracie Station, New York 10028   N2

Please send me all advance announcements and catalogues or replicas to be issued by the Museum during the next 12 months. One dollar to cover mailing costs is enclosed.

NAME

ADDRESS

ZIP

The question one has to ask is, has the Metropolitan Museum ever been any more than that? There are many reasons why one should say, 'No', chief among them the fact that during the first quarter century of its existence, it showed America what could be done to develop a museum by enlisting public support in a wide range of ingenious ways, and by good management. As a result of this, it played an important part in determining the manner in which the American museum was going to establish itself in the twentieth century. One could, of course, avoid the issue by pointing to the Museum's remarkable peripheral successes, its huge and amazing enterprise – it would be an insult to refer to the Museum's 'shop', its reproductions, its catalogues, its film shows, its lectures, its guided tours. But these must be considered fringe activities, although it has been said that, so successful have the Metropolitan's commercial ventures been, the Museum might now rightly be considered an annexe to what, taking our courage in both hands, we will call the Shop.

The central question remains, however, 'What contribution of any consequence has the Metropolitan made to the art and science of museology? What new insight has it provided into the purpose and function of art?' That it is the greatest treasure house in the Western Hemisphere or even in the whole world we may perhaps concede, although it seems that in California the J. Paul Getty museum empire must by now be running it close. We may also agree that, for Americans who wish to study the worldwide history of art, there is, thanks to the Metropolitan, no need to step outside New York. But, in a hundred years' time, when the history of museums comes to be written yet again, will it be said that the Metropolitan Museum's chief claim to be

Top left 1872. Humble beginnings. The Metropolitan Museum's first home at 681 Fifth Avenue.

Bottom left Edward Steichen's portrait of J. P. Morgan, President of the Trustees of the Metropolitan Museum, 1904.

Top right Grandeur on Fifth Avenue. The Metropolitan Museum's main entrance.

Bottom right The Great Hall of the Metropolitan, as it was in the 1920s.

Opposite top Museum feeding in style. Restaurant in the Lamont Wing of the Metropolitan, showing sculpture by Carl Milles (1875–1955).

Opposite bottom 1982. Gallery of Oceanic Art of Melanesia, in the Michael C. Rockefeller Memorial Wing at the Metropolitan.

Alfred H. Barr, the first Director of the Museum of Modern Art.

mentioned and remembered is that, in the twentieth century, it really did beat the European museums hands down at the old nineteenth-century game of adding Italian picture to Italian picture, Greek vase to Greek vase, and piece of French furniture to piece of French furniture? Was it enough? Was it worth all the effort? But there will surely be general agreement on at least one point, that the Metropolitan is and always has been a quintessentially American museum.

It is natural to turn now to the other New York art giant of this century, the Museum of Modern Art. Founded in 1929, it was described by the *New Yorker* in 1953 as 'the world centre, institutionally speaking, of the modern movement in the fine and applied arts',[28] a claim which the French, since their establishment of Beaubourg in 1977, are no doubt anxious to dispute. It had as its first director, Alfred H. Barr, who was appointed when he was 27 and held the post for fourteen years, after which he became the Director of Collections, and had much to do with determining its policy and shaping its style. He has been described both as the soul and the pituitary gland of the Museum during its formative period, but he himself once defined his task, and that of the Museum, as 'the conscientious, continuous, resolute distinction of quality from mediocrity'. The tradition of frenetic activity certainly stems from him. That the Museum has been immensely successful among a surprisingly wide range of people there can be no doubt at all, partly because of its exciting building, partly because of its atmosphere, which suggests artists – a classless breed – rather than art historians, whose unseen presence has a remarkable ability to antagonise the common man, and partly because 'the entire place is a veritable oasis in the drab, grey city'. It is a place of refreshment in more senses than one. For years, its elegant and imaginative cafeteria, opening out on to the sculpture garden, has been sufficient reason in itself for visiting the Museum.

It now has considerable assets in the form of its site, its building and a stock of works of art which have greatly appreciated in value over the years. Its Trustees have included representatives of many of the leading American dynasties – Crane, Field, Ford, Guggenheim, Rockefeller, Warburg, Whitney, but, curiously enough, never a painter, although Lord Duveen, the celebrated art dealer and collector, was at one time on the Board. The Trustees have always had a more important rôle in the affairs of the Museum of Modern Art than they have in those of most museums, even in America. Many of them have been enthusiastic collectors themselves and their taste for and in modern art has certainly been influential in building up the market, both in their own country and among the international circle of wealthy art-fanciers. 'Few Americans', noted the *New Yorker*, with the usual infinite wisdom, 'care to argue with a hundred million dollars.'

The Museum, apart from a grant from the New York State Council on the Arts for its exhibition programme, has had to be self financing and has had to pay for and maintain its own building. Its endowments cover only a small part of its expenses, and it has consequently been very dependent on the financial support of its Trustees.

Crowds outside the Museum of Modern Art for its Italian Masters exhibition, 1940.

They provided the money for the building, on a site presented by the Rockefellers, they have made large gifts for running expenses and they have given the Museum most of its pictures. The Museum arrived at an opportune moment. American interest in modern art was building up, not least because this type of painting was appreciating in value faster than any other and, strangely, there was little opportunity to see modern art in New York – the Metropolitan had very little and gloried in the fact – or, for that matter, in the United States as a whole. At the beginning of the 1830s, fourteen European cities had museums wholly devoted to modern art, compared with exactly one, the Museum of Modern Art in New York, in the United States. Sixty-six European museums, more than thirty of them in Germany, contained galleries of modern art. In America, the total was twelve.

During the fifty-seven years of its existence, the Museum of Modern Art has had an enormous influence, not only in America, but worldwide, on public taste and

The façade of the Museum as it was in the 1960s.

prejudice, on art teaching and on museum practice. It has been a leader in the movement to promote art museums, which have long ceased to be the quiet, take-it-or-leave-it places they were in the twenties. It was largely responsible for introducing the thought that a museum might be a community centre, a place of activity, rather than merely a home for collections. It could be fairly said to be the best club in New York, with the most members. It was also a pioneer, because its financial circumstances forced it to be, of the notion, strange in the museum world, that its collections were capital on which the management had to earn a dividend. It has functioned as

The large new gallery space in the Museum's renovated East Wing features painting and sculpture of the last few decades.

a design centre almost as much as an art gallery and it has broken away from the idea that once pictures were on display, there they stayed. It is a place of constantly changing exhibitions, with the kind of building which makes showmanship easy. Walls are removed and re-erected, the shape of galleries changed, décor re-created to suit the job in hand. With the opening of its new West Wing in 1984, the Museum was able to double its display space and expand its facilities. It now has more than a million visitors a year and up to 7,000 a day.

When the extensions and refurbishment had been completed, the Museum issued, on 7 May 1984, a public stocktaking of what had been achieved during its eventful life. 'Since its foundation,' it said, 'the Museum has assembled an unparalleled collection of 20th century arts: painting and sculpture, drawings, prints, photography, film, architecture, industrial and graphic design. These collections tell the story of modern art. They have been instrumental in introducing the art of our time into the mainstream of cultural life. And they have indeed provided New York with the greatest museum of modern art in the world.'

Perhaps the biggest tribute that can be paid to the Museum of Modern Art is to say that it has produced some very vigorous and intelligent children. The Metropolitan

Museum, impressive monolith though it is, has had no children, unless one excepts the Getty Museum, which is, so to speak, carrying on the Metropolitan tradition of buying up the world. There are those who would say, with some justice, that the main influence of the Metropolitan and Getty Museums has been to force up art prices to a point at which no other museum, or at least no other museum outside America, can afford to buy anything, and to have been the greatest art removal men since Napoleon is a doubtful distinction.

With the Museum of Modern Art it has been different. Its influence has been not so much in the collecting of works of art as in making use of them, in building activities around them. It would be something of an exaggeration to say that every museum of modern art in the world has been trying to establish itself as a smaller version of what New Yorkers have been able to enjoy for more than fifty years, but no overstatement at all to suggest that every such museum is unable to forget that New York is there as the great pioneer. Most of them are willing and even glad to acknowledge this. The Museum of Modern Art is not a parent of which to be ashamed, and one can see everywhere evidence of the power and stamina of its spirit, at Louisiana in Copenhagen, at the Miró Museum in Barcelona, at the Museum of Contemporary Art in Dunkerque, at the Museum of Modern Art at the Centre Pompidou in Paris. All these places have a common quality: they have succeeded in creating an atmosphere in which the art historian plays only a small part, whereas in the world's traditional art galleries the art historian is present all the time, disciplining both the pictures and the public. The Museum of Modern Art has every reason to be proud of its achievement in bypassing the art historian and in placing the emphasis firmly on the creative people: the artists, architects and designers. Like the European museums mentioned above, it has used this approach in order to tap a new public, a public which is not class-bound or examination-bound, a public which realises that one gets most out of art when one decides not to take at least some of it too seriously, when one enters into the spirit in which the artist worked. I remember, about twenty years ago, being among the Picassos at the Museum of Modern Art in New York, in the days before the 'Guernica' had been returned to Spain. Four middle-aged ladies, agreeable representatives of the gallery-devotee type, were close to me. 'Excuse me, sir', said one of them, on behalf of the group, 'could you help us, please? We understand the message of the "Guernica", but we can't get the message of these other Picassos.' 'Madam', I replied, 'they have no message. They are simply Mr Picasso enjoying himself and wanting other people to do the same. Why not try? A great deal of modern art is just a frolic. A great deal of art always has been.' I felt that the Museum was encouraging me to say that, because it was what it was trying to say itself.

Chapter Four
Man, nature and the environment

Natural History Museum, London: *'A substantial research effort is needed to sustain the essential purpose of any museum'*
Northern Animal Park, Emmen: *'A zoo's only right to existence is derived from its educational role'*
Senckenberg Museum, Frankfurt: *'A science museum which aims at reaching the visitor's emotions as well as his intellect'*
ulandris Natural History Museum, Kifissia: *'The awakening of a feeling for natural history in Greece'*

Sir Ashton Lever was an eighteenth-century country gentleman. He was born in 1729 and was educated at the University of Oxford. His home was at Alkington Hall, near Manchester. As a young man, he made a hobby of collecting live birds, and in 1760 he was credited with having the finest aviary in Britain. He subsequently widened his interests to include shells, fossils, ethnographical material and the inevitable 'curiosities'. He welcomed visitors to see his collections which, by 1774, had become so large that family life at Alkington Hall had become a little difficult. Sir Ashton therefore transferred the exhibits, by this time all dead and stuffed, to his London residence, Leicester House, where he opened a museum for the general public, charging for admission in order to cover at least part of his costs and to control the number and the quality of visitors.

Susan Burney visited the exhibition and wrote about it in a letter to her sister, Fanny:[1]

> Saturday morning we spent extremely well at Sir Ashton Lever's Museum. I wish I was a good Natural Historian, that I might give you some idea of our entertainment in seeing birds, beasts, shells, fossils, etc., but I can scarce remember a dozen names of the thousand I heard that were new to me. The birds of paradise, and the humming birds were, I think, among the most beautiful. There are several pelicans, flamingos, peacocks (one quite white), a penguin. Among the beasts a hippopotamus (sea horse) of an immense size, an elephant, a tyger from the tower,[2] a Greenland bear and its cub, a wolf, two or three leopards, a Otaheite[3] dog (a very coarse, ugly-looking creature), a young crocodile, a roomful of monkeys – one of them presents the company with an Italian song, another is reading a book (and these alive, perhaps?), another, the most horrid of all, is put in the attitude of Venus de Medicis and is scarce fit to be looked at. Lizards, bats, toads, frogs, scorpions and other filthy things in abundance.

Sir Ashton Lever's collection was in no way scientific. It is best described, perhaps, as an assembly of objects, mostly within the field of natural history, which had been brought back to England by sailors and travellers. Sir Ashton regarded them as exotics and curiosities, not as material for study, and he obviously enjoyed putting his stuffed animals into the absurd positions described by Susan Burney. For a private individual, his collections were unusually large, but a number of his contemporaries included this kind of material in their general collections of oddities, rarities and curiosities. To consider such people 'natural historians', in Susan Burney's phrase, is both misleading and flattering, since most of them were unacquainted even with such principles of classification as were available at the time. They were accumulating interest-collections, not study-collections.

When Sir Ashton Lever opened his museum in London, in 1774, the pioneering work of the great Swedish botanist Linnaeus had been accessible to scholars, through his published works, for about forty years. He began forming his systematic collection in 1732, at the age of 35, and the books which formed the basis of the modern classification of plants and animals appeared during the following twenty years.[4]

In 1741 he became Professor, first of medicine and then of botany, at the University of Uppsala. After his death, his books, manuscripts and collections were sold to Sir J. E. Smith, who founded the Linnaean Society in 1783, and are preserved at the Linnaean Society's premises at Burlington House, London.

The British Museum, which had the largest natural history collections in the world during the nineteenth century, was steadily building up its resources throughout the post-Napoleonic period and arranged them more or less along Linnaean lines. It was exceptionally well placed to do so, because British trading and military interests covered the globe, and for natural history and ethnology, as well as for archaeology, scientific specimens in great profusion came back with the merchant ships and the Navy. The Dutch had similar advantages, although not on such an extensive scale, but in Germany the situation was quite different. In an important article published in 1907, the German museologist F. Römer pointed out that the idea of a display collection (Schausammlung) in a natural history museum was very recent in Germany. The two largest museums, in Berlin and Hamburg, had had such collections for no more than twenty years and nine other provincial cities had entered this field even more recently. The majority of museums of all types had been founded in the early nineteenth century, 'at a time when Germany was poor'. Many collections had been formed by natural history societies, 'whose means were also restricted'. Even the State museums had only a small budget for purchasing animals, and there were very few posts in museums for zoologists. Trading links with overseas countries hardly existed and any collecting trips which societies or private individuals might organise for themselves, were extremely costly and difficult to arrange.[5]

The outcome of the Franco-Prussian War and the rapid build-up of the German

Navy brought about a radical change.

> The great upswing in the German economy after 1870, combined with
> the growing rise in the standard of living, provided not only the
> financial means for new enterprises, but also an enthusiasm for scien-
> tific work, especially in the natural sciences.
>
> The large number of merchant ships and naval vessels which we now
> have gives thousands of people every year an opportunity to travel the
> world: numerous government officials are now resident abroad and our
> colonies attract many young people to the tropics and bring them into
> close touch with the wonderful natural environment of these regions.
> Before they leave Germany, colonial officials and army officers are
> specially instructed as to the needs of our museums and are required,
> as a matter of duty, to carry out tasks on their behalf. The German
> Empire finances and equips major expeditions. Warships are often
> given scientific assignments, and private individuals, at their own
> expense, are now in a position to undertake research and collecting
> abroad.[6]

But, as we have already noted, the British got there first and, in museums as in all
other fields, those who begin later are able to profit by the mistakes and experiences
of the pioneers. For most of its nineteenth-century existence, the Natural History
Department of the British Museum suffered from three serious disadvantages,
appallingly cramped accommodation, an obstinate and reactionary Director, and an
inadequate theoretical base for its work. The second and third disadvantages were
closely linked, and both concern the theories of Charles Darwin.

Before Darwin published what is popularly known as *The Origin of Species*[7] in 1859,
there was no dynamic theory to account for change and development in the natural
world. Botanists, zoologists, palaeontologists and geologists, and therefore
museums, were able to classify and describe their specimens, but they were in no
position to understand or to explain to the general public why changes had occurred.
There was no realisation that one form of life had led to another, that the evidence
had to be arranged and thought about as a series. In his insistence on the serial view
of change, Darwin performed much the same kind of service for natural history as
Pitt-Rivers did for ethnology and archaeology, although Pitt-Rivers' theories never
aroused the same ferocious opposition as Darwin's. The reason for the difference is
not far to seek. Pitt-Rivers did not have to contend with accusations that his theories
undermined the traditional basis of Christianity. Those who condemned Darwin
insisted that, on the evidence of the Bible, God had created man complete and
human. Adam and Eve were the same in all essentials as Victorian people. They
were human from the start. Not so, said Darwin. The Victorians and the apes had a
common parentage. It was a very long way back, but there was ample evidence to
confirm it.

Sir Henry Flower, who became Director of the Natural History Museum in 1884 and rescued it from anti-Darwinism.

In the violent public debate which ensued from *The Origin of Species*, Darwin's theory was strongly and successfully supported by Professor T. H. Huxley. It was consistently opposed and ridiculed by Sir Richard Owen who, in addition to being the President of the Royal Society, was the Director of the Natural History Department of the British Museum. While he ruled, as he did until 1884, when he was in his eighty-first year, the chances of Darwinism making any substantial inroads into the Museum were slight.

His successor, Sir William Henry Flower, was a man of quite a different order. Born in 1831,[8] he qualified as a doctor and, in this capacity, went with the British Army to the Crimea. In 1861 he was appointed Conservator of the Hunterian Museum of the Royal College of Surgeons. He remained in this post until 1884, by which time he had completely reorganised the Museum along scientific lines. In 1884 he succeeded Sir Richard Owen as Director of the Natural History Museum, which had moved to its new building in South Kensington three years earlier. Owen had been in charge of the collections since 1856, when they were still in their old cramped quarters in the British Museum at Bloomsbury.

Flower was almost certainly the greatest museologist in Britain during the Victorian period, with a sharp, original mind and first-class organising ability. Sir Henry Cole, whose work has been discussed in the previous chapter, was perhaps the better impresario, but he was an essentially practical man and lacked Flower's theoretical ability. Five years after he took control at the Natural History Museum, in his Presidential Address to the British Association at its 1889 Meeting,[9] Flower took stock of the situation he had inherited at the Museum and told his listeners what he had done in order to begin creating a scientific museum of which the country could be proud.

There was first, he said, the problem of deciding what natural history was. Where did it begin and where did it end? What, for that matter, was a 'naturalist'? The meanings of both words had certainly narrowed considerably during his lifetime. Natural history at one time had been applied to 'the study of all the phenomena of the universe which are inedependent of the agency of man'. Then, with the introduction of terms like astronomy, chemistry, geology for the new specialised sciences, 'natural history' had gradually narrowed down in most people's minds 'into that portion of the subject which treats of the history of creatures endowed with life'. In many quarters, however, botany had split off from natural history, so that a naturalist and zoologist had nearly become synonymous terms. With the introduction of the new and more scientific-sounding term, 'biology', 'natural history' had been 'practically eliminated' from scientific terminology. 'Natural history' should not, however, be allowed to die. It was too useful a link between the scientist and the general public. So, 'since it is certain to maintain its hold on popular language, I would venture to suggest the desirability of restoring it to its original and really definite signification, contrasting it with the history of man and of his works, and of the changes which have been wrought in the universe by his intervention'.

This was the principle which had been followed when the decision was taken to move the Natural History collections to South Kensington. What was man-made stayed behind in Bloomsbury: what was not, went. But it was a very rule of thumb approach and it failed completely where anthropology was concerned. If man was nothing more than physical structure, he clearly belonged to South Kensington, but anthropology, the study of man, means far more than that: 'It includes his mental development, his manners, customs, traditions and languages. The illustration of his works of art, domestic utensils and weapons of war are essential parts of its study.' It was no answer at all to say that anthropology was concerned only with

The New Natural History Museum, South Kensington by A. Waterhouse, A.R.A., Architect. An engraving, in *Building News*, 14 February 1879, from Alfred Waterhouse's watercolour of the Museum.

those human beings who were the closest to animals, 'savages and prehistoric people', and that consequently anthropology belonged properly to the Natural History Museum. Such an attitude was, he felt, 'utterly unscientific'.

The only answer to such problems would have been 'one grand institution – an ideal institution such as the world has not yet seen, but into which the old British Museum might at one time have developed'. But this dream of a comprehensive museum, which Prince Albert had tried to realise at South Kensington, had been brought to nothing, partly by a shortage of money and partly as a result of sectional interests and empire-building in the academic world.

'Professors and curatorships of this or that division of science are founded and endowed', he said, 'and their holders are usually tenacious either of encroachment upon or of any wide enlargement of the boundaries of the subject they have under-taken to teach or to illustrate, and in this way, more than any other, passing phases of scientific knowledge have become crystallised or fossilised in institutions where they might least have been expected. I may instance many European universities and great museums in which zoology and comparative anatomy are still held to be distinct subjects taught by different professors, and where, in consequence of the division of the collections under their charge, the skin of an animal illustrating the zoology, and the skeleton and teeth, illustrating the anatomy, must be looked for in different and perhaps remotely placed buildings.'

These comments were remarkably far-sighted, since the situation is in many respects considerably worse now than it was in 1889. Sir Henry went further in his analysis of the problem, when he said that the majority of the museums were failing in their

The Eastern Dinosaur Gallery at the
Natural History Museum as it appeared
between 1805 and 1910. The display
system was advanced for its time.

The central hall of the Museum as it was
when it first opened.

public duty by confusing their two completely separate functions: to provide facilities for research, which might well be highly specialised, and to organise displays for the general public, which should put objects into a much wider context. What he called 'exhibitions' were not for experts and study collections were not for the general public. It was foolish to try to combine the two, yet most museums attempted to do so.

Flower returned again and again to this. The 'instruction of the people' was a matter of the greatest importance, but it was being sacrificed to the interests of scholars, but without providing scholars with the facilities they really needed. To make proper provision for both groups was something that he referred to as 'the new museum idea' and, in his Presidential Address to the Museums Association in 1893, he regretted that he had found little sign of it in operation at the Natural History Museum when he took it over in 1884. It had received powerful support from many distinguished figures, among them T. H. Huxley, 'but Owen, whose official position made him the chief scientific adviser in the construction of the new National Museum of Natural History, never became reconciled to it, and, unfortunately, threw all the weight of his great authority on the opposite side'.[10]

In the public galleries, he believed, the prime duty of the curator was to produce exhibitions which would be attractive to 'all who wish to obtain that knowledge which is the ambition of many cultivated persons to acquire without becoming specialists or experts'.[11] For a natural history museum, and probably other kinds as well, this required that certain clear principles should be observed. Flower summarised them in this way. 'The number of the specimens must be strictly limited, according to the nature of the subject to be illustrated and the space available. None must be placed either too high or too low for ready examination. There must be no crowding of specimens one behind the other, and with a clear space around each. If an object is worth putting into a gallery at all, it is worth such a position as will enable it to be seen. Every specimen exhibited should be good of its kind, and all available skill and care should be spent upon its preservation and on rendering it capable of teaching the lesson it is intended to convey. Every specimen should have its definite purpose, and no absolute duplicates should on any account be admitted. Above all, the purpose for which each specimen should be exhibited, and the main lesson to be derived from it, must be distinctly indicated by the labels affixed, both as headings of the various divisions of the series and to the individual specimens.'[12]

All this might appear fairly obvious, but it was revolutionary in its day, with the great majority of museums looking more like storerooms than exhibitions. The saddest element in the situation was that during the last quarter of the nineteenth century the money and the will to build large scientific museums had arrived just in advance of the theories which would allow such museums to be used properly. In London, Paris, Berlin and Vienna, the principal capital cities of Europe, large new buildings were created almost simultaneously to house collections which had long outgrown their previous accommodation, only for their owners and users to discover that they were seriously out-of-date as soon as they were opened. If it had been possible to delay them for a few years, the results would have been a great deal more satisfactory. As it turned out, however, the history of these grand and expensive Victorian buildings has been one of continuous compromise. The situation in the United States was a good deal better, partly because there was a greater freedom from traditions and restrictions and partly because the new buildings came a crucial five or ten years later than their counterparts in Europe. The National Museum in Washington, for example, was designed from the start in a manner which allowed 'the study series' and 'the exhibition series', in Flower's terminology, to be kept separate.

There have been many attempts to design museum buildings which would meet Flower's requirements. The plan favoured by Pitt-Rivers was for a system of concentric circles.[13] Flower's own scheme was linear, in a rectangular building which had the public galleries running along the front of the building, with the reserve or study collections in a windowless area immediately behind that and the rooms for staff and students at the back, where plenty of window space could be provided. In the nineteenth century such museums were not built, but in the twentieth, both ideas have been fruitful.

The Natural History Museum in London was certainly the most influential museum of its kind during both centuries. Its importance was due almost entirely to the genius of Flower, who had the advantage of being able, for many years, to combine the posts of Director and Keeper of Zoology, which ensured that his aims were realised quickly and in the manner in which he had conceived them. His plan was always the same as the one which he had originated at the Royal College of Surgeons: to illustrate natural laws and the facts of evolution, 'and to deal with every modification of form in logical series. He added to this later some striking examples of the leading facts of variation, under domestication, protective colour and form, and the structural laws of plants. Classification was also illustrated, and any striking, if simple, fact, if not generally known, was also illustrated, as, for instance, by raising the feathers of the head to show that a bird has an external ear.'[14]

One of his most appreciated achievements, so far as the general public was concerned, was to wage war against incompetent taxidermists. After visiting many museums, including his own when he took it over, he felt able to refer to 'the sadly neglected art of taxidermy, which continues to fill the cases of our museums with wretched and repulsive caricatures of mammals and birds, out of all natural proportions, shrunken here and bloated there, and in attitudes absolutely impossible for the creature to have assumed when alive'.[15]

That very large numbers of people visited, and still do visit, the Natural History Museum and other similar museums throughout the world is an undisputed fact, but it is more difficult to decide why they come. A few, no doubt, are there for much the same reason as the visitors to Sir Ashton Lever's museum: to see curiosities and wonders and to enjoy the exotic, but many more for the excellent reasons that they find natural history fascinating and the specimens beautiful. Sir Frederic Kenyon, Director of the British Museum in the 1930s, thought there might be another very important cause of the popularity of natural history museums and of zoos, too.

'The need for such museums', he suggested, 'in their popular as distinct from their scientific function is to a large extent the outcome of the growth of great cities. Till less than a century ago, man throughout the ages lived in the presence of nature. Even the largest towns were not so large but that their natives could reach the country when they chose. Now, many square miles of country are covered with houses and time and money and labour must be spent if a townsman is to see more than the trees of the streets and the sparrows and pigeons which follow the haunts of men. To an industrial country such as ours, and in hundreds of great towns in Europe and America the Book of Nature is closed to a large proportion of the population and a great source of refreshment, humanism and inspiration is cut off. If such a nation is to preserve its soul and its sanity, it must take steps to make the wonders and beauties of nature known to the town population. Increased facilities for locomotion and the multiplication of holidays are important agencies to this end, but museums of natural history have a great part to play.'[16]

The idea that the natural history museum provides the countryside at second hand is an interesting one and there may be something in it, although probably motorcars have made it less true now than when Sir Frederic was writing, but it is surely reasonable to ask, 'whose countryside?' The collections of any large museum are worldwide and English children could hardly expect to see lions and birds of paradise in rural Devon or, for that matter, brontosaurs in any country district anywhere today. But one could at least agree that plants, birds and animals are not paving stones, houses and department stores, and to that extent the natural history museum symbolises the world beyond the city limits. One could also argue that town-dwellers became more cut off from nature when cars, lorries and buses replaced horses. But, cutting through all these considerations is the undeniable fact that in Sir Henry Flower's day, museums, zoos and botanical gardens had the field to themselves. His successors have had to compete with television, and to assume and absorb it. To a large extent, the public judge them by how well they succeed in this. That television has profoundly influenced design and presentation techniques in all museums can hardly be in question.[17] The phenomenal success of natural history programmes on television is the background against which museums in this field now have to operate.

One very important effect of television is that it has widened the gap between the back and the front of the house or, in Sir Henry Flower's terms, between the public galleries and their visitors on the one hand and the reserve collections, students and research workers on the other. Up to at least the outbreak of the Second World War, both sets of people were assumed to be serious-minded, although on different levels, and for both the emphasis was heavily on what were always referred to as 'the specimens'. A lively presentation of the exhibits was neither expected, nor given, a fact which can be easily checked by looking at almost any pre-1900 museum gallery – and there are a surprising number still about. The style was, to say the least, sober. What has happened since then is that everything behind the scenes is still sober, but what is in front, on the stage, uses display techniques which mark it off clearly as being for public consumption only.

As an illustration of the enormous change which has taken place, consider the language of a book about the Natural History Museum[18] which was written for children and published shortly before the First World War. The author was a member of the Museum staff and a Fellow of the Zoological Society. He refers to 'the wonderful array of specimens' and says that a comparison of 'the several varieties of domesticated fowls' and 'jungle-fowl, the stock from which all these most-unlike varieties have been raised' contrive to 'bring home, in as graphic a way as possible, the leading facts of that great theory of evolution formulated by our most illustrious countryman, Charles Darwin – the greatest interpreter of Nature whom the world has yet seen'. As a result of the skill of the museum, 'what was before a case of stuffed birds becomes a casket of wonders'.[19]

No modern writer on museums or natural history, or at least no writer in English, would find it possible to use such highly-coloured, hard-selling language. He would rely on his pictures to make the point. He would not need to say of his stuffed birds and animals, 'They were once alive', because, through films and television, visitors to the museum would already have seen them flying, running, jumping, eating and mating in their natural habitat. The museum, in this sense, has become very much a second-best, but it has gradually come to see that it has advantages of another kind. It can, so to speak, stop the film, in order that one can study a particular animal or bird for as long as one likes. One cannot study its behaviour, because behaviour implies movement, and this is the essential difference between a museum and a film or, for that matter, a zoo. The first excels when understanding demands that the subject shall be motionless and in three dimensions, the second when movement and the effects of movement form the basis of the study. From this point of view, a photograph is inferior both to an original object and to a film. It might be described, perhaps, either as an inferior object or as a poor man's film.

During the nineteenth century, a natural history museum and a zoo had little to fear from one another. One might be said to have increased the appetite for the other. It is doubtful, however, if television has increased the appetite either for natural history museums or for zoos. It has tended to create its own appetite and to feed on it and to find its own customers.

There is a more than half-implied assumption in the remarks by Sir Henry Flower which we have quoted above that all museum visitors are potential, if not actual students, with the amateurs differing from the professionals only in the intensity and single-mindedness of their studies. The modern museum curator is more likely to think of his public as being curious and interested, rather than studious. The spirit of the age has changed, not necessarily for the better, and, if one wants to obtain a feeling for the seriousness of both purpose and atmosphere which characterised the average Victorian museum, one could hardly do better than visit a Russian museum today.

It is difficult to decide quite how seriously the curators of nineteenth-century zoos expected their visitors to regard the animals, or how far they were disappointed. A zoo has always overlapped to a greater or lesser extent with a circus, especially among children, who have formed a high proportion of the zoo-going public. A child does not make a sharp distinction between an elephant in a zoo and an elephant in a circus, except to feel, perhaps, that the second is cleverer than the first, a superior kind of elephant, because it can perform tricks, and that, as we know, is a highly unscientific attitude. But a child is not, of course, a scientist, and it is perfectly possible for a zoo, like a natural history museum, to interest scientists and members of the general public, of any age, in quite different ways.

The first modern zoo, that is, a zoo the policy of which was rooted in the scientific study of wild creatures, was the Zoological Gardens in London. This world-famous institution owed its existence to the Royal Zoological Society of London, which was founded and received its Royal Charter in 1826, mainly as a result of the efforts of Sir Humphry Davy, a chemist and President of the Royal Society, who wrote poetry for relaxation, and Sir Stamford Raffles, one of Britain's leading colonial administrators in the early nineteenth century. Sir Stamford was the Royal Zoological Society's first President, and unfortunately died soon after his election.

From the beginning, the Royal Zoological Society has been a scientific body, with the appropriate apparatus of Fellows, a learned journal, monographs and research papers. But, also from the beginning, it has been a place of enjoyment for the public, and it is a fairly safe bet that few of the many thousands of people who have gone there each year have known or cared a great deal about the scientific work on which the displays rest. Displaying and studying animals have, of course, always been closely interconnected. Exotic creatures are valuable property and it is important that they should remain alive and healthy. This involves careful attention to diet and habits, so that a wish to keep the zoo's stock in good condition for display must, in itself, result in steadily increasing biological and environmental knowledge. The survival and progress of zoos has demanded continuous investigation of the way animals behave in their native habitat and how they react to captivity.

A further consideration has necessarily been the attitude of the public to the animals in the zoo's care. In the England of 1826 this was very different from what it is today. All animals, wild and domestic, were treated with a brutality and lack of sympathy and imagination which is found only in rare instances in Britain now, although it is, unfortunately, still all too common elsewhere. It can hardly be a mere coincidence that the Royal Society for the Prevention of Cruelty to Animals was founded at almost exactly the same time as the Royal Zoological Society, in 1824. The belief that it is cruel to keep wild animals in the wholly artificial environment of a small cage has developed only gradually during the present century.[20] The pioneer in displaying animals in comparatively natural surroundings was Carl Hagenbeck (1844–1913), who inherited and enlarged his father's collections and founded Hagenbeck's Zoo in Hamburg in 1907. The zoo is still run by the Hagenbeck family. The first United States zoo, in Philadelphia, was created, as in Britain, by a Society. It was opened to the public in 1907.

It is curious that what would seem to be a natural and inevitable development, the hybridisation of a zoo and a natural history museum, should have been so slow in arriving. The reasons for the delay were partly physical, partly philosophical and partly a matter of empire-building. The major natural history museums were in the centre of cities, where there was no adjacent land on which to create a zoo, running a zoo suggested a degree of showmanship from which the more academic and influential zoologists shuddered, and the blending of a museum with a zoo involved merging two empires into one, a process which always, and in any field, leads to fierce resistance.

Throughout the twentieth century there have been many partial attempts to bridge the two kinds of institution, especially in order to arouse the interests of children, but the first thoroughgoing venture was at Emmen in the Netherlands where, since 1970, the Noorder Dierenpark – Northern Animal Park – has been a centre of experiment and innovation which has influenced theory and practice throughout the world.

In 1935, when Willem Oosting established a small zoo in the garden of his family home, Emmen was still an agricultural village. After the Second World War it was designated a Growth Town by the Government, and the thirteen acres of parkland which was and is the home of the Animal Park is now completely surrounded by buildings. A rural zoo has become an urban zoo. By 1968, when the expansion of Emmen was well under way, the zoo was experiencing serious financial problems. The number of visitors had seriously declined and the money required for maintenance and development did not exist. At that point, the enterprise was converted into a limited liability company of an original kind. Half the shares are still owned by the founder's family and half by the Municipality of Emmen. The company is controlled by a Board of Governors, half of whom are Municipal Councillors. The Municipality agreed to underwrite the loans contracted by the zoo, on condition that it gave prior approval to all borrowing. The management was taken over by Mr and

'African Savannah' in the Noorder
Dierenpark, Emmen.

Mrs Rensen-Oosting, the daughter of the original proprietor and her architect
husband, and the situation was rapidly transformed.

The Northern Animal Park, as it now exists, is very much a child of Europe's
economic differences during the past fifteen years. It is a commercial venture, in that
its operating costs are not subsidised from public funds. However, the town is
situated in an area of high unemployment, so that it has been government policy to
assist non-profitmaking organisations to invest in new, job-creating projects. The
zoo has made good use of this opportunity and three-quarters of the construction
costs of its new buildings have been met in this way.

The zoo at Emmen is now financially viable, with nearly a million visitors a year, a
remarkable figure for an institution which is a long distance from any large con-
urbation. It attributes the turnround in its fortunes to the new policy which it
adopted in 1970, and from which it has never departed, that in today's world a zoo's
right to existence can be derived only from its educational rôle. This does not mean
that the recreational aspect should be ignored. On the contrary, the philosophy at
Emmen is that the most effective education is that which is experienced as recreation.
In the opinion of the management, a prerequisite of the education process beginning
to operate is the proper presentation of the animals. A great deal of knowledge can
be transmitted unconsciously by 'exhibiting' – Emmen does not like the word –
animals or groups of animals of different species in an environment which is as close

A temporary exhibition in the
Africanium at the Noorder Dierenpark.

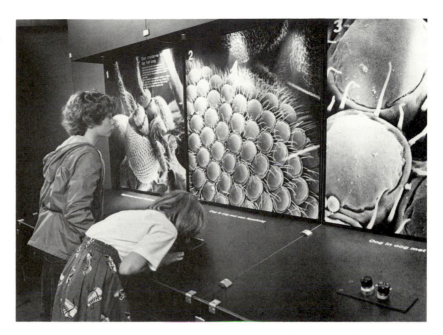

as possible to the real thing. For this reason, a geographical layout has been adopted. There is, within the zoo area, an African, a South American and a European 'region', with sub-regions within each – an African savannah and lake district, islands for monkeys, special quarters for cheetahs, and the Africa House, which is arranged to give an impression of the tropical rain forest in western central Africa.

In the Emmen philosophy, education does not consist only in presenting the animals in a meaningful way. The zoo makes extensive use of all types of visual aid in order to stimulate its visitors' interest, to provoke and answer questions and to help people to arrive at useful conclusions. It takes great pains to avoid static situations. Themes are changed regularly, nearly always annually, and each theme is developed throughout the zoo, with films, exhibitions, games, puppet-plays and publications all focussed on it.

In 1980 the zoo opened its Museum of Natural History which, together with the adjoining Africa House, is called the Africanium – the word 'museum' is deliberately not used. Here, the annual theme is dealt with in considerable detail by means of six exhibitions. In 1985, for example, the theme was Reproduction. Within the Africanium, a small ethnographical museum was created, to make clear that man cannot be thought about or studied in isolation from nature as a whole. Also in 1985, Biochron was added to the educational facilities of the Dierenpark, a new and important museum which tells the story of life on earth and which forms an introduction to the zoo. It is now possible to weld the museum and the zoo together. The aim has been clearly stated – 'Anyone visiting a zoo and seeing all those animals from every corner of the world will be amazed at the immense variety of forms. The question will inevitably arise as to why there is this incredible wealth of species. In order to answer this question, it is necessary to go way back in time to the moment when life began and then to follow the trail up to the present day. This incredibly exciting journey can be made in the Biochron. A voyage of discovery through 4600 million years compressed into a lightning visit of ± 4600 seconds.'[21]

What the Noorder Dierenpark has been attempting to do is to bring cohesion and point to its collections, and to do so in a way which appeals to a generation which has been reared on television and accepts its methods as normal. Its distinction has been in the thoroughness of its approach. It has thrown away the traditional division between a zoo and a museum as irrelevant, it has taken the best scientific advice, in the knowledge that efficient popularisation must rest on a foundation of sound scholarship, and it has employed first-class designers in order to make the message attractive. In this programme, living animals are both collection and media.

To a greater or lesser degree, every zoo and every natural history museum in the world has been trying to accommodate itself to changing attitudes on the part of the public and in the process it has had to reconsider the task it is trying to accomplish. The problem with which all old-established natural history museums have found

The entrance hall to Biochron, at the Noorder Dierenpark. An exhibition about the geological timescale of the Earth.

Biochron. A reconstruction of a carboniferous forest, 300 million years ago.

'The Rise of the Reptiles' in the Biochron. A life-size reproduction of the flying pteranodon in the exhibition.

themselves faced during the past thirty or forty years has been basically the same, to take steps to end the fragmentation and over-specialisation of knowledge. In the case of the Natural History Museum in London, this has amounted to a return to the original nineteenth-century plan, to present 'a comprehensive, philosophic and connected view' of natural history. In the course of time, the Victorian aim got lost. Dr Roger Miles, who has played a major part in the recent reorganisation at South Kensington, describes the Museum's fall from grace in forthright terms.

'What resulted', he says, 'was not a connected and philosophic view of biology, but a narrow-based, incoherent and fragmented one. Over the next ninety years[22] there was no thoroughgoing attempt to relate the various galleries to one another, or to place them in the context of biology as a whole. Little attempt was made to go beyond

The Natural History Museum in the television age, with a public which is 'curious and interested', rather than 'studious'.

Left The new Human Biology section. How do we grow up? Why do our bodies change? An introduction to chemical messengers.

Right The Origin of Species. On arrival at this part of the Natural History Museum, visitors are faced with the basic question which Darwin tried to solve.

the appearance of organisms and explain their significance in nature. Thus as biology developed, the Museum became less and less what it was intended to be. Visitors and objects were juxtaposed, but nothing was done to help visitors organise or extend their knowledge.'[23] Since 1970, the exhibitions have been completely reorganised and redesigned, in order 'to make the Museum an exciting place where the layman can explore and discover natural history'.[24] This has involved following what one might call the Emmen approach, but without, of course, the live animals. 'The complete set of new exhibitions will cover all forms of life – including man, who was largely excluded from the subject-matter of the original displays. However, it will do more than just demonstrate the diversity of the living world. It will show how living things interact with one another, and introduce major concepts of modern biology, such as that of an eco-system. It will describe the chemical and physical processes which maintain life, and ideas such as that of natural selection. It will thus stress four clearly-defined themes of modern biology: (a) man, (b) ecology, (c) life processes and behaviour, and (d) evolution and diversity.'[25]

That the fulfilment of these aims has transformed and rejuvenated the Natural History Museum to an extent which would have been almost unimaginable even ten years ago is hardly a matter for discussion, but the Museum should not be given too much credit for what has, after all, been a worldwide movement.[26] The Natural History Museum in London has been responding to international pressures as well as returning to the faith of its founding fathers. Nevertheless, its size and immense prestige have certainly constituted a guarantee that its change of heart and innovations would be taken seriously and would have a considerable influence among museums of a similar kind elsewhere.

Yet, despite the wind of change that has blown through its galleries, the British Museum (Natural History) has remained politically cautious, at a time when a number of biological topics have been the cause of great controversy. The eco-system to which it is now dedicated includes only faint signs of a political dimension. Its eco, one might say, is not fully eco, certainly not to the extent that one finds elsewhere. There are certain aspects of biology in which it has shown itself disinclined to be involved. It has remained, one might say, a *Times* rather than a *Guardian* museum.

One could reasonably contrast it, in this respect, with the Senckenberg Museum in Frankfurt. This has a history rather longer than that of its London counterpart. The Naturmuseum and Forschungs Institut Senckenberg was established in 1817. Since then, it has always been, like the Natural History Museum, an internationally important research institution, with a public museum attached to it. Bombed and largely destroyed during the Second World War, it was forced to consider the form in which it wanted to re-establish itself and soon realised that to make the new a replica of the old was out of the question. Attitudes and aims had changed, and the Museum had to adapt itself accordingly. One wonders how the Natural History Museum, similarly placed, would have reacted.

Until it was bombed, the Senckenberg was a stolid, conventionally Victorian type of museum. It had excellent collections, particularly within the fields of palaeontology and geology, and its research work had an international reputation. The quality of research continues, but the appearance and organisation of the museum is now entirely different. Like the Noorder Dierenpark, it devotes constant attention to making its collections visually attractive and to arranging stimulating special exhibitions on matters of social importance, such as population control and the pollution and degradation of the environment. It achieves this partly by adopting a clearcut, unmistakable and not infrequently provocative position and partly by blending art and scholarship in the most skilful and enthusiastic manner, employing a combination of both in order to increase the impact and significance of the information that it is trying to communicate. The result is something which would have seemed utterly strange forty years ago, a science museum which aims at touching the visitor's emotions as well as his brain, or perhaps one should say, a museum which believes that the intellect is more likely to function if it is encouraged by the emotions.

It would be idle to pretend that a German, Dutch or Scandinavian museum concerned with either natural history or ethnology which had not adopted something of this stance during the past twenty-five years would not have found itself in some difficulties with younger visitors, who expect to find marked evidence of social responsibility in all public institutions. Once again, it is tempting to allow one's fancy to roam and to speculate on how the British Museum (Natural History) might have developed during the post-war period if it had been a country other than Britain.

Museums are, inevitably, conditioned, in their aims, their atmosphere, their appearance and their sense of priorities by the country in which they find themselves. A

Room 5 at the Senckenberg Institute,
c. 1915.

Part of the section devoted to fish at the
Senckenberg Institute, 1985.

The founders of the Goulandris
Museum of Natural History,
Angelos and Niki Goulandris.

textbook illustration of this truth is provided by the Goulandris Museum of Natural History, at Kifissia, on the northern outskirts of Athens. This large museum, housed in a building designed for the purpose, is a private foundation. Conceived, created, paid for and administered by Mr and Mrs Angelos Goulandris, it has been developed over the past two decades and is devoted to the study of the Greek natural environment. It is still the only museum of its kind in the country – apart from a branch museum very recently established in Corfu – and, although it is an entirely private venture, it finds itself functioning, *faute de mieux*, as the State Museum of Natural History, a situation which is unparalleled anywhere else in the world. The Goulandris found a vacuum and they have done their devoted best to fill it. The work which they have carried out and financed in the encouragement of research and in the awakening of an interest in natural history, especially among schoolchildren, deserves the gratitude of their own country and the admiration of Europe as a whole. An interest in natural history of any kind is outside the Greek tradition. Children do not keep pets and the study of wildlife is not considered a suitable subject for schools. This attitude is reflected throughout society. Both the Greek government and the Greek people have paid scant attention to the conservation either of the landscape or of wild creatures. Domestic and farm animals are treated with indifference, if not actual cruelty. Professional ornithologists do not exist in Greece.

What the Goulandris have therefore created is not so much a museum as a beacon in the darkness. Completed in 1983 with the opening of its Ornithological Gallery, it now presents the full range of plant and animal life in Greece, together with its rocks, minerals and palaeontology. With its large library, its herbaria and its documentation centre, the Museum offers excellent research facilities. It has a carefully planned educational programme for children, while at the same time providing for the scientific and technical training of its staff. It is also carrying out an important series of nature conservation projects.

In all matters regarding the natural environment, the Goulandris Museum is the conscience of the nation. There can surely be no other museum in the world, of whatever kind, which is in quite that position. By comparison, the British Museum (Natural History) seems a positive luxury. The Goulandris Museum could perhaps be described as the national powerhouse for generating an interest in natural history throughout the country, and a sensitivity to the forces which menace the environment. To be effective, this kind of interest must be widely distributed. It cannot be centralised and the need for it is worldwide. What may well be a pattern for progress in the developing countries can be found in Kenya, where the growth and popularity of local Wildlife Clubs during the 1970s and 1980s has been a most encouraging feature of the educational scene. Many of these clubs have small museums of their own, usually in schools, and these, with their combination of natural history and archaeological displays, complement at the local level what the National Museum is doing in Nairobi. There are already signs that something similar is beginning to happen in Greece.

Entrance to the Goulandris Museum of Natural History.

View from the entrance hall to the botanic galleries. A three-dimensional model of a plant-cell illustrates photosynthesis, the sole means of maintaining life on our planet. Enlarged or natural-scale models of fungi, lichens, algae, mosses, ferns, gynosperms and angiosperms enable the visitor to understand the importance and interrelationship of these groups in the plant kingdom.

Goulandris Museum of Natural History.

Diorama of mountain animals.

Part of the museum's display of aquatic birds.

Chapter Five
Science, technology and industry

National Museum of Technology, Paris: *'A public depository of machines, models, tools, drawings, descriptions and books of all the arts and trades'*

Science Museum, London: *'The discoveries which have changed the life of every member of the community'*

Deutsches Museum, Munich: *'A museum of masterworks of natural science and technology'*

Museum of Science and Industry, Chicago: *'Intense involvement of visitors through hands-on participation'*

Palace of Discovery, Paris: *'Its great thrust in scientific demonstrations and minimising of artefacts'*

Municipal Museum, Rüsselsheim: *'Allowing the historical dimension within the objects to become visible again'*

In pre-industrial societies, such as are still to be found in many parts of the world today, craftsmen work in public, so that every member of the community can see and understand the processes and techniques of production. Making things is part of everyday life. One can wander through the artisan quarters of India or Cyprus, for example, and watch technical skills being practised. Today, in Western countries, these activities are usually 'hidden behind factory walls, where only the specialised factory worker enters',[1] and even most industrial workers themselves are well informed only about what goes on in their own particular factory, and not necessarily in every part of that. For more than a century and a half, the museum has therefore had an important social rôle to play in explaining different branches of technology to people who might otherwise remain in ignorance of them, a function which has been accepted and developed in more recent times by films and television.

The first museum in this category to be established was what is now the National Museum of Technology – Musée National des Techniques – in Paris. It was, like the museum in the Louvre, a child of the French Revolution. The idea itself was not new. In the early seventeenth century René Descartes had suggested the creation of a museum of scientific instruments and of the mechanical trades. What he had in mind was something much more enterprising than a mere collection of objects. A skilled person was to be attached to each category of exhibits – the arrangement would be by trades – in order to answer visitors' questions and to explain how the various processes were carried out. Nothing, unfortunately, came of the plan. However, in 1794, when France was being governed by the Directory, a Decree[2] was passed by the National Convention which brought Descartes' proposal closer to reality. It began as follows:

> Article 1 – There shall be formed at Paris, under the name of the Conservatoire des Arts et Métiers, and under the instruction of the Commission of Agriculture and the Arts, a public depository of

The National Museum of Technology, Paris:

Top left Steam waggon designed by Cugnot in 1771.

Bottom left Lathe constructed for Louis XVI by Mercklein in 1780.

Top right Pascal's calculating machine, 1652.

Bottom right Model of a carpenter's workshop, made by Étienne Calla and commissioned by the Comtesse de Genlis.

machines, models, tools, drawings, descriptions, and books of all the arts and perfected inventions ['machines inventées et perfectionées'] shall be deposited at the Conservatoire.

Article 2 – The construction and use of tools and machines employed in the arts and trades shall be explained there.

It was some time before the Decree was put into force, but in 1799 the museum was installed in the medieval Priory of Saint-Martin-des-Champs, which had ceased to be used for religious purposes in the previous year. Several collections of models, machines and scientific instruments were brought together there, including especially those of the celebrated inventor, Jacques de Vaucanson.[3] The Priory buildings were restored and enlarged at various times during the nineteenth century and eventually came to consist of a number of narrow exhibition halls, in parts of which the lighting was so poor that the contents of cases placed along the walls were almost invisible.

Museographically, the National Museum of Technology can hardly be described as avant-garde, and the educational possibilities of its collections have never been properly realised, but during the nearly two centuries of its life it has accumulated a treasury of historically interesting objects, ranging from Pascal's 1652 calculating machine to early photographic equipment, and from apparatus used by Lavoisier to one of the finest collections of clocks and watches in the world. Its collections, however, conceal the original purpose of the Museum, which was to use them in order to communicate to students, teachers and the general public the most import-ant aspects of contemporary science and technology. It was not conceived as an historical museum, but it gradually acquired that rôle as its collections inevitably became historic with the passage of time. Like other early technical museums, it became largely the national repository of technical objects from the past, a museum of history rather than of education in the principles and practice of science and technology.

The entrance to the Museum of Patents, South Kensington, a watercolour by J. C. Lunchenik. The building was later dismantled and taken away to become the Bethnal Green Museum.

Yet it was of great importance in the development of museums, because it helped to swing the attention of the public and of governments away from its obsession with art and antiquities and towards more solid and practical matters. By existing, under government patronage, and by collecting, conserving, valuing and publicising useful, as distinct from merely pleasant and beautiful things, the National Museum of Technology did much to make this new type of museum reputable.

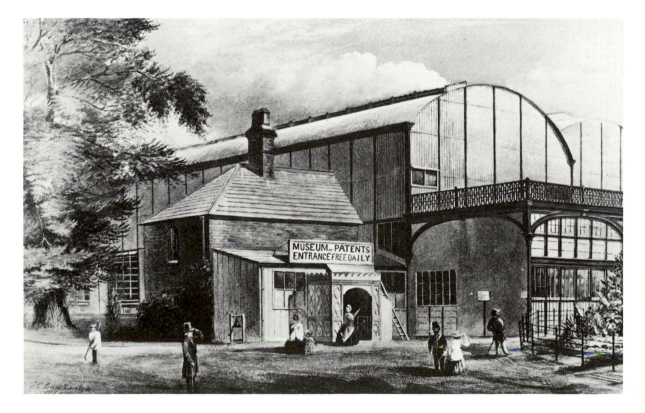

The influence of the Science Museum in London has been of a different kind. Its origins were much vaguer than those of its predecessor in Paris. It grew, in several stages, out of the broadly-based South Kensington Museum, which was opened in 1857, with a strange hotch-potch of industrial and artistic collections. At that time there was no concept, in England or elsewhere, of a Museum of Science in the modern sense. The idea of pure science was only just beginning to develop in the public mind and at South Kensington the Museum, on the science side, was primarily an educational institution, attempting to provide teaching in basic principles for teachers and skilled workers. It was an instructional body and its collections were gathered together mainly for this purpose.

During the 1860s and 1870s, other buildings were put up on the South Kensington site. One of them housed the Patent Museum, which was not altogether what its title suggested. It contained, for example, Stephenson's 'Rocket' and 'Puffing Billy' locomotives, an early reaping machine, Richard Arkwright's original spinning machine and the apparatus used by Wheatstone in the development of the electric telegraph. The collections were not confined to patented inventions, although these were well represented and, although this was probably not intended, what eventually resulted was a museum of technical devices.

In 1874 a Royal Commission was formed 'to enquire into the State of Scientific Instruction', and museums were included in its terms of reference. In its final report, the Commission recommended 'the formation of a Collection of Physical and

Part of the Educational Collection at South Kensington *c*. 1860. This shows the interior of the Museum of Patents building.

Mechanical Instruments', and went on to say that 'we submit for consideration whether it may not be expedient that this collection, the collection of the Patent Museum, and that of the Scientific and Educational Department of the South Kensington Museum should be united and placed under the authority of a Minister of State'. What then happened provides a classic instance of the reluctance of the British Government and Civil Service to let anything happen too quickly.

By a Minute dated 22 January 1875, the Lords of the Committee of Council of Education approved a proposal to form a Loan Collection of scientific apparatus, which was to include not only apparatus for teaching and research, that is, modern apparatus, but also 'such as possessed historical interest on account of the persons by whom or the researches in which it had been employed'. This step could perhaps be described as encouraging, rather than enthusiastic. Some progress was, however, being made. In 1876, the Science and Art Department organised a Science Exhibition, which was a great success. Scientific instruments of many types and from many countries were displayed, lectures were given on current scientific progress, and the public was shown how these new developments were affecting their own lives. The man in the street had never before had the tools and methods of pure science presented to him so systematically and in such quantity. But, sadly, this did not result in the Museum being given authority to build up a comprehensive collection of scientific material, which would be kept continuously up-to-date. There were additions from time to time, some of them important, but the Museum was not organised in a way which would have made it possible to take advantage of them.

What followed was half a century, if not more, of inadequate accommodation, absurdly small budgets and what appeared to be official indifference, both to the Museum and to science. It was not until 1909 that a Departmental Committee of the Board of Education concluded that new buildings were both essential and urgent. They would, it declared, 'be of incalculable benefit alike to intellectual progress and to industrial development', and would allow the Museum to be 'an institution of which the country may well be proud'. But the results were hardly spectacular or excessively rapid. Building began in 1913 and, with interruptions caused by two wars, continued sporadically until the 1970s, but the facilities are still completely inadequate and the Museum today has a somewhat tired and run-down appearance, which is eloquent evidence of a chronic shortage of both funds and inspiration.

Why, then, should one include it in a select list of Museums of Influence? There are two good reasons for this, one relating to the 1860s and 1870s, and the other to the 1920s and 1930s. In the first of these periods the South Kensington Museum was the most important focal point in Britain for the efforts of those who were battling to persuade the Government to devote more attention and more money to education in science and technology. Its symbolic value was undoubtedly greater than its actual quality. The fact that it existed and that it was slowly but steadily building up its collections and developing its educational work gave heart to those who were con-

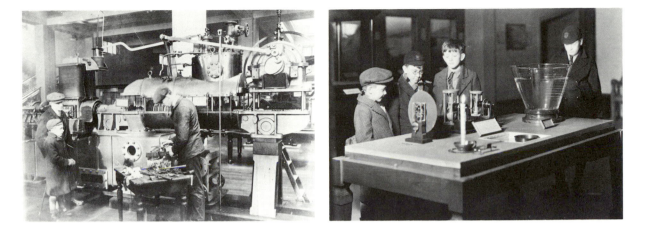

Left Early 1920s. Visitors watching work on a Parsons turbo-generator in the East Gallery of the Science Museum.

Right Working exhibit at the Science Museum, 1950s.

vinced that Britain's survival depended largely on its ability to produce sufficient scientifically-minded people. The influence which the infant and adolescent museum had on this crusade can hardly be over-emphasised. But it was essentially a domestic crusade. Such international influence as the Museum has had came later, and mainly in the interwar period. At the present time, many of its methods of presentation have a markedly old-fashioned flavour and are unlikely to have been widely admired and imitated in the Western world for many years. There have been more lively and more inspiring models available.

But in the 1920s the situation was different. In 1925, Charles R. Richards wrote *The Industrial Museum*. An American, he had been visiting European museums whose collections came within this field and his book was produced mainly to show his fellow-countrymen what was going on in the world outside and to encourage them to do something similar. It is interesting to observe what it was about the Science Museum that evoked his enthusiasm.

Firstly, there was the not unimportant matter of the collections. 'The Science Museum', he reported, 'is extremely rich in original material and models associated directly with great inventors and pioneers, such as Watt, Arkwright, Stephenson, Maudslay, Bessemer, and with men of science, among whom may be mentioned Babbage, Herschel and Kelvin. Models and drawings of early engines of Newcomen and Watt, a locomotive of 1813, Stephenson's "Rocket" and other locomotives of 1829, Arkwright's first spinning frame, a replica of Hargreaves' spinning jenny, Maudslay's first screw-cutting lathe, and other milestones of the Industrial Revolution are numbered among the technical treasures.'[4]

The preservation of such items bordered on the miraculous, and it was due in no small part to the fact that the Science Museum had been there to receive and care for them. Without a national depository, the survival of such important material would have been much less likely.

Display of 'Puffing Billy' and other
steam locomotives, 1939.

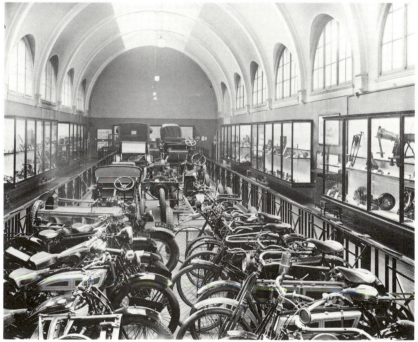

Gallery 18 of the Science Museum in
1930. A masterly example of how not to
do it.

Richards found another great merit in the Science Museum. 'Of late years', he told his readers, 'much attention has been paid to the elucidation of the exhibits from the educational standpoint. A large number of the technical models have been arranged to operate mechanically, and diagrams and other explanatory matter have been effectively introduced. Much care has been taken with the labels attached to the exhibits. These labels present not only the historic facts regarding the exhibits, but describe their construction and operation.'[5]

But, and it was an important qualification, 'the arrangement of material in progressive series to illustrate industrial evolution is not a conspicuous feature of the museum'.[6] It was a serious defect and one from which the Museum still to some extent suffers, although the Museum's publications during the past fifty years have done much to compensate for shortcomings in the displays. The Science Museum publications might almost be said to have constituted an influence in their own right.

The Director of Chicago's Museum of Science and Industry, Victor J. Danilov, has suggested that museums of science and technology have passed through three major stages of evolution, 'with the first two phases taking place in Europe and the third receiving its greatest impetus in America'.[7] This division seems reasonable enough, providing that one allows a museum to have more than one life. The Science Museum in London, in its Victorian clothing, belongs clearly enough to Phase One, the stage of regarding the collections mainly as teaching material, where the National Museum of Technology also has to be placed in its early years. But the Science Museum described by Charles Richards in 1925 was at least partly a Phase Two museum, in its use of working models and diagrams to show how machines and processes functioned.

The Science Museum's publications desk in April 1928. The small size of the desk illustrates the low priority given to museum sales at this time.

Oskar von Miller (1855–1934), founder of the Deutsches Museum. The photograph was taken in 1925.

The curiously named German Museum (Deutsches Museum) in Munich was not only a Phase Two museum, but the first true representative of the category. It came into being at the beginning of this century, largely through the imagination and stupendous energy of one man, Dr Oskar von Miller. Dr von Miller was a distinguished engineer who specialised in the generation and transmission of electricity. In 1903 he produced a plan for what he called 'a museum of master-works of natural science and technology', and presented it to a gathering of government and city representatives, academics and industrialists in Munich. What he had in mind was a museum which would illustrate the development of science and technology, especially in Germany, and at the same time show how progress in these fields had influenced the character and quality of the life of the people. He was successful in obtaining the enthusiastic support of prominent industrialists and scientists and, what was equally important, of the city and central government. The Association of German Engineers (Verein Deutscher Ingenieure) was also solidly behind the project.

For the first twenty years of its existence, the Deutsches Museum had to content itself with accommodation in the old building of the Bavarian National Museum, but in 1911 the City decided to make the island in the River Isar available for the construction of a new museum, which was completed two years later. It cost fourteen million marks, of which the City of Munich contributed one million, the Bavarian State Government two million, the Central Government (Deutsches Reich) two million and German industry rather more than two million. Most of the building materials were obtained as gifts, and the construction and installation work was carried out either without charge or at cost. The railways conveyed all building supplies free.

The Deutsches Museum was possibly the most complex community enterprise the capitalist world has ever seen. Although there have been many examples, especially in the United States, of more straightforward partnerships between a local authority, which provides and maintains the museum building, and some form of independent organisation, which owns the collections and runs the museum, the complexity of the public and private support for the Deutsches Museum must surely be unique. With the German example to hand, one wonders why nothing similar was attempted in the case of London's Science Museum, where an adequate building early in the present century would have been an immense advantage. There were probably two fundamental reasons for the difference – the low prestige and poor organisation of professional engineers in Britain, and the extreme individualism of British industrialists.

Unfortunately, the outbreak of war in 1914 made it impossible to install the collections and open the museum until 1925. The formal inauguration was on 6 May 1925, which was Oskar von Miller's seventieth birthday.

A little earlier, the Deutsches Museum had been visited by Charles Richards, during his tour of similar institutions in Europe. He was greatly impressed by the

Replica of George Stephenson's
locomotive, 'Puffing Billy' (1813),
photographed in the Deutsches
Museum in 1939.

The first motorcar built by Carl Benz,
in 1886.

Reproduction of a coal-mine in Upper
Bavaria showing techniques in use in
1900.

The aviation collection of the Deutsches
Museum, in its first home in the
National Museum, 1921.

care that had been taken to make the exhibitions interesting. 'A large part of the apparatus in the collections is in working condition', he noted, 'Many of the models are connected with electric motors, and may be actuated by visitors or guides'.[8] The important features of industrial and mining processes and of transport systems were made clear to the visitor. 'The typical method that is pursued is to illustrate the development of every art by first showing the primitive beginnings, through actual apparatus, models or representations. From this starting point the museum shows in sequence the important progressive steps that have taken place.'[9]

Even before the war, the attendances at the Museum had been very encouraging. In 1910 the total reached 300,000, but these figures need to be interpreted with some care. Not all the visitors came voluntarily. From the earliest days, every schoolchild over the age of 10 in Munich had to attend the Museum at least once a year under the guidance of either a teacher or a member of the Museum staff. There were guided tours, too, for adults, conducted by the 'engineers' in charge of the various sections. Public lectures were frequently arranged in the evenings.

A special fund was created to allow factory workers and older students from technology-based schools (Realschulen) and grammar schools (Gymnasien) from all over Germany to spend four days at the Museum. 300 such places were available each year. Those who came were required to write reports on what they had seen and learnt and about six diplomas each year were awarded to those who were judged to have sent in the best reports.

All visitors had to pay for entry. A single visit cost twenty pfennigs, an annual season-ticket three marks and a group ticket for fifteen students one mark. The income from these sources was substantial, but it amounted to no more than a subsidy towards the costs of running and maintaining the Museum. The genius of Oskar von Miller lay primarily in his great ability as a fundraiser, and especially in the skill with which he mixed private and public funding. Exhibits and financial support were obtained from the leading industrial concerns, the City of Munich provided free heating and lighting, academic institutions seconded staff, either part- or full-time. Oskar von Miller was a strong personality, with a well-developed sense of public relations and, although it would be unfair to say that the Deutsches Museum received more credit than it deserved, the entrepreneurial nature of the Museum made sure that its achievements were not disregarded, either nationally or internationally. For a great many people in all countries during the 1920s, which were probably the Museum's golden age, the Deutsches Museum was a model of what a museum devoted to science and technology should be. Its influence in the United States, which had yet to set up similar museums, was certainly considerable.

In the course of time, however, certain weaknesses in its organisation and philosophy became apparent. One arose from the design of the building, where the solidity of the construction and the division into subject areas imposed a rigidity on the internal arrangement and made it difficult to modify the system of display as fashion and new types of technology demanded. The dependence on industrial money also brought serious disadvantages, especially in the matter of setting industry and technology within their social context. Any suggestion that capitalism might not always work for the common good or that industrial relations in Germany had ever been other than faultless would not have been tolerated by the paymasters on whom the Museum depended, a consideration which became even more important as the National Socialist Party increased its control over the life of Germany. Under these circumstances, the temptation to concentrate on 'pure' technology and to disregard the social implications of technical change were very great. The Deutsches Museum yielded to the temptation and, as it did so, its influence outside Germany faded.

But its organisational framework and its methods of financing have stood the test of time. The Museum has been bound into the industrial, commercial and political fabric of Germany with remarkable skill. The administration, apart from the Museum's own full-time staff, is at two levels, in the usual German fashion, with a Supervisory Board and an Advisory Board. The Supervisory Board is composed of nominated members from the Länder; the Cities of Berlin, Bremen, Hamburg and Munich; the principal Academies of Science; industrial and professional associations, and representatives of leading industrial concerns. The Advisory Board includes people from industry, the banks, the technical press and the universities. It is difficult to think of a major organisation within the industrial, commercial or scientific fields which does not send its representative to the Museum's annual meetings.

Each year German industry makes valuable and important gifts of both historic and modern technical equipment, as well as loans for special exhibitions. The firm of Carl Zeiss finances the supervision and operation of the Planetarium, Siemens looks after the repair and maintenance of the Communications section, and other industrial firms give similar help. There are frequent gifts of materials, furnishings and working equipment, and the main publishers provide free copies of any books which come within the Museum's orbit. During the eighty years of its history, the Deutsches Museum has become probably the best-provided of the world's technical museums.

It has reached this position by making sure that the people who run German industry feel that it is 'their' museum and that they have an almost automatic duty to finance it. So far, this policy has worked well but, since one cannot know what the political and economic future of German industry may be, it would seem prudent to widen the basis of the two Boards in a way which would allow for the possibility that future government may be further to the Left than is the case at the present time. No harm would be done by making the policy-making and governing bodies look a little more like the community as a whole, rather than merely the more prosperous and more conservative sections of it. The same could, of course, be said of the Trustees of most American museums of all types.

That is for the future. So far as the past is concerned, there is no doubt that the Deutsches Museum was the big name among museums of science and industry in the years between the wars. Partly because it was much less well publicised, its near-contemporary, the Technical Museum in Vienna, has always tended to be under-rated. Its history has been, to say the least, unfortunate. Conceived while Vienna was the centre of a great empire, built just before the First World War,[10] and opened in 1918, when Vienna had been reduced to the capital of a small, defeated, impoverished country, what the world eventually saw was a museum which would have been avant-garde in 1913, which was modern and still somewhat adventurous in 1918, but which, because of scandalous underfunding, had to be forced to allow the Deutsches Museum to occupy the centre of the stage during the inter-war years. Today it has a sadly old-fashioned look and a degree of imagination is needed in order to recapture the feeling of excitement it created when it was first opened and when national morale was at its lowest ebb.

Architecturally, it was a more intelligently planned building than the one which the Deutsches Museum came to occupy. The ground floor consisted of a single large space covering the whole site. There were no separate or closed exhibition rooms, so that not only were changes in the layout of the exhibits relatively easy to make, but the visitor was able to get a feeling of the links between one branch of technology and another. In some ways, however, the museums in Munich and Vienna were very similar. Both had plenty of working models, both aimed at showing how industrial processes worked and how machines had developed. Both had obtained an undertaking from the educational authorities that schoolchildren should visit the museum once a year. Both were using films in the early 1920s as a means of illustrating technical processes. In all these respects, the two museums were considerably in advance of any others. Both were pioneers of the same new ideas and practices. The problem is to decide which museum is to be given more credit for arriving at these new ideas in the first place and for publicising them in a way that would draw international attention to them and, taken as a whole and for the various reasons given earlier, the Deutsches Museum would seem, with hindsight, to be entitled to the prior place.

It is not difficult to understand why Victor Danilov considered both the Deutsches Museum and the Technical Museum in Vienna to be Phase Two museums. Both were concerned more with the past than with the present and the future. Like the Science Museum in London, they were essentially history-of-technology museums. They might deal with modern developments, but these were principally in the nature of postscripts to their main story. Every Phase Two museum was a storehouse of historical artefacts. An important part of its function, probably the most important, was to collect and conserve objects.

This being so, it is curious that Danilov places the Palace of Discovery (Palais de la Découverte) in Paris within his Phase Two category, since its aims from the begin-

Exhibits and demonstrations in the Palais de la Découverte.

Top Distillation of liquid air.

Centre left Electro-magnetic levitation.

Centre right Demonstration of static electricity.

Bottom Special exhibition on radioactivity.

ning were quite different from those of the Deutsches Museum. Created in 1937 in part of the Grand Palais by the Nobel Prize winner, Jean Perrin, in collaboration with some of the most eminent French scientists of the day, its emphasis has always been strongly on the present.[11] It has described itself as 'a scientific cultural centre' and as 'a dynamic museum'. Every day, university students demonstrate a large number of scientific experiments to visitors, explaining them in language which is intelligible to people with no specialist knowledge of the subject. The preservation of artefacts has never ranked high in its list of priorities, and because of this it has sometimes been reckoned unworthy to be thought of as a museum at all, a consideration which has not bothered its Director and his staff in the slightest, since they have never claimed such a title for their institution. They operate the Palace of Discovery, not the Museum of Discovery, the museum side of French science and technology being catered for by the Museum of Arts and Trades, which we have already discussed.

Yet the official catalogue of French museums, compiled with the authority of Les Musées de France, regularly includes the Palace of Discovery, apparently without any misgivings, and there is a strong case for classifying it as the first of a new line of museums of science and technology which have become important during the past forty years and which, as often as not, are called Science Centres rather than Science Museums. To complicate matters still further, most of the older-established museums of science and technology nowadays incorporate many of the features of the science centre, without, however, abandoning their interest in the history of the subject.

The Palace of Discovery has always been an unashamedly didactic museum, run by people who are convinced of the importance of making as many of their fellow-citizens as possible aware of the principles and applications of science. It has been mostly state-funded, but industrial concerns have been persuaded to sponsor special exhibitions, partly in order to stretch the Museum's budget and partly to indicate the career opportunities which exist in science and technology. Its success has been due to the enthusiasm of the members of its staff, who have improvised and made do in the most remarkable and praiseworthy manner, during a period when science was a poor relation to the humanities in France, much as it was in Britain in the second half of the nineteenth century. In mid twentieth-century France, the Palace of Discovery helped to maintain public interest in science, especially among young people, very much as South Kensington did in late nineteenth-century Britain. During the past twenty years, the situation has completely changed, and the new prestige of science and technology in France has been recognised by the creation of a new museum colossus on part of the site of the old cattle-market and slaughterhouse at La Villette, a Palace of Science to rival the Palace of Arts already existing in the form of the Centre Pompidou. Whether, magnificently funded and housed, it will have the same atmosphere of excitement and democratic involvement as the old Palace of Discovery remains to be seen.

But, as we have already noted, Victor Danilov felt able to relegate the Palace of Discovery to Phase Two status and to insist that the founding of his own museum, the Museum of Science and Technology in Chicago, 'launched the third major stage in the science museum movement'.[12] In so far as the Museum of Science and Industry was established in 1933 and the Palace of Discovery in 1937, this may possibly be true, but it ignored one not unimportant fact, that the Paris museum was almost wholly concerned with what one might call contemporary science from the beginning, whereas for many years Chicago combined the past and the present. Chicago did not become almost entirely Phase Three until well after the Second World War.

What it certainly did do from the day it opened was to make its visitors part of the show, through what Danilov describes as 'hands-on participation', that is, by giving them plenty of opportunity to set exhibits in motion and to follow through the results. This had, of course, already been done elsewhere, notably in Munich and Vienna and at the Science Museum in London. Chicago, however, made such activity central to its operations, and in the process earned itself a further claim to distinction. It made the noisy museum respectable. In the 1960s, the Museum of Science and Industry was fully entitled to the title of The Noisiest Museum in the World, except on Thursdays, when school parties were not admitted. Now, in the 1980s, there are many other museums with which it would have to share the honour.

At the Ontario Science Centre in Toronto, for instance, it was realised from the beginning that, by aiming at 'active participation' and 'emotional experience with intellectual satisfaction', a quiet museum was not only an impossibility, but undesirable. 'A much more permissive attitude toward visitor behaviour is possible than is the case in conventional museums', wrote its Director, Douglas Omans. 'We are not custodians of unique and priceless artefacts or works of art, which must be protected at all cost. Our visitors may shout, romp and play, and as long as they are not interfering with the enjoyment of others, or endangering themselves, we want them to react as they please.'[13] The Centre was 'an elaborate teaching machine' for 'a public with a very broad spectrum of interests'.

The Museum of Science and Industry was responsible for another museum innovation of considerable significance. The Deutsches Museum had shown twenty-five years earlier that it was possible to persuade industrial concerns to subsidise a museum of this kind by giving it money, machines and apparatus. Chicago went one step further, by getting sponsorship for whole sections of the museum. Telecommunications, for example, have been sponsored by the Bell Telephone System, and agriculture by Massey-Harris. This obviously relieves the Museum of a great deal of worry and expense, but it would be idle to pretend that it does not bring a different set of problems.

To begin with, a museum in which each major department has a different sponsor

The Museum of Science and Industry, Chicago. Note the size of the car park.

cannot achieve a uniformity of style. Every sponsor will arrange matters as he thinks best, using his own designer and making sure that the exhibit is as beneficial to him as possible. This is not to say that the work will not be well done, nor that certain guidelines will not be followed. Nor does it mean that visitors will dislike the results. It is simply to state an obvious fact, that it will not be possible to have an overall style or approach. This is another way of saying that visitors to the Museum will find something very reminiscent of a trade fair or international exhibition, a series of stands. There is irony in this situation, since the core of the Museum is a building in the Greek style originally constructed to house the Fine Arts exhibition at the World's Columbian Exposition of 1893.

There are other consequences of the sponsorship approach. One is that the sponsor will inevitably be identified with that particular branch of technology. Bell will be telecommunications, General Motors will be automobiles, Kodak will be photography, and the exhibit will inevitably take on something of the character of an advertisement for the company. It may well do more than this. It may also function as a recruiting agency or a careers advice bureau – 'Fill in this form if you are interested in working for X'. To a non-American these considerations are probably less of a shock, after twenty years of television advertising, than they would have been in the 1960s. This is the kind of compromise which the private enterprise–large corporation economy makes inevitable, and there is no reason why museums should remain immune to it.

But another result of sponsorship in this type of museum, where industry is the theme of the museum and its major source of funds, is more serious. It has already been mentioned in discussing the Deutsches Museum. It cannot be even hinted that

105

The Transparent Anatomical Manni-kin, 1937, the first in an American museum. The Museum now has a more modern, slimmer version.

The 16-foot walk-through heart, part of the health and medical exhibit area at the Museum.

the technology in question has been anything but an unmixed blessing. One does not look a gift horse in the mouth. New means better and size means efficiency. The automobile has to be unquestionably a good thing, word-processors necessarily imply progress, the chemical control of weeds has brought only benefits. It is perfectly true that not all the sponsors at Chicago have been industrial firms. They have included trade associations, universities and government departments. But the influence of these bodies has operated in the same direction as that of the manufac-turers. The voice that comes out of the Museum of Science and Industry is unmistak-ably the voice of the Establishment. It could hardly be otherwise.

And it is a voice that speaks to a great many people. A survey carried out in 1979 in the United States by the Institute of Museum Services showed that 45 per cent of all museum visits were to science museums, compared with 24 per cent to history, that is, cultural history, museums and 12 per cent to art museums. North America, that is, the United States and Canada, now has nearly forty museums devoted to contem-porary science and technology. Very few were founded earlier than 1946. Chicago is both the oldest and the biggest, with more than four million visitors a year. Ottawa, established in 1967, and Toronto, 1969, each have getting on for two million, and the Exploratorium, 1969, in San Francisco, rather less. Nearly all of them face the same fundamental problem. Because, at least in the United States, they have only marginal financial support from the Government, they have to depend for their existence on the money which they are able to attract from the public and from industry and commerce. In order to succeed in this, they have to create what is termed 'a favourable climate for support'. This usually means two things, showing that the museum is useful to the community and making it clear that it holds Establishment values. It cannot afford either to become involved in controversy or to appear a luxury. This is mainly why the emphasis is on today's, rather than yesterday's science, on 'visitor-participation exhibits', on industrial exhibitions and on educational programmes, not on the historical development of science. Another and not unimportant reason is that America has a great deal of contemporary science and technology to display and, by comparison with Europe, very little from the past. Chicago was the first to hit on the perfect recipe for providing what was required, and from that point of view, its influence has been very great. But this does not, as Victor Danilov suggests, make it the first Phase Three museum of science and technology. It would have been more accurate, perhaps, to have said 'the first Phase Three museum of the now-classic North American type'.

It is, of course, perfectly possible to have a Phase Three science museum financed from public funds, as an element of high priority in the educational system. The Singapore Science Centre, opened in 1975, is such a museum. Planned and run by the Ministry of Science and Technology for 'the dissemination and popularisation of science among the lay public and the secondary and tertiary student population',[14] it had, oddly enough, a British, not an American consultant.[15]

It was keyed into the Government's programme of modernisation and industrialisation. The population had to become more science-minded, and 'with the aid of three-dimensional models and participatory exhibits, the Centre will be in a unique position to bring to life the difficult and abstract concepts of science'.[16] The traditional type of science museum, with its bias towards the collection and display of historical objects, was not suited to the urgency of the task. It was, the Government felt, a luxury institution, which only a wealthy country could afford. But it was realised very clearly that the Science Centre breed of museum could run away with itself. The medium could all too easily become the message, so that visitors would come in great numbers and thoroughly enjoy themselves, without necessarily learning anything at all, a truth which many of the enthusiasts for 'visitor-participation' museums have been reluctant to recognise.

Sometimes a modern science museum has gone to considerable lengths to encourage seriousness of purpose. This has happened at the National Science Museum, Tokyo, which in 1974 set up a Study Room, a self-teaching laboratory for people who want to study and carry out research on their own initiative. This aspect of the Museum's work is linked to its programme of graded exhibitions. Excellent laboratory facilities are provided, too, at the Natural History Museum at Chur, in Switzerland.

Danilov's analysis stopped short at Phase Three, but there has in fact been a clearly developed Phase Four, which is of increasing importance at the present time. Phase Four consists of museums which place science and technology firmly in their social

Adam Opel, as he was *c.* 1880.

context, without any a priori assumption that they are Good Things, museums with a social conscience. They are not necessarily crusading museums, but they leave the visitor in no doubt that the industrial museum which concentrates entirely on machines and processes and ignores the people whose lives are affected by these things has an essential dimension missing. Phase Four museums are, perhaps not surprisingly, a creation of Western Europe – they demand the right kind of political climate – but there are signs that they are beginning to spread elsewhere.

The first uncompromisingly Phase Four industrial museum, and one that has had an enormous influence on subsequent museum development, was the Municipal Museum at Rüsselsheim, near Frankfurt, in Germany. It was new and pioneering because it was organised around the concept of industrialisation rather than of industry. Rüsselsheim is Opelstadt, where Adam Opel established his manufacturing base in the 1870s, making first sewing-machines, then motorcycles and then motorcars. Like Detroit, it has been an automobile town for many years, with its economy dependent on this one product.

In the early 1970s, the Municipality decided to have a new museum, and restored part of the old Rüsselsheim Citadel for the purpose. A young Director, Peter Schirmbeck, was appointed, and it was generally expected that he would create what would have been, in effect, an Opel Museum, showing how the town had grown with the Company. What actually happened was rather different. Peter Schirmbeck belonged to a new generation, which was unable to see industry in what one might call Deutsches Museum terms. A factory, in his view, was not simply a technological unit: it was part of the society within which it operated. It conditioned that society and, in its turn, was influenced by it. So, to attempt to represent Opel independently of the people who had become dependent on it for their livelihood was both foolish and misleading. One could not keep an industrial museum separate from a museum of cultural history. To try to do so was to create a meaningless museum, a museum of half-truths.

The political situation within which he proposed to set up the new museum was somewhat delicate. The Social Democrats, SDP, had a majority of one seat on the Town Council. So long as that balance, precarious as it was, was maintained, he was reasonably safe, but if it were to change in favour of the Christian Democrats, CDU, the Museum and all it stood for was highly vulnerable. However, the feared disaster did not occur and the plans went ahead. The scheme was to divide the Museum into two parts, each concerned with a different period in the history of the town and the area immediately surrounding it. Upstairs was to be 'From the Middle Ages to the Beginnings of Industrialisation', and downstairs, 'Industrialisation'. The two sections were opened in reverse order, 'Industrialisation' in 1976, and 'From the Middle Ages to the Beginnings of Industrialisation' in 1979.

For the earlier period, there was a good deal of material available from the town's old

Left The Rüsselsheim reconstruction of a wheelwright's shop.

Right A middle-class sitting room *c.* 1900.

museum, but for what followed the collections were, for Peter Schirmbeck's purpose, far from satisfactory. 'Only the products of industry, the chocolate-covered side of industrialisation, had been preserved. What was missing were objects documenting the working conditions of industry and their evolution (machines, factory regulations, "sacks" in which the workers received their pay) and documents from the workers' movement. There were new collection areas that we had to build up from scratch.'[17] What existed, in fact, were the typical contents of a motor museum anywhere in the world, a historical collection of cars and motorcycles, together with examples of the sewing-machine which represented Adam Opel's first steps as a manufacturer. These, so far as Rüsselsheim was concerned, were 'the chocolate-covered side of industrialisation'.

Schirmbeck knew that his task was to recreate, in museum terms, the totality of local industrialisation. To achieve this, one had to make use of a very wide range of evidence and to show the district as it was before Opel arrived. One could not show what the factory system had done to the traditional life of the people unless one first explained what that traditional life had been. The two floors of the Museum were interdependent and equally essential. Together, they aimed at providing visitors with many windows into history. If the results were sometimes disturbing and even shocking, so much the better. One of the Museum's main functions was to help people to escape from historical clichés and, for that matter, from museum clichés as well. 'The mixture of objects with different origins, for example, machines placed alongside works of art, makes it possible for us to attract visitors who have different areas of interest and to make history itself interesting to people who have not been drawn to it previously. With the documentation system used, the visitor interested in the technical aspects of machines learns about the conditions facing the factory workers who have to operate them. Those who were previously too shy to set foot in an art gallery can find works of art hanging among familiar objects.'[18]

People are more likely to achieve what Peter Schirmbeck calls 'an expansion of historical consciousness' if an historical process is presented in local terms. 'Industrialisation', as a general concept, has little meaning for most people, but 'what the Opel factory did to and for the families living in Rüsselsheim' communicates much more quickly and more surely. Similarly, 'the links between National Socialism and German industrialists' is altogether too vague and general a concept to make much sense to those who have not studied the subject in some depth but, by placing close together in the Museum the Nazi flag hanging down one wall of the Opel factory administration block, an armoured car made at the works for the re-equipment of the German army in the 1930s, and a letter written by an Opel worker during the war from prison in Berlin to his family in Rüsselsheim, the point is made dramatically and unmistakably and in a manner which would be impossible for the Deutsches Museum or, if it had been historically minded, for the Museum of Science and Industry in Chicago, dependent as these two institutions are on attracting and keeping the goodwill of industrialists. The Museum is full of such imaginative touches, which serve as a constant reminder that machines and processes need people to operate them, and that these people had lives and feeling which are just as much a part of industrialisation as machines and products. Perhaps the most celebrated feature of the Museum in Rüsselsheim, and the one which expresses the philosophy of its Director in the most unmistakable fashion, is the pair of group photographs of Opel workers, one taken in 1876, not long after the factory opened, and the other in 1902. The photographs have been greatly enlarged for display purposes and Peter Schirmbeck has described the difference between them in this way.

'The one taken in 1876', he says, 'shows the qualities of the artisans' tradition. Confident and casual workers display a traditional masters' pride. Their clothing is individual. The men in the front row are seated on Biedermeier chairs; the whole group is together in a pyramid form, with the apprentices lying on a rug in front. The workers centre round one product, the upper part of a shoemaker's sewing-machine. Their interlocking gestures reveal that individual colleagues communicate with one another.

'Although taken only twenty-six years later, the second Opel photo (1902) gives a completely different impression of the workers. Pride and self-confidence are no longer evident. Instead, the workers appear oppressed. The photo mirrors the monotony of industrialised piece-work in the factory. The men have placed themselves in straight rows, rather than in a pyramid. Almost all wear a standard work-uniform. There are no individual poses. Apprentices are seated on wooden boxes. The communicative gestures have almost entirely disappeared. A finished product

Opel workers in 1876. 'A traditional masters' pride'. The sections of the photograph rotate, in order to form the second picture, seen below.

Opel workers in 1902. 'The workers appear oppressed'.

– the sewing-machine – is placed in front of the group. The individual workers hold machine parts in their hands.'[19]

He could have added that a number of the men in the first picture have beards, whereas there are none in the second. Or that two men in the first group are smoking pipes and six have hats. Or, even more impressive, that several of the men in the 1876 photograph have mugs of beer in their hands and that the group has formed itself around a beer barrel. But there is no need to labour the point. The 1876

111

workers had been recently recruited from the world of individual craftsmen free to organise their own lives. The 1902 generation had been tamed, disciplined and brought to heel.

It is possible to argue that what has been created at Rüsselsheim is a museum of social history, not a museum of industry or technology. Peter Schirmbeck would answer that it is neither the one nor the other, but a river fed by many streams, a museum of industrialisation. The product has certainly been found attractive, both by other museums and by the museum-going public. The recipe is being widely followed elsewhere[20] and there is no reason to suppose that the momentum is weakening.

It would be unhelpful to end this chapter without making four points. The first is that the Rüsselsheim type of museum is possible only within what the Americans call, quite rightly, the Free World. The museum must not be inhibited from seeing the past as a whole and from illustrating its theories in any way it chooses. The second point is that it is possible to be extremely inhibited even in a Free World country. An industrial or commercial sponsor can impose a discipline quite as strict as that which results from a political dogma. Thirdly, the fact that a museum is new does not necessarily mean that it is new-wave. It may, as we have already seen in the case of art museums, simply be doing the old thing in a fresher, more sparkling, more attractive way. Many Phase Three museums are still being established in what is more and more decisively a Phase Four period. In today's world, a museum of science and technology which does not encourage its visitors to think of the human and social consequences of new developments is acting in a singularly irresponsible and out-of-date fashion. To worship Progress uncritically may suit the manufacturers and advertisers but it is not in the best interests of humanity.

The fourth point is so deliciously obvious, yet so important, that one wonders why such a strict taboo has been placed on any discussion of it. It is this. For forty years, country after country, especially the United States, has been setting up museums to explain the latest developments in science and technology. Eventually, these exhibits become out-of-date, that is to say, historical, and are replaced. What happens to the items that are superannuated? Are they stored, filed away as back-numbers, or simply destroyed? If it is the former, then invaluable collections of technical artefacts must be building up, which will become the raw material for a second generation of museums which will, in due course, start a new fashion for showing how machines and processes evolve, and we shall be back at the situation in which the Deutsches Museum and the Science Museum found themselves at the beginning of the century. Unless everything is destroyed as soon as it becomes obsolete, which is, of course, always possible, today's science centres must inevitably become tomorrow's science museums and the wheel will have turned full circle.

Chapter Six
The history and customs of the homeland

Museum of the Army, Paris:	*'History is mainly a matter of wars, generals, admirals and treaties'*
Skansen, Stockholm:	*'A pocket edition of the Sweden of old'*
Beamish, Stanley:	*'A picture of the past Northern way of life'*
National Museum of Popular Arts and Traditions, Paris:	*'Life and society in France before industrialisation'*
Museum of the History of the City of Warsaw:	*'A history of life in the city in all its aspects'*
Museum of German History, Berlin:	*'An agreed philosophy of history'*
Museum of the Jewish Diaspora, Tel Aviv:	*'We exist to tell a story, not to collect objects'*

Perhaps the only way to define history is to decide that it consists of the past, as processed and interpreted by historians. It is certainly not sufficient to say that history is the past. The past is the raw material of history, re-sifted and re-assessed every generation, if not even more frequently.

Most museums which purport to be museums of history are in fact little more than storehouses and displays of the historian's raw material. The collections may be arranged in a logical sequence and they may demonstrate how one thing led to another but, with few exceptions, they lack the unifying touch of philosophy which would turn them into history. On paper, facts are not history and, in museum terms, objects are not history. To become history, the facts and the objects must tell a coherent and intelligible story, and the decision to tell that story is, in the Western world, an act of considerable courage, because there is no agreed philosophy of history to make sense of it all and to act as a bridge between professionals and the general public. In the socialist part of the world, the situation is very different, and the task of the museum correspondingly easier. For better or for worse, a political faith indicates which items are important and which are not.

Consider, for example, the National Museum of History and Technology in Washington D.C., an intriguing colossus, established as recently as 1904, with huge collections. Alphabetically, these collections are studied and presented to the public under the following headings: agriculture; archaeology; astronomy; business history; ceramics; costumes; folk-lore; furnishings; general, i.e. the unclassifiable, a fascinating rag-bag; glass; graphic arts; industrial; manufacturing; marine; medical; military; mining; music; naval; numismatic; philatelic; photography; political; presidential; science; technology; toys; transportation. These categories undoubtedly provide a framework for appreciating what Americans have achieved during the past two hundred years. They are the clues to American history, a giant notebook of survivals but, in themselves, they are not American history.

There are those, of course, who believe that a museum can do no more. It is there to collect and preserve objects, but not to assess their cultural or political value. Each visitor and each scholar must perform that duty for himself. One sympathises with the wish to appear 'objective' and 'scientific', but such an attitude is in fact dishonest. The decision to acquire and display a museum object is both philosophical and political. Its relative importance is the result of a set of beliefs and a scale of values, both of which are being constantly modified, as society itself changes. And, with very few exceptions, the values which museum curators hold are establishment values. By this, one does not necessarily mean what one might term the values of the Grand Establishment, that is, those held and propagated by people in positions of social and political power. They may be those of, for example, the medical establishment, the archaeological establishment or the art establishment. But they will rarely be heretical. Most museums throughout the world are very conformist places and, in the case of western museums which deal with national history, in one form or another, an essential part of conformism consists of making it plain to all and sundry that the selection and presentation of the exhibits is based on no kind of ideology. It is 'scientific'.

In deciding, within the limits of the present chapter, which museums can fairly be considered Museums of Influence, one has to begin by looking at certain fundamental changes in the concept of what is and is not 'history' which have occurred during the period with which the book is concerned. One can distinguish four stages of development. In the first, which extended throughout the eighteenth century and well into the nineteenth, there was considerable interest in the history of Greece and Rome and of the Middle East during the Biblical period. Early in the nineteenth century, a passion for medievalism spread throughout north-west Europe, being particularly influential in France and Germany. It was concerned especially with the decorative arts of the Middle Ages, rather than with philosophy, political history and social life. In France, Alexandre du Sommerard formed a great collection of furniture, woodcarving, pottery and metalwork of the medieval and early Renaissance period, which he installed, in 1832, in part of the fifteenth-century Hôtel de Cluny in Paris. After his death in 1843, the Hôtel de Cluny and its contents were bought by the Government and opened as a museum. It was essentially a museum of relics and mementoes, rather than of history. The collections, subsequently greatly enriched, were chiefly French and must have served, at least in part, to interest visitors in the history and achievements of their own country.

Something of the same kind was happening in Germany, where the Romantic Revival was bringing a keen and widespread interest in national traditions and achievements. This interest was highly romantic and was characterised by a passion, amounting to an obsession, for heroic legends and myths. Its first expression in museum terms was the collection of 'German antiquities' formed from 1832 onwards by Hans Freiherr von und zu Aufsess and set up in his Bavarian castle, Burg Aufsess. It led directly to the establishment of the German National Museum in Nuremberg, in 1852, which expanded throughout the century. Broadly speaking, its field could be described as 'anything made in Germany from palaeolithic times to the end of the eighteenth century' and included paintings, sculpture, weapons, furniture, costumes, agricultural implements and domestic equipment. This remarkable collection expressed what is called in German 'romantischer Historismus', a concept that is extremely difficult to translate, if its full flavour is to be recaptured. 'A romantic attitude towards our national past', or 'the history of our romantic past' get somewhere close to it.

Both in France and in Germany, 'romantischer Historismus' was a perfect foundation for developing nationalism and militarism. The heroes of yesterday were brought out of the shadows in order to inspire those who were anxious to lay down their lives for the Fatherland or Motherland today. But, for this process to reach maturity, it was necessary first to have a series of patriotic wars, the Franco-Prussian War of 1871, the Crimean War, the Boer War, the First World War, partly in order to have a plentiful supply of heroes to commemorate, and partly to build up a good stock of battle relics on which a new kind of museum, the military museum, could be based. The military museum is a twentieth-, not a nineteenth-century development. Its prototype was the Museum of the Army, in Paris, opened in the Invalides in 1905. It was formed by merging the old Museum of the Artillery and the Ministry of War's Historical Museum, a collection of relics which had been steadily accumulating since the late seventeenth century. By the mid-1920s, every nation in Europe had something similar, in character, if not in size. Possibly the most important effect of these museums was to equate history with politics and military campaigns, an attitude which has had a powerful hold on the popular imagination for at least three generations, and from which we have only recently begun to break free.

If the second stage of historical awareness was characterised by nationalism and by a romantic attitude to war, the third could perhaps be defined as the period during which the common man began to emerge from the shadows. In the early stages of this movement, of which one is beginning to see strong traces in the 1860s, it was only the rural common man, the peasant, who was thought to be interesting. The turn of urban, industrial man had yet to come. The reasons for this highly selective attitude towards the lower orders are not difficult to find. As Europe moved into the second half of the nineteenth century, industrialisation was beginning to undermine the traditional rural way of life which had been the norm for many centuries and, as peasant culture began to be eaten away by the new industrial and commercial values, so it was seen to be an object of urgent concern. The peasant was suddenly interesting, not because he was average and undistinguished, but because he could be seen to be on the way to disappearing. Soon, he might well become a rare animal and his habits consequently had to be documented while they still existed.

Hôtel des Invalides, Paris, home of the
Museum of the Army. The Cour
d'Honneur.

The Salle Turenne as it was *c.* 1870.

Below left The Salle des Emblèmes,
formerly the Salle Turenne, in 1980.

Below right Part of the collection of
armour in the Salle Henri IV.

The fourth stage of history, if one can put it that way, has rested on two beliefs, first that everything that has happened in the past is potentially interesting and significant and, second, that what has taken place locally is as valuable a means of understanding the thinking and activities of our ancestors as were the great sweeps through national and international events and trends which still passed for history fifty years ago. It follows from what has just been said that significant and influential museums of history are not to be found before the last quarter of the nineteenth century, although the growing sense of history was being fed much earlier by museums of a different type, especially those concerned with art, antiquities and archaeology.

We begin with the view, widely and even normally taught in the world's schools until at least the 1950s, that history is mainly a matter of wars, generals, admirals and treaties, a pattern of thinking reflected in the National Museum of the Army in Paris. The Museum occupies one of the most prestigious sites in the capital, the East and West Wings of the Invalides, which is not so much a building as a shrine, a temple in honour of the French army. If one follows the visit through in a logical sequence, one begins with a gallery where one is shown the various methods of military attack and defence which existed from prehistoric times until the Middle Ages. From there, one moves into the Francis I Gallery, which is devoted to weapons and armour from 1066 – the choice of date is interesting[1] – to 1598. The treasures here include the armour of Henry II and Francis I. The Henry IV Gallery, which follows, contains armour used in jousting and tournaments, and for parades. Mural paintings depict notable feats of arms during the reign of Louis XIV. There follow three galleries in which one can see fine collections of swords and firearms of the eighteenth, nineteenth and twentieth centuries and another filled with Oriental weapons.

All this constitutes, so to speak, the hors-d'œuvre. We are then served with the principal courses of the military meal in the West Wing, the First and Second World War Galleries, with weapons, uniforms, documents, battle-plans and memorabilia of the leading commanders. Audio-visual displays are much in evidence throughout.

Over in the East Wing, we go further back in time. In the Turenne Gallery, also known as the Gallery of Flags, there are hundreds of flags and trophies, shown against a background of murals illustrating the campaigns of Louis XIV. Also here are a number of Napoleonic relics, including his 'petit chapeau' and the sword he carried at Austerlitz. Next in line is the Vauban Gallery, with eighteen full-size mounted figures, showing the uniforms and equipment of the French cavalry since the days of the Consulate.

One proceeds upstairs to galleries dealing with the Ancien Régime, the First Republic and the Empire. Napoleon Bonaparte receives generous treatment here, with his campaign tent, complete with its original furniture. Here, too, are exhibited scenes

from the major battles and daily life of the Grande Armée. From there, one pro-
gresses to Napoleon's period of exile on St Helena. The room in Longwood House,
where he died in 1821, has been recreated, with its original furnishings, the
Emperor's personal possessions and his death-mask. The tour ends with exhibits
devoted to the activities of the French army in Africa.

This is what one might describe as traditional history-book history, history built
around armies and their leaders, and the Museum is its focal point. Nothing quite as
pure-blooded exists in other countries. Although military museums are widespread
and in some places quite large, they nearly all feel as if they are on the fringe of
society, taken seriously by the initiates, but by few others. The National Museum of
the Army in Paris is mainstream. In France, one makes jokes about Napoleon at
one's peril, but in England Nelson and Wellington are permitted to be much more
human and fallible, respected rather than revered or deified. The atmosphere
surrounding the Nelson relics in the museum at Monmouth or those of the Duke of
Wellington at Stratfield Saye is very different from what one finds at the numerous
Napoleonic museums scattered over France.

What, then, can the influence of the National Museum of the Army be said to have
been? The presence and prestige of this, the first modern military museum, has
made it easier to establish other and smaller museums of the same type. It has
also made it possible to develop two parallel and contradictory philosophies of
history, one militaristic and chauvinistic, the other conditioned by modern attitudes
to society and to the place of individuals within it. Internationally, the Museum has
produced one highly enjoyable caricature of itself, in Brussels – an early twentieth-
century military museum, frozen and preserved virtually intact, and a number of
pale shadows and faint echoes, collections of military relics, organised and presented
on very small budgets by people who only half believe in what they are doing.
England, Spain and Italy, to take only three examples, nowadays feel half-guilty
about having armies, and therefore military museums. France, like the Soviet
Union, does not. Yet, paradoxically, Britain has more military museums than any
other country in the world, including the USSR. This is a product, not of militarism,
but mainly of the British system of county regiments, most of which eventually
developed their own museums.

A fact which neither the National Museum of the Army in Paris nor any other
military museum known to me mentions, let alone emphasises, is that nearly all the
private soldiers recruited into the armies and navies of the European warlords up to
the time of the First World War came from peasant families, for the very simple
reason that the population of every European country, other than England, continued to be overwhelmingly rural throughout the nineteenth century. The ranks
were filled by tough people, accustomed to living hard and on a simple diet, with
little spendable money, and at best semi-literate. The cultural gap between them and
their officers was enormous. To have presented a full picture of the army, a military

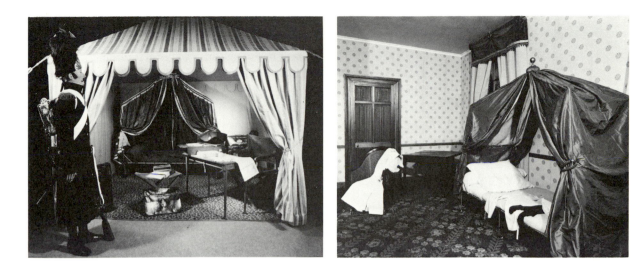

The Salle Boulogne at the Museum of the Army, Paris.

Left Reconstruction of Napoleon's campaign tent.

Right Reconstruction of the room in Longwood House where Napoleon died in 1821.

museum should therefore have concerned itself a good deal with social history, but in fact this dimension has always been missing. Perhaps the most powerful and lasting influence of the museum in Paris was that it presented the French army in a social vacuum, as an organisation with its own values and its own forms of motivation. Military museums in other countries followed suit.

One has therefore been faced with the absurdity of having the same kinds of people presented separately in two distinct types of museum. The ethnologists and folklore specialists took one part of their lives and the military historians took another. Even a modern museum as intelligently researched and planned as the Museum of Popular Art and Traditions in Paris, which will be discussed later in this chapter, failed to bridge the gap between the two. A soldier or a sailor, like a convicted criminal, was regarded as a different species of animal, a being temporarily or permanently withdrawn from civil circulation.

There was, I am sure, no plot, no planned operation, no theory which brought about this state of affairs. Anyone who studies Britain's National Maritime Museum at Greenwich objectively will very quickly perceive that, in those sections devoted to the Navy, what he is in fact looking at is a museum of the British Naval Officer, in which ratings are little more than theatrical props, accessories to the main story. There has been a great temptation, when presenting history in museums, to follow the tradition of seeing and interpreting the past in terms of the leading actors. What is nowadays called 'social history' is a twentieth-century creation. G. M. Trevelyan defined it, negatively, as 'the history of a people with the politics left out',[2] and, positively, as 'the daily life of the inhabitants of the land in past ages', pointing out that this has to include 'the human as well as the economic relation of different classes to one another, the character of family and household life, the conditions of labour and of leisure, the attitude of man to nature, the culture of each age as it arose out of these general conditions of life, and took ever changing forms in religion, literature and music, architecture, learning, and thought'.

It is not necessary that social history should be concerned with a nation as a whole. A village community is a perfectly respectable and rewarding subject for the social historian to study and write about. What is essential, however, is that the particular community shall be looked at as a complete unit, with no element excluded as unworthy of consideration, and that the historian shall be aware of the existence of other communities which impinge upon it. The local historian who is obsessed by his chosen microcosm is a menace both to himself and to his readers.

The main problem is, of course, that when the existing balance of attention is so manifestly absurd and unjustifiable, the temptation to put one's emphasis overwhelmingly on the other side is often difficult to resist. Pioneers have a way of being single-minded people, and this is both a strength and a weakness. Artur Hazelius, the founder of Skansen and the Nordic Museum in Stockholm, both unquestionably museums of influence, is a good illustration of this.

Hazelius, the son of a regular army officer who eventually became a general, was born in Stockholm in 1833. His father considered it very important that his son should be brought up in the country and sent him to live in a rural vicarage. Artur Hazelius eventually became a teacher, specialising in the Scandinavian languages, and was something of a Nordic fanatic, campaigning for, among other causes, the 'purification of Swedish from foreign loan words'. He travelled extensively in Sweden, where he noticed, even in the 1850s and 1860s, that the traditional forms of village life were disappearing, as a result of the growth of industry and the development of the railways and of postal and telegraph services.

The beginnings of Skansen: the Bollnäs House in 1898.

He soon convinced himself that, if future generations were to be able to understand what Sweden had been like before these far-reaching changes took place, collections had to be formed quickly, while the material still existed. 'During my travels,' he wrote, 'I have become only too well aware of the disappearance, now rapidly taking place, of our Swedish national costumes and the handicrafts and artistic skills of former generations. These impressions, and the inactivity of the authorities, make me consider it to be the duty of each private citizen to preserve for the future all that can be preserved of these and other things.'[3] He himself started buying such objects during the early 1870s and in 1872 he put on a small exhibition of them in Stockholm, to stimulate public interest. At the 1878 International Exhibition in Paris, he broke new ground by displaying what he called 'living pictures', scenes from country life, with models dressed in Swedish folk costumes placed against accurate representations of peasant rooms. During the following decade, he developed this idea further by showing not only interiors but complete houses.

The first part of the site known as Skansen was bought in 1891. Two wooden and one stone cottage were brought there, together with a Lapp camp and two charcoal-burners' huts. In 1892 the area was increased and funds had been raised to build up a collection of wild and domestic animals. During this decade, further buildings were added, including complete farmhouses with their fittings, equipment and implements, roads and terraces and a mountain railway were built. The process of extension and development has continued throughout the present century, with the purchase and re-erection of houses, farm-buildings, workshops and mills from all

Sagaliden, Skansen's first restaurant, opened in 1897. It operated until 1914.

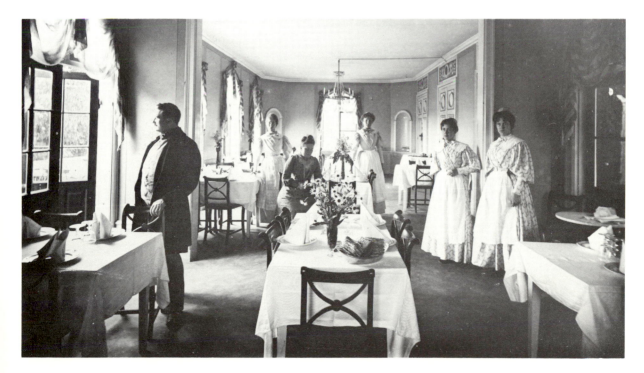

over Sweden. An open-air theatre was added in 1911 and a folk-dancing area and 'the longest escalator in Europe' during the 1930s. In 1938 Skansen attracted two million visitors, a remarkable achievement for such a small country.

The Museum has always aimed to provide relaxation as well as education. Its first café was opened in 1892 and there has been much development in this direction since then. The latest restaurant, Solliden, opened in 1952, seating 800 people inside and, in summer, a further 1,000 outside on the terraces.

By the time of his death in 1901, Hazelius had the satisfaction of knowing that he had established the first open-air museum in the world, that it was in a thriving condition, and that it was extremely popular. He had also been responsible for setting up the Nordic Museum, in which the history of Scandinavian, mainly Swedish, culture could be presented within a more normal kind of museum building. In retrospect, his ideas may seem somewhat naïve and romantic – there has been a certain folksiness about Skansen, which has not been to everyone's taste – but there can be no doubt at all that what Hazelius created had a profound influence on museum development, not only in Scandinavia, but throughout the world.

It is clear that his aim was not merely to invent a new kind of museum. 'He wanted to create a symbiosis between culture and nature, an environment where Swedes for generations to come would be able to see how their forefathers had laboured to cultivate the land with the help of – but also in battle with – the forces of Nature. This is also one of the reasons why the wild animals of the Nordic region have been given a place at Skansen.'[4] He wanted, too, to 'recreate old traditions in a living environment', that is, to provide a suitable environment for performances of folk-dancing and folk-music, and for dramatic performances, and to make Skansen a recognised centre for national celebrations.

One could say, with confidence, that if someone with similar aims were to set out to create the equivalent of Skansen today, he would not attempt to do the job in the same way, and in that sense, the direct influence of Skansen has certainly faded. Skansen was and is the country brought to the city, but Stockholm today is very different from what it was in the 1890s. It is much larger, much more sophisticated, and much richer. In 1891 Sweden was a poor country, with thousands of its people emigrating each year in search of a better living in the United States. Many Swedish peasants became farmers in America, taking their traditions, their agricultural techniques and even their style of farm buildings with them. Swedish rural history was continued on the other side of the Atlantic, a fact of which one would be unaware, if one had only Skansen as a guide.

The cultural context of Skansen has, in fact, changed radically during the ninety-five years of its existence. The difference between what is inside Skansen and what is outside, both in Stockholm and in Sweden as a whole, is much greater today than it

A street in Skansen's Town Quarter. In the buildings there are workshops, with craftsmen demonstrating their trades.

Below left The eighteenth/nineteenth-century Delsbo farmstead from the province of Hälsingland.

Below right A farmworker's cottage at Skansen as it was in the 1920s. The picture was taken in 1975. The man is a museum attendant and, like his colleagues in all the other buildings, is dressed in accordance with the period, with the social level of the original occupants and with the area from which the building came.

was in 1891. This makes Skansen more exotic, more of a museum now than it was then. A much greater effort of imagination is required of the modern visitor than of his grandfather or great-grandfather. He needs more help, in order to understand the full significance of the exhibits that are presented to him. A very simple example will help to make the point clear. Nowadays, it is very rare in any Western society for someone to have to earn his living by carrying heavy weights on his back or shoulder. When Skansen was established, it was not only common, but normal. Men, and not infrequently women too, shifted sacks of corn, flour and potatoes in this way, and loaded ships and carts without any form of mechanical power to help them. It was also normal to walk long distances to work, to school, behind a plough, to church. All these things are wholly exceptional today and to that extent unintelligible. Yet, without the old dimensions of strength, exhaustion, anxiety, skill, pride and fortitude, the objects themselves, however well preserved, are largely meaningless. They are fossils, which no amount of folk-dancing and farm animals can bring to life.

Artur Hazelius himself could hardly have been expected to have been aware of the problem, since the old virtues and attitudes were still to be found at the time when he was laying the foundations of the museum. The traditional rural society lingered on in Sweden, as elsewhere in Europe, until the outbreak of the First World War. The main problem, as he saw it, was to save objects from destruction and to build a new kind of museum around them, and the value of the Skansen–Nordic Museum complex in this respect can hardly be exaggerated. But one has to stress 'complex'. Skansen grew out of the already existing Nordic Museum (Nordiska Museet), which Hazelius had set up in 1873, in temporary premises[5] on the basis of his own rapidly growing collection of ethnographical objects.

'Undoubtedly', says G. B. Thompson, in an important assessment,[6] 'Skansen represented a new museum form in which full-scale traditional buildings, with appropriate furnishings and fittings, were displayed in natural surroundings, but its function was to *amplify* a subject already institutionalised in Nordiska Museet, to bring it an enlarged dimension and, for the first time, to incorporate into the museum environment the sky, the clouds, the weather and the seasonal cycle. To honour Hazelius merely as the founder of the open-air museum is to do him less than justice; he merits fuller acknowledgement as one who recognised the social value of serious and organised folk life study and who helped to pioneer its establishment as a permanent, institutionalised discipline.'

Thompson has no doubt as to what the value of folk-life study was in Hazelius' time and what it is still today, to turn the attention of historians and the public attention away from 'constitutional affairs and the political means by which they were generally determined and conducted'[7] and towards 'man's day-to-day affairs'. From this point of view, one might regard the Nordic Museum and Skansen, and their descendants, as balancing agents to the museums inspired by the Museum of the

Army in Paris. But, as Thompson pointed out in the paper to which we have already referred, the folk life movement contained what seem now to have been two in-built weaknesses. The first was that to transfer material of this, or almost any other kind, to a museum is almost inevitably to romanticise it. It is cleaned up, tidied up and put into good repair and there is no suggestion of the more unpleasant associations which these carefully preserved buildings once had for the people who lived in them. In a Skansen building there was nobody dying, nobody ill, nobody quarrelling, nothing smelling disagreeable, nothing dirty, nothing broken. What was provided for the enjoyment and instruction of visitors may have been authentic, but it was not realistic.

The second flaw in the folk-museum, open-air museum approach was that, although it certainly presented information about the day-to-day lives of ordinary people, they were a special kind of people, rural people. The people who lived in towns and worked in manufacturing industry or in urban commerce were not represented at all. One realises why this was so. Although Hazelius himself was interested in the common people as a whole, he felt that evidence for the history of country folk was in the greatest danger of disappearing so, naturally enough, he decided to concentrate on that. There was a practical advantage in doing so, since most of the traditional rural buildings of Norway, Sweden and Finland were built of wood, which made them much lighter, cheaper and easier to transport and re-erect than masonry structures would have been.

Many, perhaps most, of the folk and open-air museums which have been set up in both Europe and America during the present century have been inspired more by Skansen than by the folk-life principles which Hazelius developed. The museums were meant to illustrate a theory, to make it easier to reconstruct the life of past times, but they finished up by being an aim in themselves. They became, in Thompson's excellent phrase, 'architectural zoos', in which one learnt a great deal about vernacular architecture, but very little of any importance about the people who lived in the architecture. For most people today, an open-air museum or a folk-museum – the terms have unfortunately become almost interchangeable – is essentially a museum of buildings.

The Netherlands Open-Air Museum, at Arnhem, illustrates the situation very well.[8] Founded in 1912, during the first flush of enthusiasm for the Skansen idea, it has the correct Hazelius aim, 'to present a picture of the daily life of ordinary people in this country as it was in the past and has developed in the course of time', and it emphasises that it is not the buildings which are important, 'but the people who lived and worked in them'. Yet in practice it has confined its attention to buildings and crafts which belong to the pre-industrial age or at least to those which have no connection with the main stream of industry. It is, like Skansen and most other open-air museums, a museum of pretty buildings and, in the modern world, the pretty building is most regrettably exceptional. Its task, even so, has been more difficult than Skansen's in one respect, in that, Holland being Holland, most of the houses, mills, workshops and other items moved to Arnhem are constructed of brick, not wood. Another important difference is that the site is much bigger. There has been more space over which to distribute the exhibits, so that it has been possible to provide a more satisfactory context of trees, grass, water and cultivated land. There is not the feeling of congestion that one has as Skansen. Arnhem is far less of what Thompson called 'an architectural zoo'.

All over Europe and North America one can see Skansen's descendants, collections of pleasant pre-industrial buildings and the contents to go with them. They give a great deal of enjoyment to millions of people each year and it is good that what they have to show has been saved from destruction. It is less good, however, that they have encouraged the belief that a 'folk-life' museum must necessarily be concerned only with the horse-and-cart age. A major cause of this misconception has undoubtedly been the word itself. In the Scandinavian and German-speaking countries, and in the Netherlands 'folk', 'Volk' or 'volk' simply means 'people', and what interested Hazelius was therefore 'the life of the people'. In English, however, 'folk' has acquired quite a different connotation, 'Merrie England', the days of happy peasants and craftsmen and self-contained village communities. 'Folk-song' and 'folk-dance' have precisely this flavour to them.

The modern preference for 'open-air museum' over 'folk-museum' represents a not very successful attempt to rid this type of museum of its folksy associations. The Poles have neatly by-passed the problem by calling folk-museums 'Skansens' and by referring to a person who is a specialist in this field as a 'Skansenologist'. But, whether they label themselves 'folk-museums', 'open-air museums' or 'Skansens', nearly all have taken great pains to avoid such contentious and potentially disturbing matters as ill-health, poverty, industrial unrest, social protest, trade unionism and political movements, which are indisputably part of the 'life of the people'. For this reason, 'folk-life studies' are not the same as social history, and a 'folk-museum' is not a social history museum. Folk-museums have a possibly inescapable cosiness about them. They certainly reflect the life of the people, but by no means all of that life.

In 1972, Frank Atkinson, the creator and director of Beamish, 'the museum of man and industry in the North-East', gave it as his opinion that 'nostalgia is going to be bigger and bigger business in the next few years',[9] and the success of his own museum in County Durham has fully justified the forecast. At Beamish, however, nostalgia is much more broadly based than at Skansen or Arnhem. During the nineteenth century and for much of the twentieth, the North-East was one of Britain's major industrial areas. Shipbuilding, chemicals, iron and steelmaking, and coal-mining were of particular importance. These industries have now largely died away, producing serious problems of unemployment and re-adaptation, and yielding vast quantities of obsolete machinery and equipment which can find a home only

Left Pitmen's cottages from Hetton-le-Hole.
Right Until recently, northern coal-miners used to take a daily bath in front of the fire. In this picture the ritual is taking place in the traditional way inside one of the cottages at the Museum.

in a museum or in the scrapyard. In such a situation, the resources of a museum concerned with these matters are both the physical relics of the past and the interest and pride of local people in their own past. If these resources are to be fully exploited, an historical museum, whether in a building or of the open-air type, cannot possibly be of the Merrie England or Merrie Sweden breed. Part at least of the nostalgia which it stimulates must come from the use of industrial material, which is another way of saying that Frank Atkinson had to develop a completely new kind of folk-life museum, one in which industrial buildings were moved to the museum site. It was to be, he said, 'a museum dealing much more in social history than folk-life'.[10]

The site had to be chosen with great care. It had to be a big site and in pleasant country – the public, on the whole, does not enjoy spending its leisure time outdoors in ugly and depressing surroundings – but, since large numbers of visitors were envisaged, it had to be reasonably close to large conurbations. Having found the site, a nineteenth-century mansion, with an estate of undulating, partly wooded ground covering about 200 acres (80 hectares), the first task of the newly appointed Director, Frank Atkinson, was to explain to his employers, a consortium of four County Councils, what he was proposing to do, since the idea of a folk-museum, whether indoors or outdoors, was not well understood in the British Isles. The Welsh Folk Museum at St Fagans, near Cardiff, had existed since 1949, but it was concerned almost entirely with rural society. The beginning had been made with open-air museums of vernacular architecture at Avoncroft, in Worcestershire, and at the Weald and Downland Open-Air Museum, near Chichester, and in Northern Ireland the Ulster Folk Museum Act of 1958 was providing the fundamental philosophy of a folk-museum, although the museum itself, the Ulster Folk and Transport Museum, was to develop only slowly during the next twenty-five years and is still by no means complete.

In 1962, Atkinson explained that the new museum would be 'one of the first in this country, although open-air museums are fairly common in Scandinavian countries',[11] and a little later he set out his policy for it. 'An open-air museum', he said, 'serves to illustrate vividly the way of life, the institutions, customs and material equipment of the ordinary people. It is an attempt to make the history of a region live, by showing typical features of that history as accurately as possible.'[12] More precisely, Beamish was to illustrate what he called 'the Northern way of life', although 'the North-Eastern way of life' would have been more appropriate. In so far as it was possible to freeze that way of life at a particular point in time, the chosen date was to be about 1900, when the prosperity of the region's industries was at its peak. It would, in other words, be concerned hardly at all with pre-industrial society, and in this respect it was striking out on a completely new path. Unlike Skansen and its descendants, which included the Welsh Folk Museum, it was not to be in the slightest degree folksy. Its open-days would present brass-band concerts and engines running under steam, rather than displays of folk-dancing and hand-weaving.

Beamish opened to the public in May 1971, although to begin with all that it was possible to offer visitors was a display of small items inside Beamish Hall and a chance to wander round the estate where the pioneering open-air museum was to be. Year by year afterwards, the grand design began to take shape. There was a coal-mining area, with a real drift-mine, which visitors could enter – there is coal on the museum site – and a complex of deep-mine surface installations brought in from elsewhere in the region. A row of pitmen's cottages, with their yards and gardens, was meticulously taken to pieces and rebuilt adjacent to the pit, with authentic furnishings and decorations. An operational tramway and railway were laid out, with a railway station, signal-box and goods yard transported to the site and re-erected. A complete town area was reconstructed, with shops, houses, a dentist's premises, a public house and other buildings of the period. The town area was provided with its park and bandstand, in which concerts were regularly given at weekends. And, in a group of nineteenth-century farm buildings, there were displays to show how farming was carried on in the region at around the turn of the century.

There is much yet to do. Two of the North-East's major industries, iron and steel and chemicals, have so far not been dealt with at all and two others, shipping and shipbuilding, will never be, at least, not on this site, since Beamish is not on the coast. But sufficient has already been done to make it 'the perfect place for a magnificent day out',[13] with a large cafeteria, a shop, an enormous car-park[14] and an audio-visual display to fill in the background. It is important to mention, too, an aspect of Beamish which the general public does not normally see, its splendid library and photographic archive, which are now important research tools for anyone studying the social history and industries of the North-East.

Typical cottage activities in the mining villages of the North-East were baking and making 'proggy mats' – rugs made from small clips of old clothing. The Museum shows visitors how this was all done.

Reconstructions of two early twentieth-century shops at Beamish:
Left a grocer's
Right a draper's

A replica of George Stephenson's 1825 locomotive, 'Locomotion', is regularly demonstrated at Beamish. Part of a rebuilt coal-mine can be seen in the background.

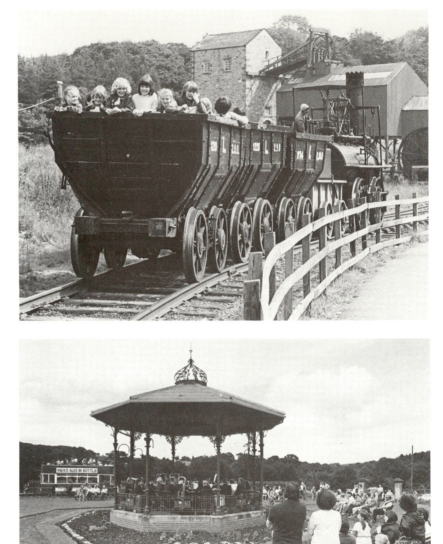

A brass band concert in progress at Beamish.

There are certain special achievements which mark Beamish off as belonging to a new generation of folk-museums – its skill in discovering private funding to supplement the money already available for capital purposes from public resources, the high quality of its publicity and public relations, its determination to make itself attractive to people of all social classes and levels of education, its political shrewdness, its realisation from the outset that most of the money required to cover operating expenses would have to come directly from the public,[15] in the form of entrance charges, shop sales and cafeteria profits. But its chief claim to be included in our list of Museums of Influence rests on its re-assertion of the Hazelius ideal in a way which brought industrial society uncompromisingly within the definition of a folk-museum. Comparisons have been made between the open-air museum at Bokrijk, in Belgium, which also has industrial exhibits, and with the Ironbridge Gorge Museum, but the three museums are in fact very different. One section of Iron-bridge, Blists Hill Open-Air Museum, does, it is true, have superficial resemblances to Beamish, but its philosophy is quite its own and its depends for its prestige and its visitors on what one could, without disrespect, call Ironbridge proper, the sites in the great Valley of the Industrial Revolution. For this reason, Ironbridge has its place in the next chapter, which is concerned with what I have called history where it happened, that is, with historical site museums. Bokrijk is different from Beamish in quite another way.[16] It is, and feels, like the Arnhem kind of open-air museum, that is, the majority of its exhibits are either pre-industrial or non-industrial, but it has added industrial exhibits as a kind of postscript.

But to refrain from setting up a museum barrier between the pre-industrial periods of a country's history is an achievement in itself, and we should be grateful for it. Rüsselsheim would certainly not describe itself as a folk-museum, despite the fact that it is deeply concerned with the everyday life of ordinary people, and it is assuredly not in any way folksy. Neither, equally certainly, is the National Museum of Popular Arts and Traditions (Musée National des Arts et Traditions Populaires) in Paris, for many years the Mecca of folklorists throughout the world, and a museum which, both for the range and quality of its collections and for its methods in displaying and studying them, has had a profound influence on other museums.

Its history goes back for rather more than a hundred years. In 1878 the Museum of Ethnography (Musée d'Ethnographie) in the Trocadéro began to collect and display French material, as a sideline to its main business of acquiring items from more distant cultures. In 1935 the Trocadéro Museum was divided into two parts, one becoming the Museum of Mankind (Musée de l'Homme) – the ethnographical museum – which is still at the Trocadéro, and the other, the Museum of Popular Arts and Traditions, which was to concentrate entirely on rural, pre-industrial France, and which eventually, in 1969, found a permanent home in a new building designed for the purpose on the edge of the Bois de Boulogne, after spending thirty-two years in the basement of the Palais de Chaillot.[17]

It is easy to be overwhelmed by the sheer size of the collections and by the facilities which are available for studying them, but the main importance of the Museum lies elsewhere, in the seriousness of its approach. Because this is a large, State-funded, academically reputable institution, the subject which it represents, by whatever name it may be called in different countries, has acquired a much higher prestige, both nationally and internationally, than it would probably have acquired otherwise, at least in the short term.

Above left 'Symbols' in the Cultural Galleries

Above right A shepherd, with his flock of sheep-bells.

Skittle collection in the Museum's Study Galleries.

Since it was first established, the Museum of Popular Arts and Traditions has pursued an energetic programme of collecting and research, greatly helped by the fact that its first Chief Curator was Georges Henri Rivière, one of the few undisputed museum geniuses of the twentieth century. A Chair of Popular Arts and Traditions, the first in the world, was created at the École du Louvre in 1937, in association with the Museum, an International Folklore Conference was organised in the same year and programmes of fieldwork were set up, which continued throughout the war years. After the war, the results of more than ten years of collecting and research were shown to the public in the form of a long series of temporary exhibitions on particular themes. Twenty-two of these exhibitions took place between 1951 and 1964 and many of them formed the basis of the displays in the new museum. They attracted much attention and admiration, both within France and abroad, and made it clear that museums of this type could no longer be dismissed as mere entertainment and romanticism.

The Museum is divided into three parts, a Cultural Gallery, which is on the ground floor, a Study Gallery, in the basement, and an area for special exhibitions. The Cultural Gallery comprises two sections, one which shows how man interacts with nature and transforms it to suit his own needs, and another which illustrates the society which he creates in the process of doing this, 'society' meaning, in this context, the society of pre-industrial France. There are three methods of displaying objects, by means of theme-displays, reconstructed settings and slide-sequences. In the first of these, the presentation is highly stylised, with the objects hanging against a black background from a nearly invisible thread. The second includes six detailed reconstructions, domestic interiors, a blacksmith's shop, a wood-turner's workshop and a fishing boat, each accompanied by a recorded explanation, and by a lighting system which draws attention to the particular part of the display which is being described at that moment.

Georges Henri Rivière, the first Chief Curator of the Museum of Popular Arts and Traditions.

In the Study Gallery, there are two sources of information – the objects, arranged according to types, and the study-booths, which offer slide-sound sequences and videotapes to illustrate processes and techniques. The objects have only classification headings and numbers. Detailed information is provided by what are called *Ethnological Guides* ('Guides Ethnologiques'), which cover such subjects as Rural Transport, Domestic Equipment and Customs and Beliefs, all of which visitors have to buy for themselves although the prices are very modest.

Now, seventeen years after the Museum opened, it is inevitably beginning to show its age a little, especially in the matter of style and technique. What was once ahead of its time can hardly be expected to give that impression for ever. The difficulty over the updating of the displays is that, since a great deal of money went into creating them in the first place, a great deal will have to be devoted to their eventual refurbishment. In museums, as elsewhere, one makes a large investment at one's peril, or rather, at the peril of one's successors. But, beyond question, it is an investment which has yielded rich rewards, by providing a worthwhile standard of comparison, against which other museums can measure themselves, and by placing folklore firmly where it belongs, within the frontiers of ethnology, so that a folk-museum can at last be understood for what it really is, a museum of the ethnography of the homeland.

The Museum of Popular Arts and Traditions quite deliberately avoided any form of chronological arrangements. It represents history organised by types of activity and belief, rather than by date. Such a system suits this kind of material very well, but it would be inappropriate and confusing if it were to be applied to other varieties of museum which are concerned to interpret the past. Museums which tell the story of a city or a town are a good case in point. The central theme here has to be the growth of the city from its earliest beginnings, but with this as the spine of the museum, holding the body together, it is possible and reasonable to develop thematic displays – the guilds, the medieval Church, shipping, and so on – as one proceeds from century to century.

Few things are more natural than the wish of a city, a town or even a village to set up a museum of clues to the local past, a temple of historical relics. 'Local history' is the most frequently found items in the contents of any museum, large or small, throughout the world, but it is usually, alas, an unflattering term. Most museum-based 'local history' consists of little more than bits and pieces from the past, telling no coherent or particularly meaningful story. The local museum is all too often the community antique shop, with all the attractions and imperfections of such an establishment. The disciplined, organised museum in which local history is given a shape and a pattern is something of a rarity. The gradual progress towards something better is described in the final chapter of the present work, but it can usefully be anticipated here by considering one or two museums which have made a successful attempt to present local history on the grand scale, the history of a capital city.

Inevitably, such a museum has characteristics which must be different from those of a provincial history museum. The capital is a curious and fascinating hybrid. It is both itself, a city in its own right, but at the same time a symbol of the country as a whole, *multum in parvo*. The museum of the history of London or Amsterdam is a place in which the threads of Britain or the Netherlands are gathered in, a centre of relics and reminiscences which are neither wholly national nor wholly local. Virtually every capital city in the world has a museum which is of this type, or which purports to be. One finds them in Buenos Aires, in Brussels, in Moscow, in Oslo, in Prague, in Paris, in Rio de Janeiro, all announcing themselves to be the custodians and impresarios of the city's past. And so indeed they are, in the sense of being the major repositories of a city's historical relics, but in most cases the relics are both too numerous and too haphazardly gathered together. They do not tell a story which makes proper sense, mainly because those responsible for the museum have not made up their minds what the story is.[18]

One of the few museums of the type which does tell a full and convincing story is the Museum of the History of the City of Amsterdam, created during the 1970s. A few years ago, I asked its Director which museum had impressed him most, taught him most, during the extensive world travels which he had undertaken while the museum was in the planning stage. Which was, so to speak, his Museum's mother, or perhaps grandmother? He answered without hesitation, 'the Historical Museum of the City of Warsaw'. The reply was both generous and fully justified, but it produces, so far as the present book is concerned, a somewhat complicated situation, which could be described in the following way. For every one foreigner who has visited the Historical Museum of the City of Warsaw during the past thirty years, at least five thousand must have visited the Museum of the History of the City of Amsterdam,

Exterior of the Museum of the History of the City of Warsaw in 1945.

Exterior of the Museum in 1980.

simply because Amsterdam is so much more accessible. It would be unfair to say that, for this reason, the Amsterdam Museum has received more credit as a pioneer than it is entitled to, but one could certainly suggest that Warsaw has not received the reward it deserves. The influence of Warsaw has tended to be exercised, not directly, but at one remove, an injustice which I propose to rectify by including the Historical Museum of the City of Warsaw in our list of Museums of Influence.

It was originally established in 1936, as the Museum of Old Warsaw, in two historic houses in the Old Market. During the Second World War, it was totally destroyed by the Germans. Soon after the end of the war, the decision was taken to rebuild the historic areas of the city in their original form and to allocate one complete side, of the Old Market, comprising eleven former houses, to a new Historical Museum. The façades of these houses had survived, although in a battered condition. The rebuilding was carried out in such a way that each house preserved its original identity, with the new Museum arranged in a series of small rooms on four floors of every unit.

The first part of the Museum was opened in 1955 and the work of conversion and installation was completed in 1965. The collections of the pre-war museum had been completely lost during the war and a new beginning had to be made to discover objects which could be used to illustrate the history of Warsaw, from its thirteenth-century beginnings up to the present day. The task was appallingly difficult, but it was accomplished by bringing Warsaw-related material back to the capital from other parts of Poland and by gifts from other museums and from private individuals. The style of exhibition was governed to a great extent by the sparse nature of its collections. Every item on display had to work hard for its living and pictures and three-dimensional objects were made to complement one another in an ingenious way.

The pre-war museum was exactly what its title indicated, a Museum of Old Warsaw. Its successor was not only much larger, but completely different, both in concept and in execution. The aim was to show life in the City in all its aspects, as it developed from the centre of a princely court to the capital of an independent Polish state, and the focal point of the struggle to achieve national independence from Swedes, Russians, Prussians, Napoleonic French and Hitlerite Germans. With military invasion and occupation, entwined with political struggle, as the Museum's core, the great variety of Warsaw's activities, decade by decade and century by century, could be fitted into place. The arts and crafts, the music, the literature and the theatre are there, but not in a vacuum. One understands who their patrons were. Trade and industry are well represented, and one sees the links between money-making activities, fine architecture and domestic comfort.

The floor-by-floor arrangement of the Museum has been carried out with great skill and imagination, so that one begins, on the ground floor, with the early days of the City and, by mounting the stairs, moves steadily towards modern times. The dreadful years of the German occupation and of the systematic destruction of Warsaw are on the top floor, together with the beginnings of the post-war reconstruction.

One understands why the Director of the Museum of the History of the City of Amsterdam felt able to say that he had learnt more in Warsaw than anywhere else. Most museums of this type display the skin and perhaps the flesh of the city: Warsaw has the blood and the nerves as well. There is an eventful and at times terrible story to tell, and the Museum tells it brilliantly.

It has been said often enough that museum directors in a socialist country have a much easier task than their colleagues in the West, at least in a museum which is concerned with history, because the political framework within which they operate provides them with a straight line through history. They are not required to make sense of history, because the task has already been performed for them. There is certainly a good deal of truth in this, but whether or not it amounts to saying that the

Top left Arms and armour at the Historical Museum of the City of Warsaw. A good example of the Museum's skill in producing an impressive effect with slender resources.

Top right Reconstruction of a middle-class sitting-room in Warsaw at the beginning of the present century.

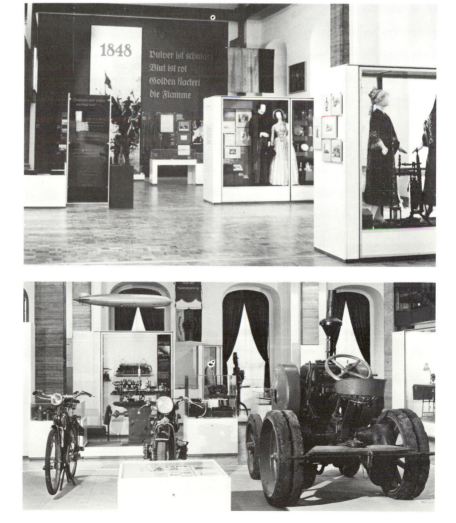

1830–48 section at the Museum of German History, Berlin. Social contrasts at the time of the 1848 Revolution.

1924–9 section at the Museum of German History. Lenz Bulldog tractor, 1925.

Class differences in early 19th-century Germany, as illustrated by rooms in the Museum of German History in East Berlin.

Reconstruction of a worker's kitchen-living room, *c.* 1900.

A middle-class sitting room, *c.* 1900.

Museum of London or the Museum of the City of New York would be better museums if the British and the Americans had an officially agreed philosophy of history is a matter for discussion. There must, even so, be some good reason why the German Democratic Republic has had a Museum of German History for more than twenty years while, on the other side of the Wall, the Federal Republic has yet to establish one.

The Museum of German History in East Berlin has earned a place on our list for a number of reasons, one of which is that it exists. In the West, it has been sometimes dismissed as mere propaganda, but this is a very superficial view, not least because it ignores the important fact that the Museum of German History is, professionally and irrespective of its politics, an excellent museum.

Before it was set up, in 1952, the decision was taken that, for the purposes of the Museum, German history should be taken as beginning in 1789, the year of the French Revolution. One can hardly imagine the French coming to the same conclusion about their own history, although one imagines that they would agree, with some confidence, that after 1789 Europe could never be, and has not been, the same again. If a point had to be selected at which the old world came to an end and the new began, 1789 is probably as good as any. One should remember that in 1952 the Berlin Wall did not exist and Germans were still able to move more or less freely between the East and the West. It was certainly envisaged at that time that the new Museum would be accessible to all Germans and that it would be what its name implied, *The* Museum of German History, not a Museum or our Museum or the Socialist Museum of German History. Its aim was stated to be 'the enlightenment of

Interior of a hut in a concentration camp, an exhibit in the section '1933–45'.

the people and especially of youth' and it was intended as 'a central example of the work to be carried out by historical museums'.[19]

With these aims in mind the Museum, accommodated, perhaps symbolically, in the former Prussian State Arsenal, was designed to present German history as a whole – the politics, industry, literature, empire-building, science, wars, music – as a series of mighty decade-by-decade sweeps. Each room had a text over the doorway, explaining the basic theme of what is to be seen inside, and there was, of course, a great deal more information attached to the exhibits themselves. Throughout the museum, there were realistic room arrangements, ranging from side-by-side recon-structions of a worker's congested kitchen-cum-living room and a more comfortable middle-class sitting-room, both dating from *c*. 1900, to the interior of a hut in a Nazi concentration camp. The presentation was simple and by 1980 a little old-fashioned, although it was almost avant-garde when the Museum first opened. The message was clear, that as German capitalism built up during the nineteenth century, the divisions between the workers and their exploiters became more marked. The rich became steadily richer and the poor steadily poorer, until a series of inevitable explosions and disasters took place, the revolutions of 1848, the First World War, the Russian Revolution, the Great Depression of the 1930s, the rise of Hitler and National Socialism, the Second World War. Around these mainstreams of misery and Valhalla, life somehow went on and German genius contrived to flourish, although never with the vigour that would have been possible had socialism been in control of the nation's destiny.

Of course it was propaganda, but where are the museums of history in the West which offer a different, yet equally simple and comprehensible philosophy, with the same quality of exhibits to support it? The Museum of German History was planned, not for intellectuals and specialists, but for the common man, and the job was well done, so far as the period up to 1945 is concerned. After that, the Museum appeared to have lost its nerve, so that the post-war years were dealt with by a series of tempor-ary exhibitions, few of which, alas, were of the same quality as the main part of the museum. Within the socialist world, the Museum of German History has undoubtedly had a considerable influence. It has been much visited, much written about and, not surprisingly, much praised, as being a model of what a popular historical museum should be. But, in the West, where it has also been widely discussed, its value and influence have been of a different kind, as ammunition for those who believe that conservation and exhibition are in themselves not enough and that the greatest of a museum's merits is its ability to tell a story.

Nowhere has this belief been more passionately held, nor more brilliantly put into practice, than at Beth Hatefutsoth, the Museum of the Jewish Diaspora, at Tel Aviv, one of the most important museums of the present century. It was fortunate in having as its first Director Jesaja Weinberg, a man who had previously been responsible for bringing Israel's National Theatre from nothing to a high point of

Rashi Chapel, Worms, Germany.
The Chapel was built in 1624 by David
Joshua Oppenheim, a leading member
of the Worms community, as an annexe
to the ancient Worms synagogue.

success. Weinberg has always emphasised that his skills lie in communication, not in preservation, and accepted the task of being the Museum's creator and first director on this understanding. His brief was twofold, to convey the essentials of the Jewish faith and to tell the story of the dispersal of the Jewish people over the world. His public was assumed to consist mainly of Jews who needed to have their faith and their confidence strengthened, and of non-Jews who knew virtually nothing about Judaism and who might well have seriously distorted ideas about Jewish history.

His first step was to decide, with the best help available, exactly what the story was that he had to tell. That achieved, he had to work out the most impressive and the most vivid ways of telling that story. Where original objects were available, he would use them. Where, as often happened, the originals could not be obtained, he used first-class replicas or models. It was impossible, for instance, that the French authorities would allow the famous figures of the Christian and the Jew to be removed from the west front of Strasburg Cathedral, in order to be put on show in Tel Aviv, so, because his story required these figures, he obtained replicas. And, since Solomon's Temple had been destroyed by the Romans, he had a model made, according to the most reliable historical and archaeological evidence. He was fre-

Model of the Jewish quarter in Lublin. The poster announces a ban on the followers of Shabbetai Tzevi.

quently offered objects from all over the world, 'for the Museum'. If they helped to tell the story, he said 'Yes', but if, as was usually the case, they did not, he said 'No'. 'We', he was fond of saying, 'are in the story-telling business, not the usual museum business'.

A great deal of money was available, and spent, and the results, by general consent, were wonderfully good. There were some particularly memorable touches, a planetarium-type display to show the course of Jewish history, a wall of portraits and biographies to draw attention to Jews who had made an outstanding contribution to the countries in which they had settled – many visitors were heard to comment that they had previously had no idea that this or that person was a Jew at all – booths equipped with computer terminals, in which one could ask for detailed information about particular subjects, the information being available as a print-out, in the language of one's choice, when one left the Museum.

Left Using computer-stored information concerning Jewish communities throughout the world.

Right Model of the Synagogue at Elkins Park, Pennsylvania, built in 1954 and designed by Frank Lloyd Wright. The tent-like structure symbolises Mount Sinai.

Jesaja Weinberg's creation gave the world museum establishment a considerable shock, from which it has hardly recovered. In Warsaw, one might perhaps forgive or, more probably, overlook a national museum which insisted on telling a story, because relatively few people went to Warsaw and a heresy which was perpetrated there could always be attributed to the fact that the museum was in the socialist half of the world. But in Tel Aviv it was a different matter. What happened there could not be brushed aside and forgotten, because the links between Israel and the United States and Europe were so close. Israel was mainstream and, in any case, its museums were known to be good. Storytelling, however, was only part of the problem. Mr Weinberg had committed two more very grave offences. He had used replicas, not only without shame, but with confidence and pride and, as the director of a museum of world importance, he had turned his back on the two sacred duties of acquisition and conservation. Men have been asked to resign from their clubs for far lesser misdemeanours.

Chapter Seven
History where it happened

Colonial Williamsburg:	*'The opportunity to buy and restore a complete town'*
Ironbridge Gorge Museum, Telford:	*'The integrated management of a group of historic sites'*
Museum of Man and Industry, Le Creusot:	*'Any object within the community's perimeter is psychologically part of the Museum'*
'Wasa', Stockholm:	*'The documentation of a seventeenth-century folly'*

In 1982 ICOM published a report called, in its English version, *Archaeological Site Museums*. Considering the French fondness for precise, legalistic terminology, the title is a little puzzling, since the report is, in fact, about site-museums in general, not merely those related to archaeology. It begins with a definition. 'A site museum', it says, 'is a museum conceived and set up in order to protect natural or cultural property, movable and immovable, on its original site, that is, preserved at the place where such property has been created or discovered.' It then distinguishes four categories of site-museum.

First, 'Ecological'. By this is meant 'museums in surroundings which, so far as one can tell, have not been changed by man'. The Museum of Yosemite National Park, California, is instanced as a museum of this type.

Then, 'Ethnographical'. This is 'a museum, whether in a place which is still inhabited or not, which illustrates the customs, habits and way of life of a community'. The report puts Ironbridge in this box, having first taken care to remind its readers, somewhat primly, that the term 'industrial archaeology' was a piece of Anglo-Saxon quaintness and that the correct expression should be 'industrial heritage' ('patrimoine industriel').

The third category is labelled 'Historical'. This refers to 'a museum at a place where, at some time in the past, an event occurred which was important in the history of a community' and, as examples, we are offered battlefields, fortresses, public buildings and the homes of the great.

The last sub-division, 'Archaeological', should be restricted to 'museums at the point where excavations have taken place'.

Given the breadth of choice allowed by the ICOM definition, a remarkably high proportion of the world's museums today could be fairly described as 'site-museums'. I am sure this would not have been the situation fifty years ago. Consider the range of such museums in the British Isles alone, a by no means untypical area. Milton's Cottage, Chalfont St Giles. Revolution House, Old Whittington, Chesterfield – an old inn connected with the planning of the 1688 Revolution. Acton Scott Working Farm Museum, Church Stretton. Wellbrook Beetling Mill, Cookstown, County Tyrone. Manx Village Folk Museum, Cregneash, Isle of Man. Darlington North Road Station Railway Museum. Roman Painted House, Dover. Osborne House, Isle of Wight. Bateman's, Burwash – the home of Rudyard Kipling. Big Pit Mining Museum, Blaenavon. Cathedral Treasury, Lincoln. North Wales Quarrying Museum, Llanberis. Wedgwood Museum, Barlaston.

Approximately 20 per cent of the 2,200 museums in the British Isles could claim to be site-museums of one kind or another, and the proportion is rising, partly because such museums are usually cheap to run, partly because they are popular with the public, and partly because, in every country, the national stock of historical sites is increasing all the time. Such a process could be halted only by an international agreement to have no more important events and no more distinguished people, which would obviously be absurd.

Site-museums have a life and a reality about them which other types of museum cannot hope to approach. The possessions of the late Sir Winston Churchill would lose much of their appeal if they were to be moved from Chartwell, the house in which he lived. The Wellington Museum at Waterloo would not have its present impact if it were anywhere but in the inn used by the Duke as his headquarters during the Battle of Waterloo. Even the most cursory of world surveys shows the rich potential of what I have chosen to call 'the museum of history where it happened', a description which I prefer to the rather dead and flat 'site-museum', which conceals the essential dynamism of such an institution. In Japan, for example, one has the evocative memorial museums at Hiroshima and Nagasaki, in the German Democratic Republic the cells and crematorium at Ravensbrück concentration camp, and in Poland the museums in what remains of the concentration and extermination camps at Lublin (Majdan) and Szlutowo. At Dresden, in Canada, is the house known as Uncle Tom's Cabin, the former home of the Rev. Josiah Henson, 'Uncle Tom' of Harriet Beecher Stowe's novel, with mementoes of Henson's work for runaway negro slaves, while across the border in the United States are numerous museums at places made famous by the Civil War, at Gettysburg, for instance, and at Harper's Ferry. The national capital in Washington D.C. has preserved Ford's Theatre as a museum, restored as it was on the evening in 1865 when Lincoln was assassinated there. Argentina has converted Manuel de Falla's former home at Alta Gracia into a museum, with the furniture, library and other material relating to the life and work of the composer, and at Leningrad visitors can tour the cruiser, 'Aurora', the warship taken over by the crew during the October Revolution and used during the attack on the Winter Palace, with the radio room from which Lenin's message announcing the final triumph of the Revolution was transmitted.

All these museums rely heavily for their appeal on the fact that the building, or the ship, or whatever, is an integral part of history. It is impossible to say that any one museum began the fashion of creating such historical shrines. If they had any definite parent, it was the medieval place of pilgrimage, for St James at Compostella, for St Thomas à Becket at Canterbury, and for all the other saints and martyrs commemorated throughout Europe. When the pilgrimage habit became secularised, one eventually had the beginnings of visits to historic houses and sites, and indeed of tourism as it is now understood. 'Tourists,' Donald Horne has said with great perspicacity, 'are the main modern pilgrims, carrying guide books as devotional texts'.[1]

There is not much point in setting up either religious or secular shrines if few people visit them, and it cannot be an accident that the enormous growth of site-museums has coincided with the advent of mass motor-travel, a development which took place earlier and more rapidly in some countries than in others. It happened first in the United States and mainly for this reason – wealth was another – all four types of site-museum identified by ICOM were widespread in America while other countries were still thinking about the possibilities. And once America had set up this kind of museum, with such confidence and such success, it became easier and more respectable for the more backward places to do the same. The term 'backward' is, of course, purely relative but, in museums, as in other fields of human activity, there is a good deal of truth in the often-repeated statement that what America does today other countries will be doing in fifteen or twenty years' time. A generalisation with equal validity is that Europe invents things and America develops them and makes them a commercial success.

It is interesting to observe that the Americans have, in general, been hostile to the idea of setting up 'Skansens'. 'Very few are the houses that now stand entirely out of their historic settings', wrote Laurence Vail Coleman in 1939,[2] 'and nearly all of these few are in one place – Henry Ford's artificial Greenfield Village at Dearborn, Michigan . . . The United States embraces too many radically different settings and such variety of local materials that house-gathering is insupportable. Our people seem able to visit historic houses wherever they stand. America's 644 scattered historic house museums are collectively her Skansen.'

The total now is considerably more than 644, probably four times that number. Local communities, especially in the Eastern states, where a high proportion of the choicest and oldest houses are to be found, have made something of a hobby of turning architecturally fine houses into museums. During the past thirty years, however, the emphasis on preservation has noticeably shifted away from buildings which are simply old and good to look at and towards those where historic associations are the principal merit. The two most important reasons for this change are the need to do full justice to the past achievements of America's black citizens and to the western and midwestern states, which were of no great significance before the middle of the nineteenth century, but very important indeed thereafter.

The Americans may have shown little enthusiasm for open-air museums in the now-traditional European sense, but they have much to their credit in the preservation of groups of buildings on their original site – pioneer strongholds, like Sutter's Fort at Sacramento, mission compounds in California, Texas and Arizona, pioneer settlements such as that of the Harmonists at Economy, and at Ambridge, Pennsylvania. But the grandest of all collections of museum houses, either in America or in the world, is in Virginia, where Williamsburg, the eighteenth-century State Capital, has been restored and reproduced in its entirety, 'the site museum to end all site museums'. The influence of the Williamsburg project within the United States has been enormous, in increasing the interest of Americans in their own past, in providing an insight into the technical problems involved, and in demonstrating how such an ambitious and costly venture can be made financially viable. Its example has been followed in many places abroad, although the debt has not always been acknowledged.

Williamsburg was the first example of large-scale conservation in the United States. It was carried through in the only way which would have been possible in America, by private philanthropy, and as the result of a remarkable partnership between the Rev. William Archer Rutherford Goodwin, who had the idea, and John D. Rockefeller, Jr, who had the money. Goodwin came to the very run-down city of Williamsburg at the beginning of this century as the rector of Bruton Parish Church, which had been built in 1715. Restoring his own church gave him both a feeling for Williamsburg and a taste for restoration. In his book, *Bruton Parish Church Restored and its Historic Environment*, published in 1907, he described Williamsburg and the surrounding area of Virginia as 'the cradle of the Republic' and 'the birthplace of her liberty'. Its buildings should be safeguarded and 'the spirit of the days of long ago' preserved. Having expressed himself in these confident terms, he left Williamsburg for a pastorate in Rochester, New York, and stayed there until 1923, when he returned to Williamsburg to become the head of the department of Bible literature and religious education at the College of William and Mary, where he had an opportunity to develop his considerable fund-raising talents by becoming director of the College endowment campaign. In 1924 he approached Henry Ford's son, Edsel, for funds to buy and restore the entire town, on the not unreasonable grounds that the Ford family had been 'the chief contributors to the destruction of Williamsburg, by encouraging the development of paved roads, filling stations, snack bars, advertising hoardings and traffic signals, all of which seriously interfered with the historic atmosphere'. Ford replied that his conscience was not strong enough to provide the funds required. An approach to John D. Rockefeller, Jr was more successful. Rockefeller visited Williamsburg and found that the opportunity to buy and restore a complete town, and to preserve it from 'inharmonious surroundings' was 'irresistible'.

Rev. W. A. R. Goodwin and John D. Rockefeller Jr.

Duke of Gloucester Street before
restoration.

After a tentative beginning, during which Rockefeller authorised only surveys and
limited purchases of land and buildings, the project gradually moved towards a
full-scale operation, which involved detailed historical research, the recruitment
and training of architects – who had hitherto shown little interest in working on
historic buildings – and the training of suitable craftsmen. An interpretation service
was set up, to meet the needs of the public, and guides appointed and trained, and
by 1934 sufficient had been done for Williamsburg to be judged fit to receive the
American public. The plan had been to demolish 300 modern structures, to restore
thoroughly more than 60 of the early buildings that remained, and to build exact
replicas of 70 that had gone, including the colonial Capitol, the court house, the
Governor's mansion, and the gaol. In 1938, Rockefeller authorised further building
work, partly in order to provide useful work for young Virginian architects, during
a period in which the long-drawn-out economic recession was making it difficult for
them to find employment. One might note in passing that a major reason for the
great increase in preservation activity which occurred throughout the United States
in the mid-1930s was the decision of the Federal Government to make money
available for the purpose, as a means of finding work for skilled people who would
otherwise have had nothing to do.

Conservation and rebuilding began again in earnest very soon after the end of the
War in 1945 and is now substantially complete. At this point, one can look back over
the past sixty years and try to assess what has been accomplished. It would hardly be
an exaggeration to say that, in the United States, Williamsburg produced something
approaching a cultural revolution, making it possible for ordinary people to gain a
reliable impression of how their eighteenth-century ancestors lived. There were, of
course, certain dangers in the organisers' devoted pursuit of authenticity, which in

Costumed interpreters at the
Governor's Palace.

Costumed staff in the Millinery Shop.

The Capitol at Colonial Williamsburg.

some ways may have achieved more than they intended. In the autumn of 1938, the distinguished architect, Frank Lloyd Wright, spoke at William and Mary College and congratulated those responsible for the restoration of Williamsburg for showing 'how shallow and little life was then in the Colonial period', which is one way of saying that there had been no attempt to romanticise the life of those times. Five years earlier, H. I. Brock had complained that the place was too tidy and too cosy, that much of the 'harshness' of life in Colonial times was missing. What exactly he meant by this is not clear, but he may well have been thinking of the absence of smells and unpleasant sights in the reconstructed town and of any sign of the slave economy on which Colonial Williamsburg had depended.

The Interpretation Department is fully conscious of this kind of problem. It realises that different generations will ask different questions about Williamsburg and that it must be ready to meet and answer them. 'We must not forget that history includes the underprivileged and the discontented', it has said. 'We must aim to discover and present a truthful and broadly based past that has relevance for all, whether or not they agree with the way things have turned out so far. Especially we must strive to show more clearly the contributions of eighteenth-century Williamsburg's black residents, who constituted about half the population and did most of the heavy work. As our research discovers more details of Negro life, our interpretation must find ways of communicating them to all our visitors, whether black or white.'[3] Few museums of whatever kind have ever made the point in such a clear and uncompromising manner. Most would probably have been frightened to do so. It is important to remember, however, that Colonial Williamsburg, like any other museum dependent on entrance fees and on profits from auxiliary activities, must please the public or perish. It must pay constant attention to the mood of the market. The more satisfied customers it has, the more prosperous it will be.

But care with interpretation has been only one of Colonial Williamsburg's virtues. It has trained hundreds of craftsmen to very high standards, and in this way created, for the national benefit, a pool of skilled labour which would not otherwise exist. It has discovered a great deal about the materials, tools and techniques used in the past. It has encouraged, more than any other single institution, the growth of a new breed of archaeologist, now known as the historical archaeologist, who works on sites

Costumed demonstrators in the Black-smith's Shop.

which belong to the historical period. It has persuaded scholars to accept buildings as historical evidence, one of the most difficult tasks it has had to perform. Through its work on the site and through its conferences, films and publications, it has provided a model for those who wish to restore and preserve buildings elsewhere. It has demonstrated to the whole world the value of preserving a site as a whole, with a master plan, instead of as a disconnected series of bits and pieces. It has experimented with ways of communicating not merely information about the past, but the atmosphere of the past. And, through its beautifully made and necessarily far from cheap replicas of eighteenth-century furniture and other items, made in its own workshops, it has enabled a great many members of the public to, in effect, take part of Colonial Williamsburg away with them and to benefit from its presence in their homes and offices. Not least, through its specialised conferences for members of the museum profession, it has shared its incomparable experience of what it calls 'historical management' with many people in many countries.

Colonial Williamsburg has been and still is a powerful seminal influence and, as with any institution which has brought about a revolution in thinking and practice, one forgets too easily, and ungratefully, what the situation was before the revolution took place. But there is no need to exaggerate the achievement, to the point of pretending that there was no innovation before Williamsburg. Fire and the wheel were not invented here, nor, indeed, was interpretation of the practice of dressing the guides up in period clothes. The idea of the 'living museum' has roots which go well back into the nineteenth century, certainly as far as the 1876 Centennial Exhibition in Philadelphia, where visitors were able to see a number of interesting folk-life tableaux. Artur Hazelius, an enterprising publicist and crusader after the Americans' own heart, had sent six of these tableaux, illustrating the habits and dress of the Swedish peasantry. There were scenes of elk-hunting, courtship, christening, life among the Laplanders, Bible reading, and the death of a little girl.

One American exhibit also concentrated on folk-life, with a 'New England Farmer's Home' and, by contrast, a 'Modern Kitchen'. The more or less official *Illustrated History of the Centennial Exhibition* contains a description of them. 'The New England Farmer's Home,' it records, 'was a plain one-storey log house, and was built and arranged in the style of the New England farmhouses of a century ago. It contained a parlor, or "settin-room", a kitchen and bed-rooms, all of which were furnished with veritable heirlooms, contributed by the people of New England.' 'Everything in the house', it went on, 'had the ripe flavour of antiquity, and the visitor might see in the place an exact reproduction of the houses that his ancestors, the Minute Men of the Revolution, left so promptly and bravely when the news of the Battle of Lexington called them to arms. The farm-house was occupied only by ladies, who were dressed in the quaint costumes of their great-grandmothers and who conducted visitors through the house, and explained to them the story and uses of its contents.'[4]

Visitors to the Exhibition were able to compare the Log House with the Modern Kitchen, and to see how it 'contained all the improvements of the present age, and showed the progress of the century in the department of domestic economy'.[5]

Costumed guides were also used at the beginning of the present century by the New England historian and antiquary, George Francis Dow, who, in 1907, installed three period rooms in the Essex Institute at Salem and later, in 1909, began America's first open-air museum on a plot of land adjoining the Institute. He bought and moved to the museum Salem's oldest house, the 1685 John Ward House, and furnished it in such a way as to present 'a truthful picture of 17th century household life in Salem'.[6] Dow aimed at realism, noting that 'where original furniture or utensils of the period have not been available, reproductions have been made. The finished result is believed to be highly successful, giving much of the atmosphere of liveableness.'[7] A year later, Dow was able to report on how the public had received his efforts with the house. 'The experiment of showing visitors about "the old house" by Miss Symonds and her two assistants dressed in homespun costumes of the time when the house was built has proved to be a great success, as the appropriately costumed figures add much to the effectiveness of the restored interior. A gentleman from New York City, who has a country estate in Virginia, has recently dressed his house servants in careful reproductions of these 17th century costumes worn by our assistants during their summer season. The old house, with costumed attendants, has also been photographed for moving pictures, and thus will be seen by many in distant cities.'[8]

Henry Ford was also an enthusiast for dressing up and for carrying out old-time activities. In 1926 he restored, at great expense, the Wayside Inn at South Sudbury, Massachusetts, celebrated in the poems of Henry Wadsworth Longfellow, and immediately it was finished held a dance in it, with everyone in Colonial period costumes. Later, he restored another inn, the Botsford Inn, near Detroit, where he had often danced as a young man. This, too, he used for evenings of old-time music and dancing. And when, in 1928, he began work on his 'pocket edition of America', Greenfield Village, he said that his aim was to recreate 'American life as lived', to 'demonstrate, for educational purposes, the development of American arts, sciences, customs, and institutions by reproducing or re-enacting the conditions and circum-stances of such development in a manner calculated to convey a realistic picture'.[9]

But, despite the millions that Henry Ford poured into it, it is doubtful if Greenfield Village has had anything approaching the influence of Colonial Williamsburg, which applied, on a scale that no-one could ignore, the recipe for 'live interpretation' which has been immensely popular in America. It developed the use of costumed interpreters and historically accurate craft demonstrations to a high degree of efficiency, and made a strong impact on other American museums which were being developed at the same time – Mystic Seaport in Connecticut, Plimouth Plantation,

Old Sturbridge Village, and the Farmers' Village at Cooperstown, New York. Costumed guides and demonstrations are frequently found too, at the Living History Farms, which are now numerous in North America. This particular aspect of Colonial Williamsburg does not seem to have had a great appeal in Europe, however, where, so far, visitors to museums seem to find costumed guides and demonstrators rather embarrassing.

These particular aids to historical awareness are found here and there in Europe but, as far as one can judge, they are not taken very seriously by the museum management. The Ironbridge Gorge Museum in England, which pioneered the large-scale industrial site-museum, makes no use of such stimulants, in the belief that, properly presented, the relics themselves are sufficiently impressive and interesting to attract visitors in adequate numbers.

Ironbridge Gorge has been described, with only a little exaggeration, as 'the birth-place of the Industrial Revolution'. More precisely, it consists of an area some three miles long and rather less than a mile wide, along both sides of a deep wooded gorge through which the River Severn flows on its way to the sea near Bristol. In the eighteenth century the Severn was Britain's most important industrial highway. At the northern end of the Gorge is the famous iron-making village of Coalbrookdale where, in 1709, Abraham Darby pioneered the smelting of iron with coke and, in so far as the Industrial Revolution could never have come to full fruition without ample supplies of cheap iron, the Industrial Revolution may be said to have begun in Coalbrookdale. During the eighteenth and nineteenth centuries there were iron-works, coal-mines and factories along both banks of the river and a bridge to bind the whole complex together was essential. The Darbys, with their immense confidence in the possibilities of the material, decided to make it of iron and what still stands there is generally considered to be the first iron bridge in the world, opened to traffic in 1779 and known to industrial historians and archaeologists everywhere simply as 'The Iron Bridge'.

Commercial iron-making is no longer carried on in the area with which the Iron-bridge Gorge Trust is concerned and only foot passengers can nowadays use the Iron Bridge. In Ironbridge itself there is the usual mixture of shops, banks, public houses, restaurants and dwelling houses that one would expect to find in a pleasantly situated village with a considerable tourist trade. The Trust, unlike Colonial Williamsburg, does not own all the property, but it does exercise, through the local Planning Authority and by its own money-making and employment-providing presence in the district, some influence over development. Its own directly con-trolled sites are both industrial and residential. They include the Abraham Darby Furnace, excavated and rehabilitated in the late 1950s by its then owners, Allied Ironfounders, and now protected by a special building; the Great Warehouse (1838), which now accommodates a Museum of Iron, a display which tells the story of the Darbys and of the community of Coalbrookdale, and the main Trust

The Great Warehouse at Coalbrookdale, housing the Museum of Iron.

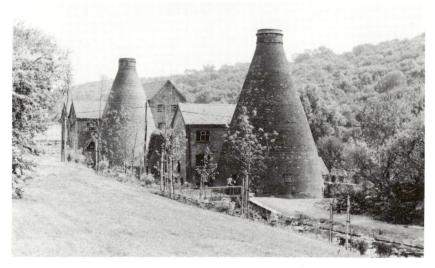

Coalport China Works Museum.

Interior of Rosehill House, the Darby family mansion.

Living room in the Shelton Tollhouse at Blists Hill Open-air Museum.

Left Demonstration of steam winding-engine at Blists Hill.

Right Re-erected steam-hammer at Blists Hill Ironworks.

shop; the Quaker burial ground – the Darbys were Quakers; Carpenters Row (1783), built by the Darbys for their employees and 'now restored to illustrate the living conditions of working families in the Dale'; Rosehill House, the former Darby mansion, now restored and appropriately furnished, with a number of original family pieces, as an ironmaster's house; four timber-framed cottages (1636), one of which now houses a working wrought-iron smithy, as it did in the past, while the others provide accommodation for staff, volunteers and research students.

The students mostly work in the Centre for Industrial Archaeology, which has its lecture and work rooms and library in a nineteenth-century building once the property of the Darbys' successors, Allied Ironfounders, who are no longer active in the area. The same building also contains the Elton Collection of books, paintings, prints and ephemera relating to the Industrial Revolution.

Moving south and west along the Gorge, one comes first to the Iron Bridge itself, the abutments of which have recently, with government help, been strengthened and restored – an interpretation centre is in the former bridge-keeper's house – and then to the remains of the Bedlam Blast Furnace (1757), the only furnace of the great period of expansion in the Shropshire iron industry of which anything substantial remains. Nearby is the Coalport China Works, which ceased operations in 1926. This has been restored, together with the adjoining part of the Shropshire Canal, and has now become the Coalport China Works Museum, which tells the story of the people and products of the Company over a period of 150 years and where the techniques of china manufacture are demonstrated in reconstructed workshops.

A separate large unit of the Museum, Blists Hill, occupies a wooded hillside site overlooking Coalport. It contains a rich variety of remains of eighteenth- and nineteenth-century industrial activity, which have been excavated, consolidated and restored. These include three early nineteenth-century blast-furnaces, together with their blowing-engine houses, a coal-mine, and the upper level of the Shropshire Canal, with the inclined plane that connected it to Coalport. Around and among these remaining-on-the-original-site items is a large and growing open-air museum of industrial items transported here from elsewhere. Among these are a sawmill, a foundry and an ironworks where wrought-iron is being made by the traditional puddling process, the only place in Britain where this can now be seen.

The Ironbridge Gorge Museum Trust was established in 1968, as a company limited by guarantee and registered as a charity. It is governed by an executive board of fifteen, which includes two members each nominated by the County and District Councils and by the Development Corporation of Telford New Town, of which Ironbridge is a part. The finance has come from a number of sources and in a variety of forms – industrial and commercial donations, local and central government grants, university help with educational work and, of course, direct payments from visitors.

Preparing vehicles for an Ironbridge Gorge Museum special event, 'Horses in Harness'.

As at Colonial Williamsburg, such a vast concept could only have been carried through by someone of exceptional imagination, optimism and determination.

Williamsburg had Rutherford Goodwin and Ironbridge had Neil Cossons. Cossons arrived at Ironbridge in 1971, when practically nothing was happening, and left in 1983, when the bulk of the work had been done and the Museum had become an international success. He saw that his main task was 'to make on-site preservation more realistic in consumer terms'.[10] This meant, broadly speaking, that the museum had to be sufficiently attractive to persuade large numbers of people to make the journey to Ironbridge. Having come, they had to feel that they were getting value for money. The Trust might be in charge of important and wonderful historical relics but, unless they were skilfully publicised and interpreted and unless what are usually called 'the visitor amenities' – car-parking, lavatories, refreshment facilities, pleasant, helpful staff – were considered satisfactory, the public would not come or come more than once, and would not recommend the Museum to their friends. Ironbridge, in other words, had to see itself not only as a business but as a well-managed business.

This concept was very strange indeed in the Europe of the early 1970s, less so in America. The term 'management' was rarely used in connection with museums, where expressions like 'productivity', 'return on capital' and 'profitability' were equally taboo. On this side of the Atlantic, Ironbridge has almost certainly done more than any other museum, except perhaps Beamish, to make the notion of museum management respectable and to suggest that working in a museum can no longer be regarded as a sheltered occupation. Many museums in Britain, the so-called 'independent museums', are in the same situation as Ironbridge, in that they will go bankrupt if an insufficient number of people visit them, but at Ironbridge there was an additional reason why management had to be good and financial controls tight. The sites which formed the museum were too numerous, too complex and too scattered to make amateurism anything but a disaster.

Cossons himself defines the task and the approach in clear terms. 'This concept of the integrated management of the historic sites of the Gorge by a single authority', he believes, 'has provided both the inspiration and the challenge of the Ironbridge project ever since. For the first time, a "purpose-built" organisation and a non-statutory one at that, has had the opportunity to plan, co-ordinate and manage the conservation and interpretation of an area which was geographically coherent and desperately in need of care and attention. The scheme, significantly and rightly conceived as a "museum", by no means satisfied the full requirements of a "national-park" type of approach, but it was practical and, with the beneficent ingredient of independent charitable status, it was also achievable.'[11]

It was achievable and it was achieved, but the very fact of its success gives rise to certain anxieties about the future of what appear, at least superficially, to be similar institutions elsewhere. The first contains a paradox: the bigger such a museum becomes, both the more protected and the more vulnerable it is, protected, because it has such a wide range of attractions to offer the visitor, and vulnerable, because such a large income is required in order to pay the bills. A ten per cent drop in annual attendances would be of little consequence – it could even be welcome – to the British Museum, which is publicly funded but it would be a serious matter at Ironbridge. If 'Ironbridge' had consisted of nothing more than the Abraham Darby Furnace and the Iron Bridge, the two great showpieces, the Museum staff need hardly have consisted of more than two people, and annual expenditure would have been very small indeed. Once the decision had been taken to grow, however, the Museum inevitably faced all the dangers and advantages of large size. There are now a considerable number of site-museums in Britain which are concerned with one form or another of industrial history and archaeology. All of them must be constantly worried as to whether they are big enough or small enough to be viable.

One important aspect of the problem is that Ironbridge and, in its different way, Beamish, have raised the expectations of the museum-going public. Both of them now offer the visitor so much that everywhere else is bound to ask itself if it is offering too little to gain its fair share of the market. In museums, as in everything else, quality costs money, and how does one compete if one has very little money? The giants of the site-museum world, such as Williamsburg and Ironbridge, are fully entitled to say that they have enormously improved standards of organisation, conservation and interpretation, providing examples for others to follow. They can also claim to have given millions of visitors an opportunity to think about the past in a different way, by confronting them with evidence of the everyday life of people not unlike themselves. The key word, however, is 'visitors'. Very few of those who come to folk-life museums, whether of the open-air kind or in a more conventional building, live in the district. They may enjoy what they see and they may go away having learnt a lot, but their own roots are not in the place where the museum is.

With their invention of the eco-museum (*éco-musée*), the French have gone about the business in a different way. The first experiments were carried out during the 1960s in very rural areas, where the aim was to present the traditional culture within the natural environment where it had flourished and developed. Further examples were added during the 1970s. The pattern varied according to the district, but two examples will indicate the general approach.

The eco-museum of Marquèze was set up within the Regional Natural Park of the Landes de Gascogne. Characteristic timber-framed farmsteads from the central part of the Landes were brought to the site, together with the domestic, handicraft and agricultural equipment used by the peasants, and the appropriate livestock. This, visitors were told, was how people in this area lived and worked until very recently. These were the ancestors of the families who live here today.

The exhibits were spread out over a large site, so as to give the impression of having always been there. Added to them is an 'environmental museum', the purpose of which is 'to bring out the changes in the environment wrought by man and the inter-actions between animal, vegetable and mineral elements within the ecological context'.[12]

Here, the intention was to create a museum which would be interesting and helpful, especially to local people. A slightly different emphasis is to be found at the Camargue Museum (Musée Camarguais), in the Camargue Regional Wildllfe Park, near Arles. This museum is run by a foundation. The Camargue is thinly populated, with only about 8,500 people living there all the year round, although a considerable number of tourists come during the summer months. The purpose of the Museum was to bridge the gap between the residents and the tourists. Jean-Claude Duclos, who had administrative responsibility for the venture, described its aims in this way. 'On the one hand', he said, 'there is the need to be able to communicate all that constitutes the originality and wealth of the natural and cultural heritage of the Camargue and the concern to protect and conserve it, while, on the other hand, it is necessary that information of this kind should be contributed, as far as possible, by the inhabitants of the Camargue themselves, by means of an exchange of ideas within the Camargue and working outwards, between the local inhabitants and their guests.'[13]

The use of the phrase 'the local inhabitants and their guests' is significant. The tourists were to be regarded as having been invited by the residents to come to the Camargue and to meet them and, for this reason, the people whose home was in the region were to take an active part in providing material and ideas for the Museum. It was to be their Museum. By making a direct contribution in this way and by being involved in the planning from the beginning, they were being given an opportunity to gain a much deeper understanding of their own traditions and environment. They would be participants, not onlookers.

The Camargue was already surprisingly well endowed with museums and the new one was required to supplement them, by providing a type of information and insight which did not already exist in the other institutions. The overall scheme had been well thought out. The Gimès Information Centre is at Saintes-Maries-de-la-Mer, the principal tourist town in the Camargue, and here the aim has been 'to inform them of the resources of the local environment and make them more aware of their fragile nature . . . and to direct them towards a range of other facilities which could provide them with more detailed knowledge of the wildlife and cultural life of the Camargue'.[14] The Park Lodge, at the Mas du Pont de Rousty, is the Park's link with the local community. It provides facilities for meetings organised by the Foundation or by local associations, and is the place where local people can obtain a wide range of information about what is going on in the area.

The Camargue Museum was designed to encourage an exchange of ideas between visitors and the inhabitants of the Camargue, on what the organisers refer to as 'the double input system'. Located in the buildings of an old sheep-farm, its displays are

The glassworks at Montcenis, as it appeared in 1820.

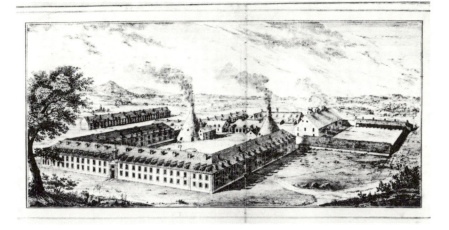

Le Creusot. The Château, with its glass cones in the courtyard and the surviving buildings of the former Schneider works in the background.

in three parts, illustrating the district as it was before 1850, the Camargue in 1850, the period of greatest vigour and prosperity before the coming of the industrial age, and the Camargue as it is today and as it could be tomorrow. Each part of the programme invites a comparison with the other two and takes a broad sweep, which the French dignify by the name of 'interdisciplinary synthesis', through every aspect of the Camargue, its geology, natural and human ecology, history, archaeology, ethnology, sociology, language and land-use. Much of the material used in arranging the exhibits was presented by local people, who in this way have a stake in the museum.

In addition to these facilities, there are two old-established museums of more conventional type. The Museon Arlaten, at Arles, was founded in 1896 by the poet and local patriot, Frédéric Mistral. It contains valuable collections of objects representing the popular arts and traditions of Provence. The Baronelli Museum, at Saintes-Maries-de-la-Mer, was established by the municipality and includes a series of dioramas illustrating the natural environment of the Camargue and a collection which recalls the work of the Marquis de Baronelli, who was a determined defender of local traditions.

All twenty-seven of the French eco-museums have broken new ground, and taken together represent one of the most important museological developments of the past fifty years. Their common features have been a determination to involve local people in their planning, thinking and operation and to consider the resources of an area as a whole, making no clear distinction between man-made features and the natural environment and between past, present and future. They have been based on the conviction that by understanding the past, one is likely to make a better job of handling the present and of organising the future.

The eco-museum which has had most influence abroad and which has exploited the 'double input system' in the most thorough-going manner is undoubtedly the Museum of Man and Industry at Le Creusot, in central France. Le Creusot had been, since the late eighteenth century, one of the most important industrial regions of France. Its prosperity had been built around the production of armaments and railway locomotives, with the Schneider family, which came originally from Eastern France, as the highly successful entrepreneurs. After the Second World War, the Schneiders fell into disgrace, as a result of collaboration with the Germans, and the manufacturing empire collapsed, leaving Le Creusot destitute. The establishment of new forms of employment was, of course, the priority, both for the municipality and for the Government, but raising the morale of the district was also important, and a group of influential people, among them the then Secretary-General of ICOM, Hugues de Varine-Bohan, and his predecessor, Georges Henri Rivière, had the imaginative idea that a special kind of eco-museum, a Museum of Man and Industry, could make an important contribution to this. What they had in mind might be described as a kind of museum therapy, in which local people would not only help to create the museum, but would themselves be living exhibits in it.

The new eco-museum, or 'fragmented museum' (*musée éclaté*), as it was also called, was to be concerned with an area of about 500 square kilometres, half industrial and half rural, divided into 25 communes, with a total of 150,000 inhabitants. It contained two urban communities, Le Creusot, which had been based on manufacturing, and Montceau-les-Mines, a coalmining town. The Schneiders had lived close to the works at Le Creusot, in a splendid eighteenth-century château, with a park and, in its forecourt, the impressive glass-cones of the Manufacture Royale de Cristaux, which had been set up not long before the Revolution, in 1783.

Left Offices of the tileworks at Montchanin.

Right The Pré-Long Pit at Montceau-les-Mines.

Work on the development of the Museum of Man and Industry began in 1971 and, in so far as one can 'open' such a museum, it was opened in 1974. Its philosophy was set out in an important paper by Hugues de Varine-Bohan in 1973. 'Any movable or immovable object within the community's perimeter', he wrote, 'is psychologically part of the museum. This introduces the idea of a kind of "cultural property right", which has nothing to do with legal ownership. Accordingly, it is not the function of the museum as such to make acquisitions, since everything existing within its geographical area is already at its disposal.'[15]

So every building, every person, every cow, every plant and every tree within the museum's boundaries was to be considered part of the collections, an object of interest and significance. The 'fragmented museum' had to be given a core, an interpretation point, and this was to be in the château, which had been the centre of the spider's web woven by the Schneiders. The old web had been brushed away and

164

the people were making a new one. The displays in the Château were to illustrate the general history and character of the area, the daily life of its people over the centuries, and its artistic and industrial products. The Château was also to serve as a base for research into industrial civilisation, so that the Museum of Man and Industry could be set within a wider context.

A distinction was made between the 'general' and the 'reserve' collections.

> Any object which still has a physical or emotional value for its natural owner must remain physically in place and for this reason should belong to the general collection. Any object which has lost both its functional and emotional value and yet has something essential to tell us about the community and its history or environment must be collected and deposited in the museum reserves, to be preserved and used there.[16]

Staffing the Museum could not follow the conventional pattern.

> It is no longer appropriate to have curators for the type of museum we see gradually evolving. It only has actors, namely, all the inhabitants in the community. These inhabitants possess, individually and jointly, the museum and its collections. They live in it. They participate in its management, in making the inventory of their common cultural wealth, and in the organisation of cultural activities. They give their opinion about programmes. Furthermore, they participate in the research work, of which they are both subject and object.[17]

It was, however, essential to have some permanent, professional staff.

> They have to infuse life into the institution and act as a catalyst. Professional museum staff are also needed for the technical side, in order to carry out research, keep catalogues up to date, organise events and complex projects, ensure continuity, co-ordinate the otherwise haphazard activities of the various sections of the community, and represent the interests of the museum in dealing with the authorities. The members of this permanent team, who must live in symbiosis with the population, must naturally be as discreet, modest and approachable as possible.[18]

The English version of these quotations, made by professional translators employed by UNESCO, does not, perhaps, always give a correct impression of what has actually taken place at and around the Museum of Man and Industry. The members of the permanent staff have been well selected and they do indeed 'live in symbiosis with the population', but, for English readers, it would have been more accurate and more helpful to say that they are friendly, democratic, easy people, who do not put on academic airs – a particular danger in France – and who believe strongly in the Museum's philosophy. They have made the scheme work and, after fifteen years, one can say without hesitation that it has been an overall success. There have, inevitably, been failures and disappointments, and the occasional failure of members of university departments to understand that the Museum does not exist primarily for their benefit, but on the whole the original objectives have been realised. It has been possible to persuade a very wide range of local people to take an active interest in what the Museum is trying to do, scholars have come to take the experiment seriously – the great reputation of the Museum's father-figure, Georges Henri Rivière proved an enormous advantage in this respect – public money has been forthcoming to support the project and, perhaps most important of all, a succession of young people who have carried out research at Le Creusot and worked there in other capacities have subsequently taken up posts elsewhere in France and abroad, where they have been able to put their experience to good use and to adapt it to different conditions.

Any discussion of the Museum of Man and Industry would be seriously incomplete without some mention of its most original features, its 'antennae'(*antennes*). These are, in effect, small out-stations, mini-museums at five places within the Museum's territory, reflecting the very varied character of the area and permitting a certain degree of specialisation and an opportunity for local initiative to express itself. The five 'antennae', as their name suggests, serve also as listening points, places from which information can be fed back to headquarters. They are:

1. The Maison du Canal du Centre, at Écuisses, where the emphasis is on the history and importance of the Canal, which was a vital form of transport for this heavily industrialised region before the coming of the railway.
2. The coalmine at Blanzy, which has long ceased to produce coal, the surface installations of which have been preserved.
3. The school-museum (Maison d'École) at Montceau-les-Mines.
4. The medieval priory at Perrecy-les-Forges.
5. The Combe des Mineurs at Le Creusot, a street of early nineteenth-century cottages, in a French version of the Welsh style, built for Welsh coal-miners and iron-workers who came to work in the area.

There are many obvious similarities between the Museum of Man and Industry at Le Creusot and the museum complex at Ironbridge Gorge – the scattered sites, the central interpretive museum, the integrated management, the well-organised research base – but the differences are equally significant. Ironbridge has, from the beginning, been designed mainly to attract and please visitors from outside the area: Le Creusot existed primarily to enrich the lives of the local inhabitants. Restoration and conversion work at Ironbridge has cost a great deal of money, but at Le Creusot comparatively little. Income from visitors is exceedingly important at Ironbridge, but at Le Creusot it did not have a high priority.

It is obvious that a museum's financial base has a great deal to do with the way in which it presents its cultural assets to the public. If admission charges and shop sales form a major part of the museum's income, greater attention will inevitably have to be paid to showmanship and to publicity. It is a nice point as to whether the costumed guides at Williamsburg and at other museums in America really make it easier for members of the public to feel their way back into history or whether they are simply a sales gimmick, but that they contain a strong element of showmanship nobody could deny. Another way of putting the same question is to ask whether having the costumes makes the story more understandable. I personally doubt this, but when I have made the point to Americans skilled and experienced in these matters, I have been told that Americans have to be conditioned to think about the past at all and that costumed attendants are merely one way of achieving this. They are the jacket that persuades one to buy the book, but they have no significant function in telling the story between the covers. Americans, one is led to believe, do not feel surrounded by the past and soaked in it as Europeans are. They need to be provided with obvious and regularly repeated bridges between themselves and previous generations and old dresses on modern bodies constitute such a bridge. The matter deserves much more careful investigation than it has so far received, bearing in mind that the problem of historical conditioning goes much beyond period costumes.

What one is really talking about is getting the public to feel involved in history, to identify themselves with at least certain aspects of the past. It is the business of a museum curator to be profoundly interested in this and to be constantly experimenting with ways of making it more likely to take place. One should certainly not ridicule or play down the power of original objects to help in the process, through a certain magic which original objects possess, once their associations are made clear. Replicas, however good they may be, cannot do this. A replica can appeal to the intellect, but not to the emotions.

That is why the discovery and raising of long-dead ships has been so important in developing an interest in maritime history. Up to a point, the older the ship, the more miraculous its survival and the greater its magic, that is, the power to stimulate the imagination. This has been most strikingly shown by the discovery and preservation of the Swedish warship, the 'Wasa', launched in Stockholm in 1628, wrecked a short distance away from the shipyard, on her maiden voyage, discovered in 1956, raised in 1961, brought to a temporary building for conservation and, properly housed and displayed on the city's waterfront, a very popular object of pilgrimage for many years. Its salvage and conservation represent the largest maritime archaeology project so far attempted. The 'Wasa' has not been brought back precisely to its original site, that is, to the dock where she was built, in the same way that Brunel's pioneering iron ship, the S.S. 'Great Britain' has, but she is close enough to that point for the imagination to work. In any case, it could be argued that the ship itself is the site, and that the great quantity of objects discovered in and around her form what any other kind of museum would be proud to call its collections.

Such a prodigious quantity and range of material in such superb condition, illustrat-

The upper deck of the 'Wasa'.

The lower gun-deck, after the mud and silt had been removed.

ing every aspect of life on board, had never previously been found in the remains of any ancient ship, and when this is combined with a great ship which is astonishingly well preserved in herself, one clearly has museum possibilities of such potential excitement that only gross incompetence could have brought it to nothing. What the 'Wasa' in fact received was the very opposite of incompetence. A great deal of money was made available, the best advice was taken from experts around the world, and the latest scientific techniques were employed. The 'Wasa' became a giant conservation laboratory, continuously visited and monitored by archaeologists, museum specialists, scientists and manufacturers drawn from many countries. Throughout the conservation period, the public was encouraged to watch the work in progress, on payment of a fee, and by looking into the hull from viewing platforms, to learn how a major ship of this period was constructed.

The interpretation could perhaps be described as excellent in detail, less satisfactory in providing a convincing overall view. One can look at the hundreds of objects on show and, with the help of the information provided, gain a good idea of how the crew was dressed and equipped, how and what it ate and drank, how it spent such spare time as it had, and how it operated the ship. But one is left very much to one's own devices in becoming aware of the prodigal felling of trees that must have taken place in order to provide the timber for such a ship, and of the foolish ambitions which caused such an absurd floating castle to be built at all. With its great carved superstructure, the ship was dangerously top-heavy. She may have looked magnificent, but in fact she was a monument to human vanity, liable to capsize at the first

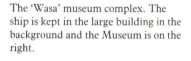

The 'Wasa' museum complex. The ship is kept in the large building in the background and the Museum is on the right.

Left Night-time in the Admiral's cabin. The officers slept two-by-two in fold-away beds.

Right A 'Wasa' sailor.

gust of a strong wind, which is precisely what she did. The museum supplies the facts, but visitors are left to draw too many of their own conclusions from them, which amounts to saying that a splendid story is not entirely well told. The main economic and political lessons are missing.

When Henry VIII's flagship, the 'Mary Rose', was raised in 1982 and brought back to Portsmouth from where she had sailed before she, too, capsized in a strong wind, comparisons were immediately made with the 'Wasa'. The 'Mary Rose' was to be the English 'Wasa' and, with certain provisos, so she is; an ancient warship brought to the surface after centuries on the sea-bed, together with a mass of objects that went down with her. She is attracting as many visitors as the 'Wasa', if not more, the conservation of what remains of her hull can be watched by the public, and there is a museum to display and make sense of the finds.

But, as with the 'Wasa', there is something missing. In each case, we can place the people on board within their own small world of the ship and the navy to which she belonged, but not within the wider context of the world outside. What was the social structure of the ship, the relations of officers to men? Why were these men there at all? Had they been forced into the job? Had they been enticed into it by a desire for adventure, or gone to sea because, despite all the risks and drawbacks involved, life on board was better than life on land? How many of them could reckon to live beyond the age of forty? How did their families, if they had them, manage while they were away? How much were these men paid and how often?

One day, no doubt, we shall have, somewhere in the world, a museum devoted to the army or the navy which faces up to its full responsibilities as a museum of social history. That day has not yet come, but the 'Wasa' and the 'Mary Rose' have brought it a good deal closer. From a museum point of view they represent an enormous advance on the how-much-is-her-cargo-of-gold-and-silver-worth attitude of the wreck-hunters around the Caribbean. Museologically, the great blessing of the 'Wasa' and the 'Mary Rose' has been that they were carrying no treasure, so that both the wrecks and their contents can be presented and thought about entirely from a technical and cultural angle.

Chapter Eight
Pointers to the future

David d'Angers Gallery, Angers: *'The artist becomes credible and the visitor remains full-size'*
Anacostia, Washington DC: *'The cultural importance of rats in a slum neighbourhood'*
The Museum House, Tacubaya: *'A museum in a vacuum'*
Brooklyn Children's Museum, New York: *'Resources no school could match'*
Sarganserland Museum, Sargans: *'The feeling and atmosphere of a district'*
House of Transport, Lucerne: *'Something more than the usual collection of railway engines, motorcars and old aeroplanes'*
Sukuma Museum, Mwanza: *'Preserving and encouraging the culture of a tribe'*

'A backward glance at museum development shows that museums only fully develop their potential for action', wrote Jan Jelinek, 'when they are actually involved in the major problems of contemporary society.' He continued with a second credo – 'Museums are institutions intended to serve society and only thus can they continue to exist and function.'[1] Dr Jelinek is a museologist with a great and deserved international reputation,[2] and anything he says should receive careful attention, but he normally writes in Czech, his native language, and translation has a way of blurring the precision of a writer's original words. Allowing for this possibility, we may reasonably ask what he meant by 'potential for action'. Does the phrase imply that museums should be taking part in a crusade or inspiring others to do so? Does 'develop their potential for action' mean the same as being 'involved in the major problems of contemporary society', or is 'involved in' perhaps no more than a synonym for 'reflect'? It is essential that one should look closely at categorical statements of this kind, especially when they come from so authoritative a source, partly in order to allow one to assess museums of the right reasons and partly to avoid the trap of confusing jargon with real thinking. 'Serving society' is a function which most people would consider praiseworthy but, assuming that free expression is permitted, there is certain to be considerable debate as to how, in any field, society is best served. 'Serving society' is not an absolute concept.

Having said this, one is not likely to find much difficulty in agreeing with Dr Jelinek to the extent of believing that, at any given time, certain social problems will appear to have a particularly high priority, and that museums, like any other media for communication, should not ignore them. If it does, it is likely to find its public

172

slipping away. But being aware of a problem does not necessarily mean that one is personally called on by God to try to solve it. Museums seem ill-adapted to be problem-solving agencies, although they may have a useful rôle to play in illustrating the nature of the problem.

Every institution which has been selected for inclusion in my list of Museums of Influence has functioned in precisely this way. It has exercised a powerful influence because the time was ripe for that influence. Skansen was created and succeeded because the development of a new industrial society produced a fear of breaking down the bridges linking the present with the past. The South Kensington Museum picked up and inspired a public which was anxious to be reassured that the factory system could be prevented from suppressing beauty and creative talent. The Northern Animal Park at Emmen provided encouragement and ammunition for those who no longer believed in man's traditional right to dominate and destroy wildlife and who wished to discover ways in which the two could co-exist more sensibly and fruitfully on the same planet. The Metropolitan Museum in New York was prodigiously helpful to the national morale, in proving to citizens of the United States and to the world that America at last possessed the money with which to buy up Europe.

In trying to forecast which museums, or what kind of museums are likely to be the Museums of Influence during the coming twenty or fifty years, one might usefully begin by considering what, on the present evidence, the greatest perplexities, yearnings, frustrations and opportunities of mankind may be. I think it very likely that Dr Jelinek chose 'problems' as an umbrella-term to cover the four words I have just used. By nature a very warm and human individual, he may well have thought that 'problems' would be more acceptable in academic circles and there seems unfortunately to be no reason to disagree with him. What then, to adopt his terminology, will the main problems be? What are they now?

I suggest five, in what I believe to be their correct order of importance. First, the degradation of the natural environment under the joint onslaught of greed and ignorance. Second, the political, scientific and financial pressures which combine to concentrate enormous, and possibly irresponsible power in the hands of the military machines of the United States and the Soviet Union. Third, the truly tragic fact that decolonisation has not worked, in the sense that the world's former colonial territories are, with only four exceptions – the United States, Australia, New Zealand and Canada – poorer, more insecure, and worse-governed than in the days when they were controlled by a European power. Fourth, that knowledge is becoming increasingly divided and specialised, and increasingly incomprehensible to laymen. This specialisation has extended to art and to music, from more and more of which the common man feels himself totally excluded. And, fifth, that persons in positions of power and influence protect themselves by sheltering behind a wall of generalisations and vague terminology. The gap between the concrete, the local, the real on the one hand and the prestigious, the theoretical, the national and the international on the other becomes steadily wider.

These five features of modern society combine to give the social and intellectual élite more confidence and the masses of the people much less. Even in those countries which now enjoy high average incomes, an intellectual proletariat is replacing the traditional type of proletariat, characterised by poverty and insecurity. The fundamental problem for museums in such a situation must therefore be to give its visitors confidence. Their influence will be directly related to their ability to carry out this function. They will be the places where the average person is not made to feel small, and the strong probability is that they will be museums of modest size. I doubt profoundly if either very large or very small museums are capable of bringing about the changes which are required if confidence in dealing with the problems of the modern world is to grow. The very large museums cannot do it, because they are powerhouses of omniscience and academic attitudes, and the very small are unlikely to achieve much in this direction, because, although their heart may be in the right place, they lack the resources. A further reason is that the bureaucracy of large museums, as of any other kind of large institution, tends to inhibit original thinking. Bureaucracies invent little and adapt badly.

What, then, does one mean by 'a museum of modest size'? One means the Rüsselsheims, the Emmens, and the Ironbridges. These three museums have already proved two points, both already clearly apparent in the nineteenth century, that outstanding museums can be produced only by outstanding directors and that, in order to produce a museum which makes a genuine appeal to a wide range of people, one has to break up the old forms and start again with a new kit of parts. It is no longer sufficient to hang paintings around walls, to fill galleries with machines raped from the surroundings where they made sense, to arrange natural history dioramas without an obvious passion to safeguard the environment from its human predators, to display the Elgin Marbles as if the political controversy surrounding them did not exist, to split off zoos from natural history museums, and museums concerned with technology from museums whose purpose is to present local history.

The extraordinarily stubborn refusal to merge agricultural and natural history museums provides an excellent example of the foolishness of which museum people have found themselves capable. Ten years ago, I described the situation in the following way, and it has changed very little since, although surely with the pressures surrounding it, it can hardly continue much longer.

> Let us suppose that we are looking at two fields in England. The first
> field contains a number of cows and a bull (agricultural museum), a
> drinking trough (agricultural museum) and a specially sown grass and
> clover mixture (agricultural museum). A flock of sparrows (natural
> history museum) is resting in one corner of the field, and a rabbit
> (natural history museum) has just vanished into the hedge (borderline,

but probably natural history museum if wild and uncared for, agricultural museum if carefully laid and trimmed). Along the base of the hedge, one can see a variety of wild flowers (agricultural museum). Between the two fields is a drainage ditch (agricultural museum), containing frogs, weeds and fish (all natural history museum). In the second field, a man is ploughing with a tractor (agricultural museum). As he turns over the ground, a number of seagulls (natural history museum) are hovering above the furrows, waiting to pick up worms and other insects (natural history museum).[3]

The ordinary person does not see the world in this artificially divided way at all. Most visitors to museums are not studying for an examination in zoology, agricultural engineering, anthropology, art history, or whatever the particular speciality of the museum may be, but until very recently the great majority of museums gave every impression of proceeding on precisely this assumption. The worst offenders have certainly been the art galleries, the backward children of the museum family, where the art historians still operate a very tight control and, consciously or unconsciously, contrive to make the average visitor feel very small, ignorant and inferior, and to frighten off people who sense that they will be put in this situation and are unwilling to subject themselves to the indignity.

In its original functional setting – a church, a temple, a private house, a guildhall – a painting or a piece of sculpture encourages a mood of relaxation, which makes genuine contemplation possible. Once it is uprooted and placed in a gallery, it finds itself in a neutral, unnatural atmosphere, where it has to compete for attention with many other works of art. In these circumstances, the emotions become anaesthetised, the intellect takes over and museums become temples of scholarship. Scholars, by temperament and training, respond with the brain, not the feelings. Connoisseurship is essentially a scholarly activity and for this reason it necessarily makes ordinary people feel inferior.

With very few exceptions, the world's art museums continue to be temples. 'How much more interesting and alive these would become if, before they saw any pictures or statues, visitors were shown how the artists' materials were prepared at different periods, how the colours were ground, the canvas or wood panel prepared, the brushes and palettes made, the stone quarried and selected. How many of the world's sculpture galleries show the tools the sculptor required or indicate how they were used? By removing the craftsman element from art and turning art museums into temples for connoisseurs, museologists have not only attempted to turn the artist himself into a rarified, intellectualised creature which he never was and never could be, but have wilfully rejected the one element in an art museum which could be guaranteed to attract and interest a wide range of visitors. The technology of art is fascinating, explicable and, above all, democratic.'[4]

The Museum of Watch and Clockmaking at La Chaux-de-Fonds, in Switzerland, allows its visitors to see craftsmen carrying out their everyday work, repairing and restoring clocks and watches for the Museum and for outside customers. There seems to be no good reason why an art museum should not do the same, why its restoration department should not be brought out of secrecy and into the public gaze, or why there should not be regular or indeed permanent demonstrations to show how artists have worked with the different materials and techniques which have been available over the centuries. One does not need to be a scholar to appreciate these things, and a practical understanding of an artist's techniques can quite easily lead to an interest in his finished work. So, too, can an explanation of the physical and economic conditions under which artists have worked at different periods, of their patrons, customers and income, of their status in the community. Equipped with this kind of information, one is beginning to have solid ground under one's feet and to feel that there might be possibilities in art museums after all. Much of the so-called educational work carried out in art museums is not, however, of this kind at all, and appears to be aimed at turning members of the general public, including children, into a reserve army of art historians and connoisseurs, which is a rather special kind of confidence trick.

For some years, I have sensed a growing feeling, especially among the younger museum professionals, that what is of prime importance is communication and that really effective communication cannot be achieved until the traditional academic barriers and compartments are swept away. This amounts to believing that every museum, of no matter what kind, is a museum of social history[5] and that, in today's world, to pretend otherwise is to court failure, if not disaster. The point has never been made more clearly or more forcefully than by the Director of the National Museum of Ethnology at Leiden in the Netherlands, Dr Peter Pott, at an ICOM meeting held in 1962.[6]

The museum director today, said Dr Pott, requires two qualities above all other, 'pluralism of interest and flexibility of imagination'. What should distinguish him from his predecessors, he went on, 'is his consideration of the interests of his potential public, rather than his own tastes and special hobbies'. He must reach this public 'as living individuals and not as an abstract audience which may take or leave what is offered to it'. He must be fully and constantly aware of the ways in which the other media approached the public. 'Nothing is more irritating to the public than to be confronted with a presentation of a subject that seems childish when compared to what it has been given on the same subject by the illustrated press, radio and, especially, television. A childish presentation immediately produces a reaction of complete rejection; people feel that, instead of receiving answers to reasonable questions asked by reasonable mature persons they have been treated like children, given a sweet and sent off to play.' What is required is 'a flexible form of representation, which draws the visitor into a personal involvement in that with which he is confronted'.

In his contribution to the ICOM seminar, Dr Pott was implying, first, that one has a duty to plan and run museums in a way which meets the needs of modern people – Dr Jelinek was saying the same – and that these needs are significantly different from those which existed a hundred or fifty years earlier. Although Dr Pott did not actually say so, the main difference between yesterday and today is that the concept of education has changed. In the Victorian age, the first great period of museum flowering, education meant primarily the acquisition of factual information. Today there is a fairly general agreement that education is concerned with the growth and development of the complete person and that the gathering and ordering of facts is only a part of this total process.

With approximately 35,000 museums in the world under the necessity of facing up to the situation just outlined, it might appear whimsical and arbitrary to single out a small number as Museums of Influence within the context of the present chapter, partly because it could be considered too soon to prove and describe their influence and partly because one might quite reasonably say, 'If A, then why not B, C, D or E?' The difficulty has to be admitted, and I have tried to deal with it in two ways, by selecting more Museums of Influence for this chapter than for its predecessors and by using each one to represent several others which may be tackling the same set of problems in a similar fashion. This solution will, I hope, be considered to be evidence of proper caution, rather than of a failure to make up one's mind. That each museum is important in itself I have no doubt, but it should also be regarded as having a certain symbolic value.

The city of Angers, in central France, has had a Museum of Fine Art for many years. It is of the conventional kind, with Italian primitives, some seventeenth-century Dutch and Flemish paintings and a quite substantial collection of works by eighteenth-century French artists. It is pleasant enough, but one would not exactly beat a path to its door. Adjacent to it, however, is something of quite a different order, the Museum of David d'Angers. Pierre-Jean David d'Angers (1782–1836) was born in Angers and became celebrated as a sculptor, specialising in large-scale monuments and in medals. He was responsible for the sculptural façade of the Panthéon and he had the engaging habit of making portrait busts of people whom he particularly admired and of sending them to his heroes as tokens of his appreciation. He bequeathed to his native city a large number of his plaster models and finished works, together with notebooks, documents, sketches and tools and, after languishing in semi-storage for many years, these have now been presented to the public in an elegant and imaginative new museum created from the ruins of a medieval church and opened in 1984.

The sculptor, David d'Angers.

Architecturally, the conversion has been brilliantly accomplished. The shell of the church was given a complete glass roof and a gallery installed in the nave. This offered possibilities for a dramatic form of display, using a combination of natural and artificial light and for remarkable views of the sculpture. But this is not merely

Left The building as converted to museum use.

Right Portrait busts in the Gallery.

a sculpture gallery. One mark of difference is the fact that it is concerned mainly with plaster models, not with the bronze or stone sculptures made from them. The models are, of course, the true originals and the finished products that the world normally sees only copies, and to introduce visitors to the artist through his models and his tools is to emphasise his rôle as a craftsman.

The whole man is here. One is shown not only how he worked, but how the commissions were arranged, what the payments were, and what kind of reception the works received from the public and from clients. We learn how the private life of David d'Angers interlinked with his professional activities and how he attempted, usually successfully, to keep a tolerable balance between the two. This sort of information is usually and foolishly held to be irrelevant to an appreciation of works of art and the refusal to provide it is the cause of a great deal of frustration and annoyance among non-professional visitors to art museums. The two great merits of this remarkable museum are, firstly, that it appeals equally strongly to the intellect and to the emotions and, secondly, that, by attempting to answer all the possible questions about David d'Angers, it puts the layman in the same position as the expert. This has two most welcome consequences, the artist becomes credible and the visitor remains full-size. The feeling of inferiority and hopelessness which is so often produced by a visit to an art gallery is wholly missing here.

It is, of course, an enormous advantage to the museum that it is concerned with only one artist. In the usual type of art gallery, the movement from one artist to another can be an exhausting business for the visitor and in most cases it leads to a superficial form of appreciation. If, on the other hand, one is given the opportunity to immerse oneself in the life, personality and creative power of a single artist, it is vastly easier to make contact with him and to understand the nature of his achievement. Other examples of what one might call the Angers treatment – the in-depth presentation of one artist in an exciting environment – are beginning to appear. Particularly good ones are to be found at St Idesbald, in Belgium – the Paul Delvaux Museum – and in Sheffield, England – the Ruskin Gallery. Both begin with three assumptions, first, that the visitor has come because he wants to, that he is genuinely interested; second, that he does not see the museum in terms of problems and difficulties and, third, that he knows nothing about the subject when he arrives and expects to receive value for money during his visit. He considers himself to be as good as the next man, and the museum does nothing to discourage the idea.

Angers began with high-prestige material and proceeded to make it intelligible to a wide range of people. At Anacostia, a museum set up in 1967 in a black district of Washington DC, the problem was precisely the opposite: to find ways of giving meaning to exceedingly ordinary and all-too-familiar objects. Anacostia, established with the help of the National Museum of History and Technology in Washington, was conceived as a local, neighbourhood museum, a type of institution of which there are many more now than in 1967, a fact which may be some measure of its influence. The chosen premises were a disused small cinema and the person appointed to plan and run the museum was a thirty-year-old black youth worker, John Kinard. What was envisaged was something which had not existed previously, a museum which grew naturally from the life of the district:

> A complete general store, just as existed in Anacostia in the 1890s, occupies one corner. In it is a post office (which we hope to get a license to operate), old metal toys, a butter churn, an ice-cream maker, a coffee grinder and a water pump, all of which can work, and any number of objects of the period, from kerosene lamps and flat-irons to posters and advertisements. There is another do-it-yourself area for plastic art, with, at present, volunteer class instruction. There are skeletons of various kinds, some of which can be put together, some disassembled. There is space for temporary art shows. There is a TV monitor system on the stage.
>
> Occupying one of the modules is a live zoo with green monkeys, a parrot and a miscellany of animals on loan from the National Zoological Park. A great success has been a shoe-box museum in an A-frame structure, full of wooden shoeboxes containing bird skins (in celluloid tubes), mammal skins, shells, fossil specimens, pictures and slide projectors for intensive handling and study. A behind-the-scenes museum exhibit of leaf-making, silk-screen techniques, casting and

Top left Anacostia Museum, the surroundings.

Top right Anacostia Museum, the entrance.

Centre left Robert Hall, a member of the staff, during a tour of the exhibition, 'Black Women: achievement against the odds'.

Centre right A member of the staff, Zora Felton, giving a silk-screen demonstration.

Bottom A performance at the Museum.

modelling, gives an additional outlet for instruction. All of this, to the tune of crashing hammers, scraping saws and slapping paintbrushes, took form in two and a half months.

The grand opening, attended by an 84-piece band, two combos, and a block party with speeches and klieg lights, took place on September 15, 1967. A local group of Trail Blazers had painted the nearby fence separating the museum from the next property with a stylish 'primitive' mural of life in Africa. The desolate surrounding lots were spruced up and one of them decorated temporarily with Uncle Beazley, the dinosaur, hero of the story, *The Enormous Egg*.[7]

There are those who have seen Anacostia as nothing more than a recipe for organised chaos, a museum version of a popular American negro church. Certainly Anacostia is as different from the British Museum as a service in a popular church would be from Evensong in Westminster Abbey or High Mass in St Peter's, but this is a superficial judgement. Any community museum will necessarily take on the flavour of the district in which it finds itself. There is no fixed pattern. Anacostia, however, must be given the credit of pioneering the concept of a museum without walls to keep it within bounds, a museum with a creative flow of ideas, exhibits and people between itself and the outside world. The objects in it do not attract the attention of international gangs of thieves. They are significant and interesting only because the ability of the organiser and designer has made them so. Anacostia can create an effective display to show the cultural importance of rats in a slum neighbourhood, but the central feature of the exhibit, a dead rat, has no market value at all.

But there are quite different ways of going about the task of setting up a neighbourhood museum. In 1972 a survey revealed that working-class families were almost completely unrepresented among visitors to the prestigious National Museum of Anthropology in Mexico City, despite strenuous efforts to persuade them to come. The decision was therefore taken to establish what might be called a museum-mission in Tacubaya, a slum area on the outskirts of the capital. Tacubaya contained 43,000 people, many of them without work and a high proportion totally illiterate. It was hardly surprising that none of them had visited the National Museum of Anthropology, or even heard of its existence.

Detailed research was carried out into the attitudes and habits of the people living in the area and, on the basis of this, it was found possible to obtain their co-operation in setting up a special kind of museum which was to be designed and run specifically for their benefit. A piece of waste ground was cleared and a group of small hexagonal buildings was erected on it. Four of them were linked together to form the museum and a fifth, with open sides, was placed a short distance away, to be used especially as a booth for projecting films and slides on to a big outdoor screen.

Objects from the main museum in Mexico City were brought out to Tacubaya and used for special displays, which remained for several months and which used the full range of exhibition techniques in order to create a museum which was lively and which could communicate with non-readers. A uniformed attendant, brought up in Tacubaya, kept a general eye on what was going on, but rules and regulations were kept to a minimum. The atmosphere was kept as informal as possible. Games were permitted within the museum area, dogs and other pet animals could be brought in and any object on display could be touched.

Not surprisingly, the museum soon became very popular. Many children spent most of the day there, using it as a kind of club. Members of the staff of the National Museum paid frequent visits to Tacubaya, to maintain contact and supervision, and to talk to local people about matters which had little direct relevance to the Museum. Within a short time, the Museum had become a general information and advice bureau, dealing with everything from health problems to marital disputes, as well as being the local cultural centre. Children were learning to read there, wives were able to escape temporarily from drunken husbands, unemployed men called in to discuss job prospects in the city. These problems should, in theory, have been dealt with by priests, teachers and doctors, but none of these had shown much interest in Tacubaya, and the Museum filled the vacuum, although it had not contemplated this rôle for itself in the first place.

The original aim, of acting as a bridge between the slum settlement and the National Museum, was to a certain extent fulfilled. Once local people had been shown the possibilities of a museum and its relevance to their own lives and once they had discovered that the museum staff were friendly, approachable people, some of them agreed to be taken by bus to the main museum and to look around it under the guidance of the experts whom they had already come to trust, but nothing else has so far been shown to work as well, in the many parts of the world, from Glasgow to Calcutta, where the missionary approach is being tried. The number of neighbour-hood museums seems certain to increase during the remainder of this century. They meet a real social and educational need.

When one uses the word 'educational' in connection with museums nowadays, one is confronted with an immediate problem. The traditional, almost classical, view of the task of a museum education department is that it provides additional information and new points of view for children who are already receiving a good basic education at school. The school, so to speak, is the dog and the museum the tail. It is doubtful if this assumption can any longer be justified. In many areas of the world, even in countries which are usually thought of as being 'developed' or 'industrialised', a great many children are intellectually deprived to quite a serious extent. They leave school semi-literate and semi-numerate – these terms are often flattering – as a result of educational theories and inadequate teaching, or else with important fields of knowledge of which they have no experience at all. Faced with this situation, museums can have a different and extremely important rôle to play. In blunt terms,

Top left The hillside community of Tacubaya.

Top right The Museum building.

Bottom left Part of the Museum interior.

Bottom right The outdoor projection building.

they can find themselves called on to remedy the deficiencies of both schools and parents. At Tacubaya, it has been a case first of motivating children to read and then of helping them to do so. In the new Regional Museum at Brindisi, in the south of Italy, children who no longer study the unfashionable and élitist subjects of Latin and history at school do their best to fill in the gaps in the Museum.

In 1899, the Brooklyn Institute of Arts and Sciences decided to establish 'a Museum that will be of especial value and interest to young people between the ages of six and twenty years old'. There were at that time about 300,000 children of school age in Brooklyn, and the purpose of the new museum was defined as follows.

> To bring together collections in every branch of local Natural History that is calculated to interest children and to stimulate their powers of observation and reflection, to illustrate by collections of pictures, cartoons, charts, models, maps and so on, each of the important branches of knowledge which is taught in the elementary schools. The Museum, through its collections, library, curator and assistants, will attempt to bring the child, whether attending school or not, into direct relation with the most important subjects that appeal to the interest of

Top Brooklyn Children's Museum. Adams Building, 1900.

Bottom left The modern entrance to the Brooklyn Children's Musem.

Bottom right The Museum building, seen from the adjoining park.

children in their daily life, in their school work, in their reading, in their games, in their rambles in the fields, and in the industries that are being carried on about them or in which they themselves later may become engaged.[8]

The Brooklyn Children's Museum was the first children's museum in the world. Its example was soon followed by other American cities,[9] but the idea of having special museums for children has not proved equally popular outside America,[10] where the tendency to set up children's departments or educational departments within general museums has been more marked. The two main objections to having Children's Museums have been that the name puts many children off coming – they

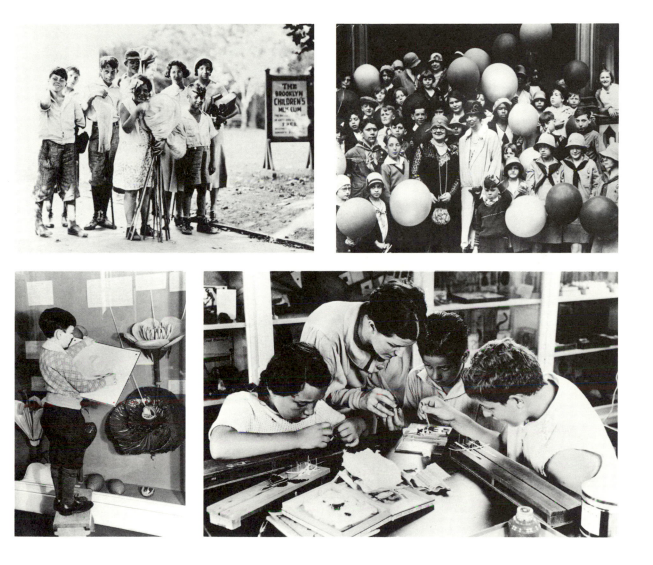

Top left Group setting out from Brooklyn Children's Museum on a field trip to Hunter's Island, 1932.

Top right Mrs Franklin D. Roosevelt, wife of the Governor of New York State, with Anna B. Gallup, Curator-in-Chief, on the steps of the Brooklyn Children's Museum, 1929.

Bottom left Sketching from a botany model in the 1930s.

Bottom right Mounting insects after a Museum field trip, 1935.

may be children, but they do not like to be reminded of the fact – and that children learn best in an adult atmosphere, which encourages them to become interested in a wider range of topics. But, in its own national and local context, the Brooklyn Children's Museum has been very successful. The original nineteenth-century mansion which housed the Museum has been demolished and has been replaced by a purpose-designed building which suggests today rather than yesterday.

Now serving the whole of the City of New York, it is financed by its own endowment income, by grants from municipal and public bodies, by corporate and Foundation contributions, and by payments and donations from the public.

Its present policy differs very little from the one with which it was launched in 1899, although the phraseology is naturally more up-to-date. Now, in 1986, it is 'dedi-

185

Children playing on the aerial bridge at the Brooklyn Children's Museum. The bridge, 52 feet high, is one of several ways in which children can reach the roof-top park of the Museum.

cated to helping children learn about themselves and the world around them through direct interaction with scientific, cultural and historical objects. The Museum's current "high-tech" facility contains more than 50,000 authentic museum objects, available for active "hands-on" experience by students of all age groups.' It has a 'portable collection' scheme, to 'bring the Brooklyn Children's Museum into classrooms throughout the City', class programmes on such subjects as 'Energy at Work', 'The Human Body: An Amazing Machine', 'Work and Play in the 19th Century', and 'Journey to Africa'. In the last of these, a very typical project, 'Visitors are invited to experience life in a contemporary African village through slides and music tapes created by Museum staff in Africa, and objects from the Museum's extensive African collection (including an Ashanti 'golden staff', a toy car from Senegal, and a Yoruba Ibeji doll). Special attention is paid to the importance of community and family life, as they are affected by contemporary African society.

There are 'Series Visits', which consist of 'three visits by the class for an in-depth experience over a three-week period of time'. Under the scheme known as 'High School and Junior High School Outreach', a Museum representative goes to the school – 'Museum instructors will visit your classroom accompanied by museum collection objects'. 'Workshops' are organised to show teachers how to use museum

An instructor, Shirley Edwards, with students at a MUSE dance workshop, 1974.

objects as a means of illustrating and enlivening their lessons – 'Teaching with objects in the classroom is a special skill that, once developed, can lead to rewarding teaching experiences'.

Without implying any criticism of the quality of the schools in the City of New York, it is obvious that the Children's Museum has resources which no school could match and that both pupils and teachers could benefit greatly by close and regular association with it. But nowadays one does not need to have something specifically called a Children's Museum or a Junior Museum in order to establish this kind of link. In many other countries, large museums and museum organisations organise similar facilities, although not on quite the same scale. How far they will be able to continue to do so, with budgets under increasingly tight security, remains to be seen. This, however, is not the immediate point. The Brooklyn Children's Museum was founded at a time when there was, at least in the Western world, a good deal more respect for formal instruction in schools than there is at the present time, and when anything which the museum had to offer was very much an extra, and a rather poor relation, to the classroom curriculum. Today the situation is quite different. Many, perhaps most, children over the age of eight or nine find classroom methods and discipline irksome and often boring. Class activities and the teachers in charge of them are in competition with television and other exciting attractions outside, and quite a high proportion of children find it easier and more agreeable to learn from the competitor than from the school. It would probably be going a little too far to say that since the Brooklyn Children's Museum has occupied its own large modern building it has increased its prestige and become a more formidable competitor to the schools it is so anxious to serve, but there is more than a grain of truth in the suggestion. It is a not impossible thought that one day in the not too distant future the Museum and the schools will change places, with the Museum as the senior partner in the learning co-operative. An alternative possibility is that the schools will survive and even prosper by becoming more like the Museum. At present any rational exploration of the situation is bedevilled by obsolete terminology. What, after all, is a 'museum', and what is a 'school'? So many changes have been taking place within the shells of both words that the words themselves have become almost an embarrassment. Fifty years ago, to have called the Tacubaya enterprise or Anacostia a 'museum' would have seemed ridiculous, but today we allow them the title because we have no other word to use.

But it is still possible to do new and adventurous things locally without departing very far from the path of tradition. There are thousands of small local museums throughout the world, many of them established a long time ago. Few of them have enough money to modernise themselves to the degree that is really needed and most are content merely to exist and to receive a number of visitors which is so paltry as to constitute a gross waste of resources. Any museum which fails to attract an average of fifty people a day should seriously consider whether it might not do better to close its doors or to merge with some other institution, yet this situation is exceedingly common, although obscured by a conspiracy of professional silence.

Any small local museum which takes proper steps to put its house in order, so that it emerges from the unknown and unvisited category, deserves both credit and publicity. The inclusion of one such establishment in our list of Museums of Influence could be of value both in indicating a trend and possibly also in intensifying the strength and speed of the trend.

Sargans is the chief town of a small region or *Land* of the same name in eastern Switzerland. Its new museum occupies a recently restored Renaissance castle, perched on a hill and enjoying magnificent views of the surrounding countryside. It is exactly the kind of site which tourists expect to find in Switzerland and are willing to seek out. The museum owes its existence to the enterprise and enthusiasm of the Sargans Historical Society. The Society possessed a small but interesting collection of local material, which was in temporary accommodation, and decided to do something useful with it. A Foundation, managed by the Society, was set up to raise funds from both private and public sources, to organise the restoration of the castle and to supervise the design and installation of the exhibits.

Sargans: the castle housing the Museum.

The exhibition style.

A scene from the audio-visual display.

Very wisely, the decision was taken at an early stage to engage a first-class designer, Hans Woodtli, who had had successful experience of shaping and presenting collections of this kind and who possessed two qualities which are at a premium in the museum world, an instinct for simple sophistication and a talent for making very ordinary objects look attractive, for grading them up visually. The money was well spent. Without these expert services, the museum would never have acquired its present style and distinction, and it would certainly not have won the European Museum of the Year Award in 1983.

Arranged on six stair-linked floors, which makes it possibly the most unsuitable exhibition in Europe for disabled people, the Museum presents the history of the Sargans region from the earliest times to the present day, against the background of the natural environment. Agriculture, industry, domestic and social life are all represented, with a pattern of unified displays, and an audio-visual presentation of exceptional quality lasting thirty minutes, aiming at making the visitor aware of the atmosphere and spirit of the region and at providing a context within which the exhibits can assume their proper significance.

There are many local history museums with collections at least as good as those at Sargans. What marks this museum off from most of the others is the discipline which has been imposed on the exhibits, so that the displays are not only extremely attractive from a visual point of view, but combine to tell the story of the area in clear terms and to communicate the special character of a part of Switzerland which is not among those most familiar to tourists. Its example, which its success in the European Museum of the Year competition has widely publicised, has demonstrated that the combination of local enthusiasm and professional presentation can result in a museum which is popular with tourists – its magnificent site and pleasant restaurant are important contributory factors – but which meets proper scholarly requirements. Sargans has become a local history laboratory, where many experiments are carried on and many lessons learnt.

The same comment could be made of the Swiss Transport Museum at Lucerne, established in 1959, and now attracting more than 650,000 visitors a year. Set up entirely with private funds, it owes its existence and its remarkable success to the determination and vision of its first director, Dr Alfred Waldis, a former employee of Swiss Federal Railways, who has devoted a large part of his life to planning and organising a museum which would be something more than the usual collection of railway engines, motorcars and old aeroplanes. The raising of the large amount of capital required to start and develop the Museum is a textbook story in itself, involving, among other enterprising feats, the diversion of State pension funds to the Museum, in return for a satisfactory rate of interest.

The buildings are modern and free from any arrogance, vulgarity or pomposity. Pleasantly situated on the edge of the lake and well surrounded by trees, they have proved very flexible and practical and easily capable of receiving large numbers of visitors in comfort. There are no monumental staircases to climb, and no lengthy corridors and vast entrance halls to light, heat and maintain. It is cheap to run, even with the extra costs resulting from a Swiss winter, and the buildings are well suited both to their essential function of sheltering the exhibits and to providing a readily adaptable shell within which displays can be rearranged with a minimum of difficulty and disruption. Large exhibits, such as a pleasure steamer which for many years carried passengers up and down Lake Lucerne, railway locomotives and aeroplanes are placed outside in the grounds but, like the trees and the grass, they are always temptingly in view through the glass walls of the buildings.

The Museum has always been known as the House of Transport (Verkehrshaus), with 'Swiss Transport Museum' added only as a subtitle. In doing this, it joins the ranks of the other pioneering museums, like Colonial Williamsburg, Ironbridge, Beamish and the Ontario Science Centre, which have tried to bypass the possibly discouraging overtones of the word 'museum'. People come to the House of Transport, many of them by the specially provided lake ferries, and discover the Swiss Transport Museum when they arrive. Inside the Museum, the story of transport is told in social as well as technical terms, so that everyone who comes is able to understand that changes in transport have brought changes in the style and possibilities of life. The House of Transport is quite different from most other transport museums, such as the British National Railway Museum at York, or the National Motor Museum at Beaulieu, for instance, where the revolution in habits caused by new forms of transport receives practically no attention at all.

The House of Transport aims to entice and please its visitors with a variety of attractions, some of which could be considered as being on the fringe of transport. These include a constant series of temporary exhibitions, a planetarium, and a section devoted to huge murals by the Swiss painter, Hans Erni, 'a chronology of the science and philosophy of the West, portraying the greatest thinkers and scientists from Thales to Einstein'. The large and well-run restaurants are an important feature of the whole enterprise. They contribute a great deal to the welcoming atmosphere of the Museum, and not a little to its income.

The Museum receives no regular subsidy from the State, and it is self-supporting as far as its running costs are cocerned. 85 per cent of the current expenditure is met by the sale of entrance tickets and from shop and restaurant profits and the remaining 15 per cent comes from subscriptions of the 20,000 members of the Association of the Swiss Transport Museum. It is a type of museum totally unknown in the Socialist half of the world, but fairly certain to become increasingly common in the West, where political and economic trends are making the entrepreneurial type of museum, often with mixed private and public funding, more and more inevitable.

The fundamental problem of such museums is not financial. What is more critical is

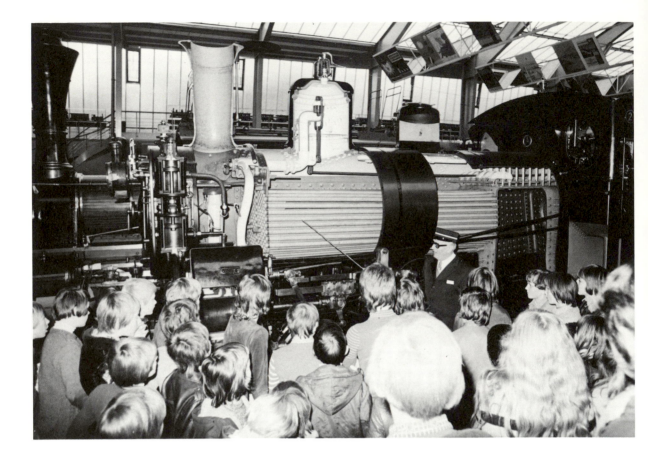

A guide at the Swiss Transport Museum points out the technical features of a locomotive.

the balance which is established between entertainment and learning, between pleasure and study. If this is not right, the museum will ultimately fail. Too much entertainment, too many 'experiences' and the museum becomes trivial, too little and it is likely to suffer from a serious shortage of visitors and this, where income is dependent on numbers, could lead to progressive decay, if not bankruptcy.

As we have seen, the word 'museum' is not universally popular, especially among those establishments which are anxious to widen the base of their public. Alternatives, however, are hard to find. It could be argued that places like Anacostia are not really museums at all, yet they seem to be something more than exhibitions. If it could be rid of the rather precious and élitist associations from which it suffers in the Anglo-Saxon world, 'cultural centre' might serve quite well. This could certainly seem to be a more suitable and more invigorating term than 'museum' for many of the new institutions which have been created in the developing countries.

There is, for example, the Sukuma Museum, near Mwanza in Tanzania. Founded in the 1950s by the Catholic Society of St Cecilia, under the leadership and inspiration of a priest who was familiar with museums in his own country, the Canadian,

Father David Clement, the creator of
the Sukuma Museum.

Father David Clement, the museum has devoted itself to preserving and encouraging the culture of the Sukuma tribe, the largest in Tanzania. The Museum has set about its task in three ways, by setting up a Cultural Research Committee to provide the necessary scholarly foundations, by arranging an exhibition of traditional Sukuma artefacts, in which individual items are changed from time to time, and by organising a school of Tanzanian handicrafts and a group of dancers who perform the traditional dances to a very high standard. The three aspects of the Museum's work are regarded as an integrated unit, the purpose of which is to help the Sukuma people to adapt their old skills, traditions and customs to the demands of the modern world. No conventional museum, no mere collection of objects, could achieve this, however brilliant the methods of presentation might be. To realise its aims, the Museum has to be a centre of activities, as well as somewhere where artefacts are preserved, and for such a concept 'museum' seems an inadequate description.

Right The Royal Pavilion at Sukuma.

Below left Helen Solanhyiwa,
potmaker, demonstrating her craft.

Below right The blacksmith's hut.

193

Left Snake dancers at the Museum.

Right A dance troupe at Sukuma performing a traditional ritual to speed and encourage work in the fields.

The Sukuma Museum is a particularly good example of its type, but similar experiments are being carried out throughout Africa and elsewhere, in an attempt to discover something which looks both backwards and forwards, which has the prestige of a museum, without its traditional inhibitions and restrictions, which grows naturally out of the national or local culture and which makes a real contribution to scholarship and understanding. To select Sukuma was to some extent an arbitrary choice, but there were two special reasons for drawing attention to its work – it was conceived and realised largely by Westerners, who knew it would be wrong to impose their own cultural forms on it, and it was developed with very little money, but immense co-operation from the people whom it was intended to benefit. It is not in European-style buildings. It feels and is African. It can function effectively with the resources of a poor country.

A study and comparison of the museums selected for this chapter would suggest certain guidelines, if not a recipe for survival and growth in the museums field during what remains of the twentieth century. First, the museum must be financially viable. It must make sense within the economy and political structure of the country in which it finds itself, and this may involve methods of funding and organisation which the purists could find distasteful. Second, it must find ways of linking itself closely and actively with the local community and of satisfying real, rather than imagined tastes and needs. And, third, it must never lose sight of the essential truth contained in the apparent paradox that successful popularisation can be achieved only on a basis of sound scholarship. We are going to see a good many fly-by-night museums fail as a result of ignoring this maxim, and it is going to be a sad process to watch, as sad as contemplating out-of-date museums fade away and eventually possibly die from a surfeit of learning, dullness, obstinacy and arrogance.

Notes

Chapter One
Fertilisation and cross-fertilisation in the museum world

1 Cecil Gould, *Trophy of Conquest: The Musée Napoléon and the Creation of the Louvre*, London: Faber and Faber, 1965, p. 13.

2 *The Life of William Hutton, Stationer, of Birmingham, written by himself*, Second edition, 1841. The first edition had been published in 1816 and conditions at the Museum had improved between the first and second editions.

3 Ibid., p. 41. The German historian, Wendeborn, who managed to visit the British Museum in 1795, experienced even greater frustrations than those described by Hutton.

4 His four-volume book, *Treasures of Art in Great Britain*, was published in London in 1854.

5 *Works of Art and Artists in Britain*, trans. H. E. Lloyd, 1838. London: Cornmarket Press, 1970, Vol. III, pp. 3–4.

6 Ibid., pp. 90–1.

7 Ibid., pp. 80–1.

8 Ibid., p. 81.

9 Ibid., p. 185.

10 *The Complete Works of Samuel Taylor Coleridge*, ed. W. G. T. Shedd, Vol. 6, *Specimens of the Table Talk of the Late Samuel Taylor Coleridge*, 1853, p. 358.

11 *Fifty Years of Public Work of Sir Henry Cole, K.C.B., accounted for in his deeds and writing*, edited by his son, Alan S. Cole, 2 vols., London: George Bell and Sons, 1884. Vol. 1, pp. 116–17.

12 Ibid., Vol. 2, p. 234.

13 The example of the Great Exhibition was followed internationally. During the second half of the nineteenth century, the main exhibitions of this kind were in Antwerp, 1869; Chicago, 1873; London, 1867, 1871; Moscow, 1872; Paris, 1867, 1878, 1889; Philadelphia, 1876; St Petersburg, 1870; Vienna, 1873.

14 Conversation with the author on 20 June 1985.

15 Ruth V. Weierheiser, 'Campaigning for a New Museum', *Museum Work*, Vol. VII, No. 2, July/August 1924.

16 For the history of ICOM, see *Museum*, Vol. XXXII, No. 3, 1980. 'Thirty-four years of co-operation between UNESCO and ICOM'.

17 Ibid., p. 154.

18 Vol. XXXII, No. 4, 1980.

19 Vol. XXXIV, No. 3, 1982.

20 *Museum Journal*, July 1909, pp. 8–9.

21 Ibid., p. 9.

Chapter Two
The antiquarians and archaeologists

1 *Boswell's Life of Johnson*, 2 vols., Oxford University Press, 1933, Vol. 1, p. 211.

2 1729–1811. Dean of Carlisle and subsequently Bishop of Dromore. His great collection of ballads, published in 1765 as *Reliques of Ancient Poetry*, was a major influence in creating an interest in the traditional literature of the British Isles and a harbinger of the Romantic School.

3 *150 Years of Archaeology*, London: Duckworth, 1975, p. 9.

4 Constituted as the Royal Society of Antiquaries of London in 1718, it received its Royal Charter from George II in 1754. But its principal journal, first published in 1770, has always been called *Archaeologia*.

5 The present Ashmolean buildings were constructed in 1841–5 and were extended in 1894, 1908 and 1967. In 1860 the Museum's natural history sections were transferred to the new

University Science Museum and its ethnographical material went to the Pitt-Rivers Museum in 1886. In 1925 the original Ashmolean Museum became the University's Museum of the History of Science.

6 Its history is described by Caroline M. Borowsky in *Museum News*, February 1963, pp. 11–21. Further information about this pioneering institution, usually reckoned to be the oldest museum in America, can be found in Laura M. Bragg, 'The Birth of the Museum Idea in America', *Charleston Museum Quarterly*, 1 (1923), pp. 3–4.

7 An assessment of this museum and its contents is to be found in an article by Richard P. Ellis, 'The Founding, History and Significance of Peale's Museum in Philadelphia, 1785–1841', in *Curator*, Vol. 9, No. 3, 1966.

8 *150 Years of Archaeology*, p. 20.

9 J. Mordaunt Crook, *The British Museum*, Allen Lane: The Penguin Press, 1972, p. 89.

10 His father, Robert Smirke, had retired in 1845.

11 The best account of Panizzi's life and achievements is Edward Miller, *Prince of Librarians*, London: André Deutsch, 1967.

12 *Minutes of the Select Committee*, para. 4951. Quoted in Miller, op. cit., p. 120.

13 Letter to Panizzi, 20 February 1861, in *Papers relating to Salaries of Officers employed in the British Museum*, p. 17.

14 *Oversyn over foedrelandets mindesmaerker fra oldtiden.*

15 In his book, *Udsigt over Nationalhistoriens oeldste og maerkeligste Perioder.*

16 *150 Years of Archaeology*, p. 41.

17 Worsaae was one of the most influential figures in the field of Scandinavian archaeology during the nineteenth century. He became Professor of Archaeology at the University of Copenhagen, Inspector of the Monuments of Danish Antiquity and, to crown his career, Supreme Director of the Museums of Ethnography and Northern Antiquities.

18 *150 Years of Archaeology*, p. 45.

19 The *Guide* was published in Copenhagen in 1836, as *Ledetraad til Nordisk Oldkyndighed*. The German version (1837) was *Leitfaden zur nordischen Alterhumskunde*, and the English (1848), *A Guide to Northern Antiquities*. Worsaae's book, *Danmarks oltid oplyst ved Oldsager* (1842) had an English translation by W. J. Thoms, *The Primeval Antiquities of Denmark* (1849).

20 Pitt-Rivers Papers, Salisbury Museum, L.846.

21 *Journal of the Society of Arts*, 18 December 1891, p. 115.

22 Ibid., pp. 115–16.

23 Fishbourne was a journalistic, as well as an archaeological project. It received a subsidy of £20,000 from *Times* Newspapers and was brought into being by the combined efforts and expertise of a journalist, Kenneth Pearson, a professor of archaeology, Barry Cunliffe, and a designer, Robin Wade.

Chapter Three
Temples of art

1 *Catalogue* to the exhibition, 'Thomas Howard, Earl of Arundel', held at the Ashmolean Museum, Oxford, 1985–6, p. 7.

2 *The Museum Age*, Brussels: Desoer, 1968, p. 16.

3 'On Art and Money', Harold Rosenberg Memorial Lecture at the University of Chicago, 1984. Reprinted in *Art Monthly*, Dec/Jan 1984/5, p. 7.

4 Ibid., p. 10.

5 Pages 4–6.

6 In this connection, one should not overlook the pioneering achievement of the Villa Albani in Rome, built 1746–63 on the order of Cardinal Alessandro Albani. The contents were entirely Greek and Roman sculpture, and the collection was arranged and presented in such a way as to concentrate attention on each item as an individual work of art, rather than on the collection as a whole which was the normal practice at the time.

7 This was the first catalogue to be aimed at the average citizen, not the first museum catalogue. The Museo Pio-Clementino in the Vatican had already, in 1782, produced a catalogue of its contents, but this was essentially for scholars. The arrangement of the sculpture galleries was interesting. The collection was entirely of Greek and Roman items, and each room was arranged around a theme or a single outstanding work.

8 A number of them are reproduced and described in Volker Plagemann, *Das deutsche Kunstmuseum, 1790–1870*, Munich: Prestel-Verlag, 1967, pp. 18–21.

9 W. Wackenrode and L. Tieck, *Herzengiessungen eines kunstliebenden Klostenbruders*, 1797. Quoted in Plagemann, op. cit., p. 25. The emotional and arch-Romantic title, *An art-loving monk pours out his heart*, is barely translatable into English.

10 Munich (1836), London (1838), Dresden (1855), Brussels (1885), Amsterdam (1885), Vienna (1891), Moscow (1912).

11 Kenneth Clark, *Other Half*, John Murray, 1977, p. 123.

12 John Physick, *The Victoria and Albert Museum: the history of the building*, Oxford: Phaidon, 1982, p. 9.

13 John Sheepshanks (1787–1863) was the son of a wealthy Leeds clothing manufacturer. He gave his collection to South Kensington because he wanted it to be 'in an open and airy situation, possessing the quiet necessary to the study and enjoyment of works of art, and free from the inconveniences and dirt of the main thoroughfare of the metropolis'. South Kensington, in 1857, was still very rural.

14 For a general account of the collections, see Ann Somers Cocks, *The Victoria and Albert Museum: the Making of the Collection*, London: Windward, 1980.

15 *Catalogue of the Museum of Construction*, 1862, p. 5.

16 The tile-makers.

17 The Albert Hall, a mile away from the Museum, was under construction at the same time.

18 John Physick, *Victoria and Albert Museum*, p. 18.

19 The decorations at the Victoria and Albert were shockingly neglected, covered over and even vandalised after the death of Sir Henry Cole. Cole's successor, Sir Cecil Harcourt-Smith, deliberately set out to remove as much of the internal decoration as he could.

20 Semper had been asked to prepare plans for a new National Gallery on the South Kensington site in London. Prince Albert himself paid for them, but the building was eventually decided to be too expensive.

21 For a good general account of these developments, see Charles R. Richards, *Industrial Art and the Museum*, New York: Macmillan, 1927.

22 Report on the Crystal Palace Exhibition, 1852, in his book, *Der Stijl*, 1860.

23 *The Museum. One Hundred Years of the Metropolitan Museum of Art*, 1969, p. 11.

24 Ibid., p. 15.

25 13 April 1870.

26 24 May 1870.

27 Aline B. Saarinen, *The Proud Possessors*, 1958. Quoted in Lerman, op. cit., p. 122.

28 12 December 1953, p. 49. This and the subsequent issue of the magazine contains a long, two-part profile of the Museum's founder, Alfred H. Barr, Jr.

Chapter Four
Man, nature and the environment

1 1752–1840, the diarist and novelist, and a member of the circle of Dr Johnson. In 1793 she married the French émigré, General D'Arblay.

2 The Tower of London, which at that time contained the Royal Menagerie.

3 i.e. Tahiti.

4 *Systema Naturae*, 1735; *Genera Plantarum*, 1737; *Species Plantarum*, 1753.

5 'Die Entwicklung des Naturhistorischen Museums', *Museums Kunde*, Band III, Heft 1, January 1907, p. 25.

6 Ibid., p. 26.

7 The full title is *The Origin of Species by Means of Natural Selection, or the Preservation of Favoured Races in the Struggle for Life*.

8 His father founded the celebrated Flowers Brewery, Stratford-on-Avon.

9 Reprinted in Sir W. H. Flower, *Essays on Museums and Other Subjects*, London: Macmillan, 1898.

10 'Modern Museums', in Flower, *Essays on Museums*, p. 38.

11 Ibid., p. 40.

12 Ibid., p. 41.

13 Explained by him in a paper presented to the Anthropological Section of the British Association in 1888 and just previously in the *Journal of the Society of Arts*, 12 December 1887.

14 Charles J. Cornish, *Sir William Henry Flower: a Personal Memoir*, London: Macmillan, 1904, p. 140.

15 Ibid., p. 17.

16 *Libraries and Museums*, Benn, 1930, pp. 96–7.

17 On this, see 'Television and the museums', *Museums, Imagination and Education*, UNESCO, 1973.

18 W. P. Pycraft, *The British Museum of Natural History*, London: Wells Gardner Darton and Co., 1910. This was in a series called *Treasure-Houses of the Nation*. The other treasure-houses were the Tate Gallery, the Zoo, the National Gallery and Hampton Court.

19 Ibid., p. 2.

20 For a useful survey of the growth of new concepts in animal management and display, see Jeremy Cherfas, *Zoo 2000*, 1984, a book based on a BBC television series with the same title.

21 Karel Jonckheers, *The Future has a Past: Biochron*, 1985.

22 i.e. since the Museum's policy was formulated by Sir Richard Owen in the 1850s.

23 R. S. Miles and M. B. Alt, 'British Museum (Natural History): a New Approach to the Visiting Public', *Museums Journal*, Vol. 78, No. 4, March 1979, p. 158.

24 Ibid., p. 159.

25 Ibid., p. 158.

26 The Zoological Museum in Copenhagen is a good example of the trend. The original museum opened in 1870 and at that time, as Bent Jørgensen has pointed out ('The new Zoological Museum, Copenhagen', *Museum*, Vol. XXV, No. 1/2, 1973), 'the main object was to show what the animals looked like' (page 63). The Museum has been completely reorganised, using dioramas 'to provide the basis for political understanding of the need to handle what remains of our environment in an ecologically responsible way' (page 63).

Chapter Five
Science, technology and industry

1 Charles R. Richards, *The Industrial Museum*, New York: Macmillan, 1925, p. 1.

2 Décret du 10 octobre 1794.

3 1709–82. He specialised in automata and machine tools. One of his lathes, built between 1770 and 1780, is in the Museum.

4 Richards, op. cit., p. 15.

5 Ibid., p. 16.

6 Ibid., p. 18.

7 'America's contemporary science museums', *Museums Journal*, Vol. 74, No. 4, March 1976.

8 Richards, *Industrial Museum*, p. 25.

9 Ibid., p. 25.

10 1909–13.

11 On its history and aims, see Jean Rose and Charles Penel, 'Rôle of Museums of Science and Industrial Techniques', *Museum*, Vol. XXV, No. 1/2, 1973.

12 Danilov, 'America's contemporary science museums', p. 145.

13 Douglas N. Omans, 'The Ontario Science Centre, Toronto', *Museum*, Vol. XXVI, No. 2, 1974, p. 76.

14 Kenneth W. Jackman and R. S. Bathal, 'The Singapore Science Centre, *Museum*, Vol. XXVI, No. 2, 1974, p. 110.

15 Dame Margaret Weston, Director of The Science Museum, London.

16 Jackman and Bathal, op. cit., p. 111.

17 Peter Schrimbeck, 'The Museum of the City of Rüsselsheim', *Museum*, Vol. XXXIII, No. 1, 1981, p. 38.

18 Ibid., p. 39.

19 Ibid., p. 36.

20 At, for example, Sheffield and Wuppertal.

Chapter Six
The history and customs of the homeland

1 The year in which William of Normandy defeated the Saxon army at the so-called Battle of Hastings and conquered England.

2 *English Social History*, 1944, p. vii.

3 *Skansen 1891–1966*, p. 1. Produced by Skansen in 1966 to commemorate the 75th anniversary of the Museum.

4 Nils Erik Bachrendtz, Arne Biörnstad, Ingmar Lioman and Per Olof Palm, 'Skansen – a stocktaking at ninety', *Museum*, Vol. XXXIV, No. 3, 1982, p. 173.

5 Its present impressive building, completed in 1907, was designed by the fashionable architect, Isak Gustaf Clason.

6 'Some considerations concerning the significance and status of open-air museums in present-day society', presented to the Conference of the European Association of Open-Air Museums, Visegrad, Hungary.

7 This situation was excellently summarised by J. H. Fabre at the end of the First World War, when he observed (*The Wonders of Instinct*, 1918, p. 291) that history 'celebrates the battlefields whereon we meet our death, but scorns to speak of the ploughed fields whereby we thrive; it knows the names of the King's bastards, but cannot tell us the origin of wheat'.

8 For a good description of the Museum and an indication of its aims, see J. M. Bos and E. M. C. F. Klijn, *Nederlands Openlucht Museum, Arnhem*, published by the Museum, 1979.

9 'Regional Museums', *Museums Journal*, Vol. 68, No. 2, September 1968, p. 74.

10 'New open-air museums', *Museum*, Vol. XXIII, No. 2, 1970/1.

11 Pamphlet, *The Village*, Spring 1962. National Council of Social Services.

12 *Policy for a Regional Open-Air Museum*. Report for a working party set up 4 October 1966.

13 Valerie Ward, 'The Beamish Museum: Giving the Past a New Lease of Life', *My Weekly: the Magazine for Women Everywhere*, 7 July 1979. Once Beamish began to get this kind of publicity, its success was practically assured, since it regards family parties as its typical visitors.

14 The absence of convenient and adequate car-parking has been a serious problem at Skansen, established as it was before the motor age.

15 Two-thirds of the total income at Beamish now comes from direct payments by the public, an exceptionally high proportion.

16 The Belgians do not always appear to agree. An article in *Het Belang van Limburg*, 4 April 1980, was headed 'Beamish: Bokrijk op z'n Engels' (Beamish: an English version of Bokrijk).

17 For an account of the Museum's history and organisation, see Georges Henri Rivière and Jean Cuisenier, 'The Museum of Popular Arts and Traditions, Paris', *Museum*, Vol. XXIV, No. 3, 1972.

18 One or two city museums have attempted to shape and discipline the history of the city by emphasising certain aspects of its development. In Helsinki, for instance, the stress has been on architectural change. (See Jarno Juhani Peltonen, 'The Helsinki City Museum, Finland', *Museum*, Vol. XXXII, No. 1/2, 1980), and in Moscow a three-stage development has been identified, Archaeology, History of Pre-Revolutionary Moscow, and Socialist Moscow (see A. Loknev, 'The Museum of the History and Reconstruction of Moscow', *Museum*, Vol. XXV, No. 4, 1973).

19 Rolf Kiau, 'Zur Entwicklung der Museen der DDR', *Neue Museumskunde*, Jahrgang 12 4/1969, p. 429.

Chapter Seven
History where it happened

1 *The Great Museum*, 1984, p. 10. One of the most original and most valuable books ever to be written about museums and museum-going.

2 *The Museum in America*, Washington: American Association of Museums, 3 vols., 1939, Vol. 1, p. 73.

3 Edward P. Alexander, *The Interpretation Programme of Colonial Williamsburg*, Williamsburg, 1971, p. 38.

4 James McCabe, *The Illustrated Centennial Exhibition in Commemoration of the One-Hundredth Anniversary of American Independence*, 1876. The quotation is taken from the 1975 reprint, by the National Publishing Company, pp. 239–40.

5 Ibid., p. 240.

6 Charles B. Hosmer, *Presence of the Past*, Putnam, 1965, pp. 215–16. In this work and in his *Preservation Comes of Age*, University Press of Virginia, 1981, Hosmer provides a definitive history of the preservation movement in the United States.

7 George F. Dow, 'Report of the Secretary', *Annual Report of the Essex Institute*, 6 May 1912, p. 16.

8 Ibid., pp. 17–18.

9 Geoffrey C. Upward, *A Home for our Collection*, Henry Ford Museum Press, 1979, p. 11.

10 'The Museum in the Valley, Ironbridge Gorge', *Museum*, Vol. XXXII, No. 3, 1980, p. 142.

11 Ibid., p. 142.

12 François Moriot, 'The Eco-Museum of Marquèze, Sabres', *Museum*, Vol. XXV, No. 1/2, 1973, p. 86.

13 'The Camargue Museum, Mas du Pont de Rousty, Arles, France', *Museum*, Vol. XXXII, No. 1/2, 1980, p. 23.

14 Ibid., p. 23.

15 'A "fragmented" museum: the Museum of Man and Industry', *Museum*, Vol. XXV, No. 4, 1973, p. 245.

16 Ibid., p. 245.

17 Ibid., p. 246.

18 Ibid., p. 241.

Chapter Eight
Pointers to the future

1 *Museum*, Vol. XXV, No. 1/2, 1975, p. 112. The entire issue was devotet to the theme, 'Man and the Environment'.

2 An anthropologist, he was the founder, in 1962, of the international journal, *Anthropos*. Director of the Moravian Museum, Brno and Head of the Department of Museology at the University of Brno, he has also served as Chairman of the Executive Council of ICOM and of the ICOM International Committee for Regional Museums.

3 *Museums for the 1980s*, 1977, p. 92.

4 Ibid., pp. 92–3.

5 See Georges Henri Rivière, 'Rôle of museums of art and of human and social sciences', *Museum*, Vol. XXV, No. 1/2, 1973. Dr Rivière points out in particular that the art museum 'offers a review of the natural and human environment as it is perceived and figured by the creative artist' (page 287).

6 His address was published as 'The rôle of museums of history and folklore in a changing world', *Curator*, Vol. 6, No. 2, 1963.

7 Paul Marshall Rea, *The Museum and the Community*, Science Press, 1932, pp. 61–2.

8 *Annual Report of the Brooklyn Institute of Arts and Sciences, 1899–1900*, p. 418.

9 By no means all the American children's museums have been successful. In her book, *Youth in Museums* (1947), Eleanor M. Moore says that the failures have been 'pasted on to a community and expected to stick' (page 9). The successes 'consider the community at the start and depend upon it to determine their course, always continuing to seek new means of usefulness through co-operation' (page 9).

10 For a stronger-worded example of the European opposition to children's museums, see Molly Harrison, *Changing Museums*, 1967, page 85.

Works consulted

General   Adams, T. R. *The Museum and Popular Culture* New York: American Association for Adult Education, 1939

Bazin, Germain *The Museum Age* Brussels: Desoer, 1968

Bell, Whitefield J. *et al. A Cabinet of Curiosities: Five Episodes in the Evolution of American Museums* University of Virginia, 1967

Coleman, Laurence Vail *The Museum in America* 3 vols. Washington: American Association of Museums, 1939

Harrison, Molly, *Changing Museums: Their Use and Misuse* London: Longmans, 1967

Hudson, Kenneth *A Social History of Museums* London: Macmillan, 1975

Kaufmann, Emil *Architecture in the Age of Reason* New York: Dover Publications, 1968

Kenyon, Sir Frederic *Libraries and Museums* Benn, 1930

Longley, Marjorie *et al. America's Taste* New York: Simon and Schuster, 1960

Malraux, André *The Voices of Silence* London: Secker and Warburg, 1954

Moore, Eleanor M. *Youth in Museums* Philadelphia: University of Pennsylvania Press, 1941

Myles, Kwasi 'Museum Development in African Countries', *Museum*, Vol. XXVIII,, No. 4, 1976

Ramsey, Grace Fisher *Educational Work in Museums of the United States: development, methods and trends* H. W. Wilson, 1938

Rea, Paul Marshall *The Museum and the Community* Science Press, 1932

Wittlin, Alma S. *Museums in Search of a Usable Future* Cambridge, Mass.: MIT Press, 1970
The Museum: its History and its Tasks in Education London: Routledge and Kegan Paul, 1949

Chapter One
Fertilisation and cross-fertilisation in the museum world

Coleridge, Samuel Taylor *The Complete Works* ed. W. G. T. Shedd, Vol. 6, *Specimens of the Table Talk of the Late Samuel Taylor Coleridge*, 1853

Fifty Years of Public Work of Sir Henry Cole, K.C.B., accounted for in his deeds, speeches and writing 2 vols. London: George Bell and Sons, 1884

Gould, Cecil *Trophy of Conquest: the Musée Napoléon and the Creation of the Louvre* London: Faber and Faber, 1965

Hudson, Kenneth *Museums for the 1980s* London: Macmillan for UNESCO, 1977

The Life of William Hutton, Stationer, of Birmingham, written by himself, 2nd ed., 1841

'Thirty-four Years of Co-operation between UNESCO and ICOM', *Museum*, Vol. XXXII, No. 3, 1980

Waagen, Gustav *Treasures of Art in Great Britain* 4 vols. London, 1854
Works of Art and Artists in Britain trans. H. E. Lloyd, 3 vols., 1838. London: Cornmarket Press, 1970

Weierheiser, Ruth V. 'Campaigning for a New Museum', *Museum Work*, Vol. VII, No. 2, July/August 1924

Chapter Two
The antiquarians and archaeologists

Bolton, Arthur T. *Description of the House and Museum on the North Side of Lincoln's Inn Fields, the Residence of Sir Hans Sloane*, 11th ed., London, 1930

Boswell's Life of Johnson 2 vols., Oxford University Press, 1933

Bragg, Laura M. 'The Birth of the Museum Idea in America', *Charleston Museum Quarterly*, I, 1923

Browning, Caroline M. 'The Charleston Museum 1773–1963', *Museum News*, February 1963

Caloo, Gudrun 'Museen und Sammler des 19 Jahrhunderts in Deutschland', *Museumskunde*, Vol. 38, 1969

Crook J. Mordaunt *The British Museum* Allen Lane: The Penguin Press, 1972

Daniel, Glyn *150 Years of Archaeology* London: Duckworth, 1975

Edwards, Edward *Lives of the Founders of the British Museum* 2 vols. London: Trübner and Co., 1870

Ellis, Richard P. 'The Founding, History and Significance of Peale's Museum in Philadelphia, 1785–1841', *Curator*, Vol. 9, No. 3, 1906

Hawkins, Desmond *Cranborne Chase* London: Gollancz, 1983

Hudson, Kenneth *A Social History of Archaeology* London: Macmillan, 1981

Miller, Edward *Prince of Librarians: the Life and Times of Antonio Panizzi of the British Museum* London: André Deutsch, 1967

   That Noble Cabinet: A History of the British Museum London: André Deutsch, 1973

Papers Relating to Salaries of Officers employed in the British Museum, Thomas Watts' letter to Panizzi, 20 February 1861 (Parliamentary Papers, House of Commons, 1866, Vol. XXXIX, p. 199)

Walters, H. B. 'Some English Antiquaries of the 16th, 17th and 18th Centuries', *Transactions of the Royal Society of Literature*, Vol. 10, 1934

Chapter Three
Temples of art

Catalogue of the Museum of Construction, 1862

Clark, Kenneth *Other Half* London: J. Murray, 1977

Cocks, Anna Somers *The Victoria and Albert Museum: the Making of the Collection* London: Windward, 1980

Fifty Years of Public Works of Sir Henry Cole, K.C.B., accounted for in his Deeds, Speeches and Writing 2 vols. London: George Bell and Sons, 1884

Gould, Cecil *Trophy of Conquest: the Musée Napoléon and the Creation of the Louvre* London: Faber and Faber, 1965

Hightown, John B. 'Are Art Galleries Obsolete?', *Curator*, Vol. 12, No. 1, 1969

Hughes, Robert 'On Art and Money', Harold Rosenberg Memorial Lecture, University of Chicago, 1984, in *Art Monthly*, Dec/Jan 1984/5

Lerman, Leo *The Museum. One Hundred Years of the Metropolitan Museum of Art* New York: The Viking Press, 1969

Little, David B. 'The Misguided Mission: a Disenchanted View of Art Museums Today', *Curator*, Vol. 10, No. 3, 1967

Physick, John *The Victoria and Albert Museum: the History of the Building* Oxford: Phaidon, 1982

Plagemann, Volker *Das deutsche Kunstmuseum, 1790–1870* Munich; Prestel-Verlag, 1967

'Problems of the Museum of Contemporary Art in the West', *Museum*, Vol. XXIV, No. 1, 1972

Richards, Charles R. *Industrial Art and the Museum* New York: Macmillan, 1927

Survey of London, Vol. XXXVIII *The Museums Area of South Kensington and Westminster* London: Athlone Press, 1975

Taylor, Francis Henry *The Taste of Angels: a History of Art Collections from Rameses to Napoleon* 1970

Tompkins, Calvin *Merchants and Masterpieces: The Story of the Metropolitan Museum of Art* Dutton, 1970

Waagen, Gustav *Works of Art and Artists in Britain* trans. H. E. Lloyd, 3 vols., 1838. London: Cornmarket Press, 1970

Whitley, William T. *Artists and their Friends in England, 1700–99* 2 vols. London: Hale, 1929

Chapter Four
Man, nature and the environment

Cherfas, Jeremy *Zoo 2000* London: BBC Publications, 1984

Cornish, Charles J. *Sir William Henry Flower: a Personal Memoir* London: Macmillan, 1904

Engström, K. and Johnels, A. G. *Natural History Museums and the Community* Oslo: University Press, 1973

Flower, Sir W. H. *Essays on Museums and Other Subjects* London: Macmillan, 1898

Jonckheers, Karel *The Future has a Past: Biochron* Emmen: Noorder Dierenpark/Zoo, 1985

Jørgensen, Bent 'The New Zoological Museum, Copenhagen', *Museum*, Vol. XXV, No. 1/2, 1973

Kal, Wilhelmina H. 'The Tropical Museum, Amsterdam', *Museum*, Vol. XXV, No. 1/2, 1973

Miles, R. S. and Alt, M. B. 'British Museum (Natural History): a New Approach to the Visiting Public', *Museums Journal*, Vol. 78, No. 4, March 1979

Penniman, T. K. *A Hundred Years of Anthropology* London: Duckworth, 1939

Pycraft, W. P. *The British Museum of Natural History (South Kensington)* London: Wells Gardner Darton and Co., 1910

Römer, F. 'Die Entwicklung der Naturhistorischen Museums', *Museums Kunde*, Band III, Heft 1, January 1907

'Television and the Museums', *Museums, Imagination and Education*, UNESCO, 1973

Chapter Five
Science, technology and
industry

Auer, Hermann 'Museums of the Natural and Exact Sciences', *Museum*, Vol. XXVI, No. 2, 1974

Chakrabosti, R. M. 'Mobile Science Exhibitions of the Visvesvaraya Industrial and Technological Museum, Bangalore', *Museum*, Vol. XXVI, No. 2, 1974

Danilov, Victor J. 'America's Contemporary Science Museums', *Museums Journal*, Vol. 74, No. 4, March 1976

Science and Technology Centres Washington: MIT Press, 1982

Greenaway, F. *A Short History of the Science Museum* London: HMSO, 1951

Greenaway, F. *et al. Science Museums in Developing Countries* Paris: ICOM, 1962

Jackman, Kenneth V. and Bhathal, R. S. 'The Singapore Science Centre', *Museum*, Vol. XXVI, No. 2, 1974

Kogan, Herman *A Continuing Marvel: History of the Museum of Science and Industry, Chicago* Doubleday, 1973

Omans, Douglas N. 'The Ontario Science Centre, Toronto', *Museum*, Vol. XXVI, No. 2, 1974

Richards, Charles R. *The Industrial Museum* New York: Macmillan, 1925

Rose, Jean and Penel, Charles, 'Rôle of Museums of Science and Industrial Techniques', *Museum*, Vol. XXV, No. 1/2, 1973

Schirmbeck, Peter 'The Museum of the City of Rüsselsheim', *Museum*, Vol. XXXIII, No. 1, 1981

Schouten, J. F. *The Evoluon: A Permanent Phillips Exhibition* Eindhoven: Evoluon, 1966

Chapter Six
The history and customs
of the homeland

Atkinson, Frank 'New Open-Air Museums', *Museum*, Vol. XXIII, No. 2, 1970/1

The Village National Council of Social Service, Spring 1962

'Regional Museums', *Museums Journal*, Vol. 68, No. 2, September 1968

Atkinson, Frank and Holton, Michael 'Open-Air and Folk-Museums', *Museums Journal*, Vol. 73, No. 4, 1973

Bachrendtz, Nils Erik *et al.* 'Skansen – a stocktaking at ninety', *Museum*, Vol. XXXIV, No. 3, 1982

'Beamish: Bokrijk op z'n Engels' in *Het Belang van Limburg* 4 April 1980

Bos, J. M. and Klijn, E. M. C. F. *Nederlands Openlucht Museum, Arnhem* published by the Museum, 1979

Coleman, Laurence Vail *Historic House Museums* Washington: American Association of Museums, 1933

de Varine-Bohan, Hugues 'A "Fragmented" Museum: the Museum of Man and Industry, Le Creusot – Montceau-les-Mines', *Museum*, Vol. XXV, No. 4, 1973

Duclos, Jean-Claude 'The Camargue Museum, Mas du Pont de Rousty, Arles, France', *Museum*, Vol. XXXII, No. 1/2, 1980

Durko, Janusz 'The Historical Museum', *Museum*, Vol. XIX, No. 2, 1966

'The Warsaw Historical Museum', *Museum*, Vol. X, 1957

Fabre, J. H. *The Wonders of Instinct* London: Unwin, 1918

Horne, Donald *The Great Museum: the Re-presentation of History* London and Sydney: The Pluto Press, 1984

Lagercrantz, Bo 'A Great Museum Pioneer of the Nineteenth Century', *Curator*, Vol. 7, No. 3, 1964

Loknev, A. 'The Museum of the History and Reconstruction of Moscow', *Museum*, Vol. XXV, No. 4, 1973

Peltonen, Jarno Juhani 'The Helsinki City Museum, Finland', *Museum*, Vol. XXXII, No. 1/2, 1980

Pott, Peter H. 'The Rôles of History and Folklore in a Changing World', *Curator*, Vol. 6, No. 2, 1963

Rivière, Georges Henri, 'Rôle of Museums of Art and of Human Social Sciences', *Museum*, Vol. XXV, No. 1/2, 1973

Rivière, Georges Henri and Cuisenier, Jean 'The Museum of Popular Arts and Traditions, Paris', *Museum*, Vol. XXIV, No. 3, 1972

Shlebecker, John T. 'Social Functions of Living Historical Farms in the United States', *Museum*, Vol. XXXVI, No. 3, 1984

Skansen, 1891–1966 Stockholm: Skansen, 1966

Thompson, G. B. 'Some Considerations concerning the Significance and Status of Open-Air Museums in Present-Day Society', *Proceedings of the Association of European Open-Air Museums* Hungary: Visegrad, 1982

Veillard, Jean Yves 'The Problem of the History Museum, with reference to the Museum of Brittany at Rennes', *Museum*, Vol. XXIV, No. 4, 1972

Zachrisson, Sune 'Agricultural Museums – the Story and Propagation of an Idea', *Museum*, Vol. XXXVI, No. 3, 1984

Chapter Seven
History where it happened

Alexander, Edward P. *The Interpretation Programme of Colonial Williamsburg* Williamsburg, 1971

Cossons, Neil 'The Museum in the Valley, Ironbridge Gorge', *Museum*, Vol. XXXII, No. 3, 1980

de Varine-Bohan, Hughes 'A "fragmented" museum: the Museum of Man and Industry, Le Creusot – Montceau-les-Mines', *Museum*, Vol. XXV, No. 4, 1973

Dow, George F. 'Report of the secretary', *Annual Report of the Essex Institute*, 6 May 1912

Duclos, Jean Claude 'The Camargue Museum, Mas du Pont de Rousty, Arles, France', *Museum*, Vol. XXXII, No. 1/2, 1980

Evrard, Marcel 'Le Creusot – Montceau-les-Mines: the Life of an Ecomuseum, Assessment of Ten Years', *Museum*, Vol. XXII, No. 4, 1980

Horne, Donald *The Great Museum: the Re-presentation of History* London and Sydney: The Pluto Press, 1984

Hosmer, Charles B. *Presence of the Past: a history of the preservation movement in the U.S. before Williamsburg* Putnam, 1965

   Preservation Comes of Age: from Williamsburg to the National Trust, 1926–1949 for the Preservation Press and National Trust for Historic Preservation in the United States: University Press of Virginia, 1981

Kvarning, Lars-Åke 'The Wasa: Museum and Museum Exhibit', *Museum*, Vol. XXXVI, No. 2, 1984.

McCabe, James *The Illustrated Centennial Exhibition 1876*. Reprinted by the National Publishing Company, 1975

Moriot, François 'The Eco-Museum of Marquèze, Sabres', *Museum*, Vol. XXV, No. 1/2, 1973

Sekers, David 'The Gladstone Pottery Museum: a New Museum of the Ceramics Industry', *Museums Journal*, Vol. 75, No. 4, March 1976

Upward, Geoffrey C. *A Home for our Heritage: the Building and Growth of Greenfield Village and the Henry Ford Museum, 1929–79* Henry Ford Museum Press, 1979

Villemure, Marcel Girard 'Les Forges du Saint-Maurice, Trois Rivières, Québec, Canada', *Museum*, Vol. XXXII, No. 1/2, 1980

Chapter Eight
Pointers to the future

Annual Report of the Brooklyn Institute of Arts and Sciences, 1899–1900

Kinard, John R. 'The Neighborhood Museum as a Catalyst for Social Change', *Museum*, Vol. CXLVIII, 1985

Kinard, John R. and Nighbert, Esther 'The Anacostia Neighborhood Museum, Smithsonian Institution, Washington D.C.', *Museum*, Vol. XXIV, No. 2, 1972

Lightfoot, Fred 'New Approaches to other Cultures in European Museums', *Museum*, Vol. XXXXV, No. 3, 1983

Lord Montagu of Beaulieu 'The National Motor Museum at Beaulieu', *Museums Journal*, Vol. 73, No. 1, June 1973

'Man and the Environment', *Museum*, Vol. XXV, No. 1/2, 1975

Ordóñez, Coral 'The Casa del Museo, Mexico City: an Experiment in bringing the Museum to the People', *Museum*, Vol. XXVII, No. 2, 1975

Rivière, Georges Henri 'Rôle of museums of art and of human and social sciences', *Museum*, Vol. XXV, No. 1/2, 1973

Rivière, Georges Henri *et al.* 'Problems of the Museum of Contemporary Art in the West', *Museum*, Vol. XXIV, No. 1, 1972

Sayles, Adelaide B. *The Story of the Children's Museum of Boston from its beginnings to November 18 1936* Children's Museum, 60 Burroughs Street, Jamaica Plain, Massachusetts, 1937

Waldis, Alfred *20 Jahre Verkehrshaus* Lucerne: Verkehrshaus der Schweiz, 1979

Acknowledgements

I should like to express my warm gratitude to two different groups of people, the thirty-seven directors who have so generously provided me with photographs and other material relating to their museums, and the much larger number of experts with whom I have discussed the project and who have given me the benefit of their advice and opinions.

Of those in the second category, I should like to thank especially: Neil Cossons, of the Science Museum, London; Barry Cunliffe, of the Institute of Archaeology, University of Oxford; David Elliott, of the Museum of Modern Art, Oxford; Jean Favière, of Strasbourg Museums; Patrick Greene, of the Greater Manchester Museum of Science and Industry; Yudhisthir Raj Isar, of UNESCO, Paris; Massimo Negri, Milan; Ulla Keding Olofsson, of Riksutställningar, Stockholm; Kenneth Robinson, of Ventures Consultancy Ltd, Beaulieu; Peter Saunders, of Salisbury and South Wiltshire Museum; David Sekers, of Quarry Bank Mill, Styal; Ray Sutcliffe, of the BBC, London; George Thompson, of the Ulster Folk and Transport Museum, Belfast; William J. Tramposch, of the Colonial Williamsburg Foundation; Ahmet Edip Uysal, of the Middle East Technical University, Ankara; Robin Wade, of Robin Wade Design Associates, London; Friedrich Waidacher, of the Steiermärkisches Landesmuseum Joanneum, Graz; Merlin Waterson, of the National Trust, London; Hans Woodtli, Zürich; Sune Zachrisson, of the Nordic Museum, Stockholm.

I am grateful to the following for their permission to reproduce the illustrations on the pages indicated: Anacostia, Washington, DC (180); Beamish North of England Open Air Museum (frontispiece, 127, 129, 130); The British Museum, London (23–4, 27); Harold Hartman (186); Brooklyn Children's Museum, New York (184–5); Colonial Williamsburg (147–51); Deutsches Museum, Munich (96, 97–8); Fitzwilliam Museum, Cambridge (25); Gallery of David d'Angers, Angers (177–8); Goulandris Natural History Museum, Kifissia (85–7); Ironbridge Gorge Museum Trust, Telford (155–8); Maritime Museum and the Warship 'Wasa', Stockholm (168–70); Metropolitan Museum, New York (57–9); Municipal Museum, Rüsselsheim (111, 108–9); Museum of the Army, Paris (116, 119); Museum of German History, Berlin (137–9); Ewald Pawlok (137); Museum of the History of the City of Warsaw (134, 135, 137); Museum of the Jewish Diaspora, Tel Aviv (141–2); Museum of Man and Industry, Le Creusot (162, 164); Museum of Modern Art, New York (60–3); Museum of Science and Industry, Chicago (105, 106); National Museum, Copenhagen (30); J. Hoepffuer (132); National Museum of Popular Arts and Traditions, Paris (132–3); National Museum of Technology, Paris (89); Natural History Museum, London (68, 70–1, 82); John Stoel (79); Noorder Dierenpark, Emmen (78, 81); Palace of Discovery, Paris (102); Pitt-Rivers Museum, Farnham (33); Raymond Thomas (37); Richard Einzig, Roman Palace Museum, Fishbourne (36); Werberi Woodtli, Zürich (189–91); Science Museum, London (90–1, 93–5); Senckenberg Museum, Frankfurt (84); Skansen, Stockholm (120–1, 123); Sukuma Museum, Tanzania (193–4); Swiss Transport Museum, Lucerne (192); Ann Nicholls (183); Victoria and Albert Museum, London (49–50, 52–3).

List of illustrations

207

Index